The Skills of Leadership

JOHN ADAIR

WILDWOOD
HOUSE

First published 1984 by Gower Publishing Company Limited, Aldershot, Hants.
Reprinted 1986 by
Wildwood House Limited,
Gower House,
Croft Road,
Aldershot,
Hampshire GU11 3HR,
England

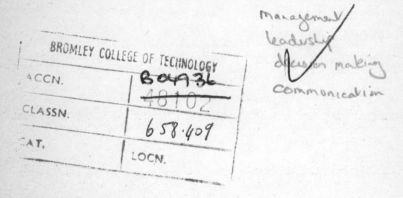

British Library Cataloguing in Publication Data

Adair, John, 1934–
   The skills of leadership – (Management skills library)
   1. Management   2. Leadership
   I. Title   II. Series
    658.4'092   HD38

ISBN 0-7045-0555-X

Printed and bound in Great Britain by
Billing and Sons Ltd, Worcester

THE SKILLS OF LEADERSHIP

Contents

Preface

Leadership is an essential ingredient in effective and successful management. Every manager therefore needs to acquire or develop the SKILLS OF LEADERSHIP. My central aim in this book is to provide some guidance to that end.

Of course, a book by itself cannot impart skills. You need practice – and more practice – before skills take shape. But you will find here the PRINCIPLES which underlie the skills, together with a range of practical hints or guidelines. Refer to them not just before you practise leadership but afterwards as well. For they will help you to diagnose accurately the reasons for your success – or limited success – in real life. It is the combination of interaction of PRINCIPLES on the one hand with PRACTICE on the other, which produces the SKILLS OF LEADERSHIP.

Readers of my earlier books will notice that this one is mainly a compilation from *Training for Leadership* (1968), *Training for Decisions* (1971) and *Training for Communication* (1973). A word of explanation. As this trilogy is now ten years old it was suggested to me that I should revise each of them and issue new editions. The difficulty is that *Training for Leadership* in particular has become something of a standard work in the field of leadership development. Although much of it, such as the descriptions of the syllabus at Sandhurst and the state of leadership training in industry, has clearly dated, training specialists and others still want to read that original book, not an up-dated version of it.

Consequently the publishers and I decided that we should keep the three *Training* books available as they are, but draw chapters from them into a new book. Here are some background thoughts on why I have chosen these particular chapters.

From the beginning I have believed firmly – and still do – that there are three main strands in the management of people, leadership, communication and decision making (together with problem solving and creative thinking). Together they form the core of 'the human side of enterprise'. Of course there are other relevant areas of skill or branches of knowledge, but these are the 'big three' – the *must knows* as opposed to the *should knows* or *might knows*. Twenty years of practical experience have confirmed my sense of the paramount importance of those three concepts. The publication of the three *Training* books as separate entities may have obscured the fact that I have always seen their subjects as part of an integrated whole. You cannot understand leadership, for example, without communication or decision making.

Much confusion about any subject springs from the failure to recognise that all our concepts tend to come in inter-related clusters. To introduce order and understanding into our theories we must often explore the entire relevant territory and deal with several neighbouring concepts at once. For me leadership, communication and decisions are not so much neighbours as members of the same family living under the same roof.

Another factor that has strongly influenced my choice of chapters is a growing desire to talk directly to managers, leaders or would-be leaders rather than to training specialists. And so I have picked out from each of the books the chapters which are concerned directly with knowledge and abilities that a leader should be aiming to master. The secondary material, which concerns training or development in the narrower sense, I have left behind in the original covers for the specialists. This book will be a success if it gives you a clear understanding of the SKILLS OF LEADERSHIP.

John Adair

PART ONE
LEADERSHIP

Introduction

The first chapter in Part One, 'The Nature of Leadership', is the foundation for the whole of the book, for the three-circles model can serve to integrate all that we should *know* and all that we should *be* and all that we should *do* as leaders. It is a written form of the first lecture I gave on Leadership at Sandhurst in the early sixties, and I am sometimes amazed when I think of all the changes in the leadership development throughout the world which have stemmed from that one address. Although I have modified it in detail it is still my message today.

Many people have told me how much they value the concrete examples or case studies of leaders given in my books. 'Looking at Leaders' contains some descriptions of leaders which demonstrate the reality of the points made in general terms in the course of the first chapter. I believe that we learn most about leadership from actual leaders, not from textbooks or training courses. They are essentially ancillary. But we should not confine ourselves to leaders we know, or even living leaders. It would be foolish if we refused to listen to Beethoven or Mozart because we did not know them personally. There are classics in leadership, too, men such as Lincoln or Eisenhower, Nelson or Montgomery, and a wise leader will study and learn from them.

The first really successful application of a group or functional approach to leadership was in the area of leadership selection, the topic of my third chapter. The skill of selecting leaders is in itself an important leadership skill. It surprises me that more industrial organisations have not followed the lead available (since 1940) from the Armed Services in this area, especially as those few who have done so have found that the

3

methods I describe do actually work in industry. Those who pass leadership tests well have been shown to have excellent records as leaders later in their managerial careers.

From Chapter 3 it is clear that the functional approach to leadership was applied successfully to the problem of selecting military leaders, but not at all (in a conscious way) to the more difficult task of training them. As a consequence of my work at Sandhurst between 1960 and 1967, however, a functional leadership course was introduced into the syllabus. Through the agency of The Industrial Society it was subsequently modified and made available to all managers.

In order to illustrate that leadership skills *can* be developed I have borrowed Chapter 4 from *Action-Centred Leadership* (1973), describing the objectives and methods of the ACL course.

1 The nature of leadership

Before the training of leaders can be discussed we must first review the different assumptions and theories upon which it might be based.

The method adopted in this chapter is to look first at perhaps the oldest and most widely held general idea that leaders are 'born not made'. From this point we shall trace the evolution of research upon the subject, sticking as closely as possible to the main highway.

The qualities approach

'Leaders are born not made.' This is perhaps the most common assumption about leadership. Those who hold it maintain that there are certain inborn qualities, such as initiative, courage, intelligence and humour, which together predestine a man to be a leader. By the exercise of will-power, itself seen as an important leadership trait, or by the rough tutorship of experience, some of these qualities might be developed. But the essential pattern is given at birth.

Although there is a positive contribution to our understanding of leadership latent in this *qualities approach,* it suffers from several disadvantages as far as training for leadership is concerned. The first of these drawbacks is that no one has yet been able to discover any agreement upon what are these qualities, that will give a man dominion over his fellows in any situation in which he finds himself. One survey of 20 experimental studies, made in 1940, revealed that only five per cent of the leadership qualities examined were common to four

5

or more studies.[1] In fact there are a bewildering number of trait names which the professional or amateur student might use to make up his portfolio. The writers of one article have listed 17,000 words used to describe qualities of personality.[2] Although there has been a continual effort to boil down the qualities to those which are essential, lengthy lists are still common. Until 1958 Eaton Hall Officer Cadet Training Unit issued one which contained 32 qualities, and at one military conference the author was handed a list of 64 leadership traits! The reader may check this lack of agreement by turning to the Appendix on page 265 where he may compare for himself the lists of leadership traits advocated by various armed services in the western world in the 1960s.

You will notice that 'courage' and 'initiative' appear in most columns in the Appendix. Do they form the core of military leadership? But, we may reflect, *all* soldiers, regardless of rank, need to be brave and resourceful. So by isolating those two qualities we are no nearer to understanding the mystery of leadership. Indeed there are plenty of examples of soldiers who possess both courage and initiative, but who by no stretch of the imagination could be called leaders.

Besides this lack of consensus as to what are the qualities of leadership, there is a second major disadvantage to this theory. The qualities approach is ill-suited to act as a basis for leadership training. Intrinsically it hardly favours the idea of training at all, and instead encourages a concentration on selection. The ability to recognise a born leader becomes all important, and attempts to 'make' leaders are viewed with suspicion.

In fact, how could the 'qualities of leadership' be used in training? The teacher or instructor might speak in the language of traits to the student, but it is difficult for the latter to know what to *do* with such remarks. If told, for example, that he lacks a sense of humour – how does he develop it? By reading *Punch* every week? No, there is nothing more serious than a young man bent on improving his sense of humour, and nothing more self-centred than this cultivation of one's own personality. And in the long run self-centredness is the one certain disqualification for any form of leadership. At the worst an unskilful teacher, using the 'qualities of leadership' language, can do incalculable harm. A comment such as 'Jones, you lack moral fibre' may take away from Jones even that self-confidence which he had.

One usually finds that students who have attempted a

self-development based on the traits approach have abandoned it after a few weeks, either in despair because they have not attained the desired qualities or (much worse) in pride because they believe they have. The pattern is often that followed by an Eaton Hall officer cadet known to the author, who resolved to practise 1-5 on the issued list of 32 'leadership qualities' on Mondays, 6-10 on Tuesdays, 11-15 on Wednesdays, etc. By Friday he had completely forgotten Monday's quota, and had become so dispirited that he abandoned the Herculean task. (Such schemes for moral self-improvement, however, if persisted in, are seldom wasted. The lives of the saints illustrate the point that when these struggles are abandoned and become hidden in a person's life, they may then bear – much later – the fruit of character.)

Therefore the qualities assumption does not form a good basis for leadership training programmes. But it does have other uses. First, it reminds us that natural potential for leadership varies in individuals. Secondly, many of us need the language of qualities to transfer our knowledge of a person's leadership ability to someone else. Thirdly, this approach emphasises the importance of what the leader *is* as a person, in an age which may be inclined temperamentally to skate over the importance of character as opposed to personality. Certainly we need more research into the qualities understanding of leadership, but until this is carried out there is no reason to make it the main basis for a training course.

The situational approach

Besides revealing the inadequacies of the traits analysis of leadership the social scientists investigating the subject in the late 1940s began to underline the importance of the situation in determining who would become a leader in a given group. R. M. Stogdill, for example, who studied the evidence for 29 qualities appearing in 124 studies, concluded that although intelligence, scholarliness, dependability, social participation, and socio-economic status were found to bear some relation to leadership,

> ... the evidence suggests that leadership is a relationship that exists between persons in a social situation, and that persons who are leaders in one situation may not necessarily be leaders in other situations.[3]

This finding expressed what might be called a *situational approach* to leadership, namely that the man who becomes (or should become) the leader in a group depends upon the particular task, the organisational and the environmental setting. Another study by W. O. Jenkins, published a year earlier in 1947, supports this conclusion. After reviewing 74 studies on military leadership the author wrote:

> Leadership is specific to the particular situation under investigation. Who becomes the leader of a particular group engaging in a particular activity and what the leadership characteristics are in the given case are a function of the specific situation ... [there are] wide variations in the characteristics of individuals who become leaders in similar situations and even great divergence in leadership behaviour in different situations ... The only common factor appeared to be that leaders in a particular field need and tend to possess superior general or technical competence or knowledge in that area. General intelligence does not seem to be the answer ...[4]

To illustrate this theory let us imagine some shipwreck survivors on a tropical island. The soldier in the party might take command if natives attacked them, the builder lead during the work of erecting houses, and the farmer might direct the labour of growing food. In other words, leadership would pass from member to member according to the situation. 'Situation' in this context means primarily the task of the group.

There are two drawbacks to this approach as far as training leaders is concerned. First, it is unsatisfactory in most organisations for leadership to change hands in this manner. At one time the Royal Air Force veered towards this doctrine by entertaining the idea that if a bomber crashed in a jungle the officer who took command for the survival operation might not be captain of the aircraft but the man most qualified for the job. But role flexibility to this degree tends to create more problems than it solves.

Secondly, an explanation was needed for the fact that certain men seemed to possess a general leadership competence which enabled them to exercise an influence over their fellows in a whole range of situations. Of course, the compilers of trait lists had been seeking, without much success, to analyse this general aptitude, and there was no denying its reality. Even so, by seeing leadership not as a quality but as a relationship, and by grasping the importance of the leader possessing the appropriate technical or professional knowledge required in the given situation, the proponents of this approach made a most valuable contribution to our understanding of the subject.

The functional approach

So far the research work described has been largely literary: the analysis and comparison of books and articles on leadership. In the late 1930s, however, more objective research commenced into the behaviour of actual small groups both in what were described as 'laboratory' conditions and also 'in the field', in an attempt to bring the scientific methods of observation, hypothesis and verification by experiment to bear upon the phenomena of social life.

These studies have produced a vast crop of papers on the social psychology of small groups, including the leadership displayed in them. From this wealth the author selected one general theory which might be called 'the theory of group needs', as having the greatest potential relevance to leadership training. By combining and developing this theory with the positive contributions of the two earlier and complementary approaches – qualities and situational – he produced a comprehensive and integrated understanding of leadership. To grasp 'functional leadership', as this approach came to be called, it is necessary first to look at the concept of 'group needs'.

If we look closely at any working group we may become aware of its distinctive corporate life, its difference from others even in the same organisation. Upon the analogy with individual human beings this could be called the 'group personality'. But, according to the theory of group needs, just as individuals differ in many ways and yet share certain common attributes and needs, so also do the corporate entities or social organisms which we know as groups. Let us now examine the most important of these group needs.

With reference to working groups, the most obvious group need is to achieve the common *task*. Generally speaking, all such groups come together consciously or unconsciously because the individuals in them cannot alone fulfil an objective. For example, one man by himself could not climb Mount Everest and survive; therefore a team is assembled for the job and co-operation becomes essential.

But does the group as a whole experience the need to complete the task within the natural time limits for it? Now a man is not very aware of his need for food if he is well-fed, and so one would expect a group to be relatively oblivious of any sense of need if its task is being successfully performed. In this case the only sign of a need having been met is the satisfaction or elation which overtake the group in its moments of triumph, a happiness which social man may count among his deepest joys.

Before such a fulfilment, however, many groups pass through a 'black night of despair' when it may appear that the group will be compelled to disperse without achieving what it set out to do. If the members are not committed to the common goal this will be a comparatively painless event; but if they are, the group will exhibit various degrees of anxiety and frustration. Scapegoats for the corporate failure may be chosen and punished; reorganisations might take place and new leaders emerge. Thus adversity reveals the nature of group life more clearly than prosperity. In it we may see signs or symptoms of the need to get on effectively with whatever the group has come together to do.

Secondly, in order to achieve the common objective the group must work as a team. Therefore it needs to be maintained as a cohesive unity. This is not so easy to perceive as the task need; like an iceberg, much of the life of any group lies below the surface. The distinction that the task need concerns things and the second need involves people does not help overmuch. Again, it is best to think of groups which are threatened without by forces aimed at their disintegration or within by disruptive people or ideas. We can then see how they give priority to maintaining themselves against these external or internal pressures, sometimes showing great ingenuity in the process. Many of the written or unwritten rules of the group are designed to promote this unity and to maintain cohesiveness at all costs. Those who rock the boat, or infringe group standards and corporate balance, may expect reactions varying from friendly indulgence to downright anger. Instinctively a common feeling exists that 'united we stand, divided we fall', that good relationships, desirable in themselves, are also essential means towards the shared end. This need to create and promote group cohesiveness we may call the *team maintenance* need.

The third area of need present in the corporate life inheres in the individual members rather than in the group itself. To the latter they bring a variety of needs – physical, social and vocational – which may or may not be met by participating in the activity of the group. Probably physical needs first drew men together in working groups: the primitive hunter could take away from the slain elephant a hunk of meat and a piece of hide for his own family. Nowadays the means for satisfying these basic needs of food, shelter and protection are received in money rather than in kind, but the principle remains the same.

There are, however, other needs less tangible or conscious even to their possessors which the social interaction of working together in groups may or may not fulfil. These tend to merge into each other, and they cannot be isolated with any precision, but Figure 1.1 will indicate their character. Drawn from the work of A. H. Maslow[5] it also makes the point that needs are organised on a priority basis. As basic needs become relatively satisfied the higher needs come to the fore and become motivating influences.[6]

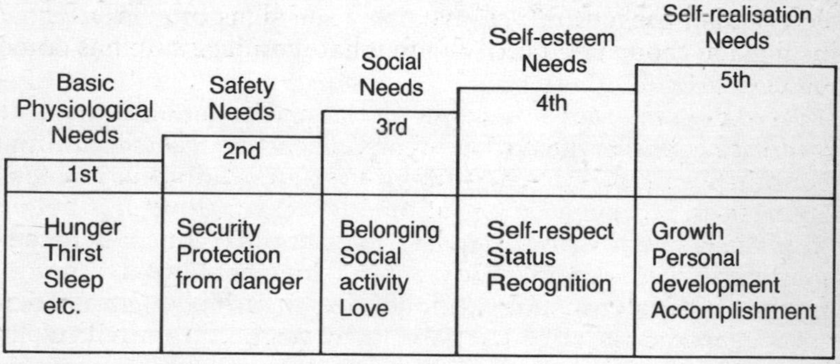

Basic Physiological Needs 1st	Safety Needs 2nd	Social Needs 3rd	Self-esteem Needs 4th	Self-realisation Needs 5th
Hunger Thirst Sleep etc.	Security Protection from danger	Belonging Social activity Love	Self-respect Status Recognition	Growth Personal development Accomplishment

Figure 1.1 The priority of needs

These needs spring from the depths of our common life as human beings. They may attract us to, or repel us from, any given group. Underlying them all is the fact that people need each other, not just to survive but to achieve and develop personality. This growth occurs in a whole range of social activity – friendship, marriage, neighbourhood – but inevitably work groups are extremely important because so many people spend so much of their waking time in them.

These three areas of need cannot be studied in watertight compartments: each exerts an influence for good or ill upon the others. Thus we may visualise the needs as three overlapping circles (Figure 1.2):

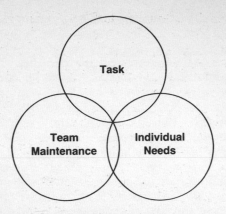

Figure 1.2 Interaction of group needs

If you place a coin over the 'Task' circle it will immediately cover segments of the other two circles as well. In other words, lack of task or failure to achieve it will affect both team maintenance, e.g. increasing disruptive tendencies, and also the area of individual needs, lowering member satisfaction within the group. Move the coin on to the 'Team Maintenance' circle, and again the impact of a near-complete lack of relationships in the group on both task and individual needs may be seen at a glance.

Conversely, when a group achieves its task the degree of group cohesiveness and enjoyment of membership should go up. Morale, both corporate and individual, will be higher. And if the members of a group happen to get on extremely well together and find that they can work closely as a team, this will increase their work performance and also meet some important needs which individuals bring with them into the common life.

These three interlocking circles therefore illustrate the general point that each area of need exerts an influence upon the other two; they do not form watertight compartments.

Clearly, in order that the group should fulfil its task and be held together as a working team, certain functions will have to be performed. By 'function' in this context we mean any behaviour, words or actions which meet one or more spheres of the group needs, or *areas of leadership responsibility* as they may also be called. Defining the aim, planning, and encouraging the group, are examples of what is meant by the word 'function'. (See Table 1.1 on page 13 for other examples.)

In most small groups the responsibility for the performance

Table 1.1 Some key leadership functions

PLANNING
- Seeking all available information
- Defining group task, purpose or goal
- Making a workable plan (in right decision-making framework)

INITIATING
- Briefing group on the aims and the plan
- Explaining *why* aim or plan is necessary
- Allocating tasks to group members
- Setting group standards

CONTROLLING
- Maintaining group standards
- Influencing tempo
- Ensuring all actions are taken towards objectives
- Keeping discussion relevant
- Prodding group to action/decision

SUPPORTING
- Expressing acceptance of persons and their contribution
- Encouraging group/individuals
- Disciplining group/individuals
- Creating team spirit
- Relieving tension with humour
- Reconciling disagreements or getting others to explore them

INFORMING
- Clarifying task and plan
- Giving new information to the group, i.e. keeping them 'in the picture'
- Receiving information from group
- Summarising suggestions and ideas coherently

EVALUATING
- Checking feasibility of an idea
- Testing the consequences of a proposed solution
- Evaluating group performance
- Helping the group to evaluate its own performance against standards

of such functions rests with the designated leader, though this is not to say that he is expected to perform them all himself. Nor can we assert that there are certain functions which must always be supplied, for this depends upon the situation in the wildest sense, including the task and the nature of the group.

By contrast with the traditional view that a leader possesses certain traits or qualities which make him stand out in any company, the functional approach stresses that leadership is essentially an interaction between leader, group members and the situation. Yet the personality of the leader is not ignored in this functional approach. It may often serve the group by representing the qualities valued both for corporate survival and the completion of the task. Thus an army officer ought to possess courage, the cardinal military virtue, although this will not in itself make him a leader. Perhaps Sir Winston Churchill in the war years afforded the supreme example in our time of the 'representative function of character', as it could be called. His bulldog demeanour and resolute speech personified the spirit of a nation, just as surely as did the youthful vigour of President Kennedy represent the mighty energies of the United States in our own day. Still, the functional approach lays emphasis not upon what the leader *is* in terms of traits, or upon what he *knows* of the appropriate technical knowledge, but upon his ability to provide the necessary functions in a manner acceptable to the group, i.e. what he actually *does* to lead in response to the three overlapping areas of task, team maintenance and individual needs.

The question of how far the designated leader should share his leadership functions with group members deserves consideration. Not many leaders consciously think this problem out; most accept the assumptions on the matter prevalent in their organisation although in some cases these are ripe for review. Supposing, however, that a leader became aware that there were alternative patterns from which he could choose, what would be the factors that he should consider before determining upon one or other of them?

In a thoughtful answer to this question two writers in the *Harvard Business Review*[7] have suggested three: the leader himself, his subordinates and the situation. Let us look at each of these in turn:

The leader

The personality of the designated leader – his interests, aptitudes and temperament – will exert an influence on the pattern of shared leadership in any group. His 'doctrine of man', as the theologians would say, determines much. If he regards people as things to be used for his own ends, pawns on the chessboard, then he will not see much need for consultation. If he is temperamentally lazy, then he may well allow group members a greater share in leadership functions than either their experience or the requirements of the situation dictate.

Perhaps the critical factor in the temperament of the leader is the degree to which he feels secure in an uncertain situation. 'The manager who releases control over the decision-making process thereby reduces the predictability of the outcome. Some managers have a greater need than others for predictability and stability in their environment. This "tolerance of ambiguity" is being viewed increasingly by psychologists as a key variable in a person's manner of dealing with problems.'[8]

'Know thyself,' enjoins the Greek philosopher. By looking at his own experience, the reactions of others to himself, and the comments of friends, the leader should gain a modicum of self-knowledge. He should be aware of any bias in his character; for example, whether or not he tends to be too task-centred and correspondingly less conscious of the needs of individuals, or whether he operates most efficiently and effectively in one pattern of shared functions rather than another. The end of such study is more appropriate action. Like a marksman archer 'aiming off' into the wind, a leader can then make allowances for these unseen tendencies in his character when he perceives that a particular situation demands a different kind of response from his normal one. Although he may feel it 'unnatural' to share out or arrogate to himself leadership functions (as the case may be) this will not be the judgment of others if he has appreciated the situation correctly.

The subordinates

The obvious question here for the leader to ask himself is how far the group members possess the necessary knowledge, experience and skill relevant to the problem in hand to participate satisfactorily in leadership functions. At one end of the scale a class of junior school-children clearly lack the qualifications to decide how they are going to plan out their work; it has to be done for them by the adult leader. On the other hand, a team of highly skilled technicians will not require this degree of 'spoon-feeding' on how to tackle a common task; the steps may become evident to all of them at once. The leader therefore should take into account the degree of 'expert' knowledge, experience and social skill resident in the group as the second main factor in his appreciation.

One note of caution, however, should be sounded at this point. Some leaders rationalise their temperamental preference for a pattern by claiming that 'their' group is incapable of being more than submissive or dependent followers. In those cases the leaders concerned lack sufficient self-knowledge to discern their own guiding motives. In fact it is rarely true that a group is so devoid in all three respects of any leadership potential that one man or woman must do it all for them; this is sometimes a fiction created as a piece of self-justification by a domineering personality. Moreover, entrusting the inexperienced with a share in leadership functions is often the only way of giving them the necessary experience, and of motivating them to acquire the appropriate knowledge and skill. There is nothing more mysterious and exciting than this ability of good leaders to transform their followers: without it, a vital element, the light and life of leadership, is missing. The great leader is always aware of latent powers in people which can be evoked and harnessed: he responds to these like a gold-diviner, thereby meeting an important segment of individual needs. Generally speaking, the more members participate in decisions, the more they feel motivated to carry them out; and the more they share in the life of the group in this way, the more chance there is that their potentialities as persons will be fulfilled.

The situation

There are, however, limits to which the leader can go in this educative process without a denial of his own responsibility, and these are set by the situation. 'Situation' in this context must again be understood in a wide sense, embracing group task and the working environment. When we think of an important (predominantly) task function such as decision making, it is clear that in certain situations life or death may depend upon the speed of a group's reaction. In such cases it is appropriate for the leader to retain or concentrate authority in his own hands rather than share it with the group. In fact some research shows that in hastily formed groups responding to crisis situations, for example serious motor accidents and forest fires, not only is a strong authoritative leadership tolerated from one man, but it is also positively expected.

Consequently, we shall not be surprised to find that groups which habitually, or characteristically, operate in crisis situations exhibit a certain pattern of leadership, with the designated leader in a fixed position of authority, and followers trained and disciplined to obey his orders promptly and without discussion. Obvious examples of such groups would include military platoons, the crews of airliners, ships' crews and operating theatre teams. But the stress element is not solely related to life-and-death; sometimes decisions must be taken promptly in order to avoid great loss to an industrial company. Time limits may not always allow the manager to share his decision-making functions with his subordinates.

Although the characteristic situation influences the general pattern it does not arbitrarily fix it on a given point. The platoon commander, for example, in barracks and on peacetime exercises will act towards his men in such a way as not to betray the residual authority he needs to command on active service, but he would be unwise to behave in those situations as if a fierce battle were raging about his ears. There is a flexibility within any pattern which the good leader will exploit according to the *specific* situation without detriment to his prime responsibility in the *characteristic* one. Indeed, a chairman of a committee may range widely with an appropriate pattern during the confines of a two-hour meeting, or even within the context of five minutes.

A decision-making continuum

The *Harvard Business Review* article already mentioned contains a useful diagram (Figure 1.3) showing the full range of sharing which might take place in any group over the general function of decision making:

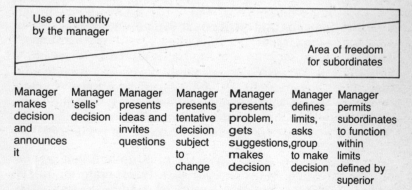

Figure 1.3 A decision-making continuum

This is largely self-explanatory. It should not be supposed, however, that the points between which a leader habitually acts on this scale necessarily describe the degree of shared *leadership* in a group. Decision making in the sense meant by the authors is but one task function, albeit a key one. We could equally well construct diagrams to illustrate the amount of member involvement in team maintenance functions. Indeed, very often a leader who exercises virtually all the task functions himself will delegate (or be expected to share) many team-maintenance functions to other members of the group. In an infantry platoon, for example, the platoon sergeant often responds to the other two areas of need, holding the men together and making sure that they get food and mail where possible. In less formal groups, a factory production team, for example, those sharing in leadership in this way may not be designated, but nevertheless they will act to complement the functions performed by the appointed leader. As a general principle, in any group larger than 7 or 8 members, some degree of sharing becomes essential: there are so many functions required for the group to work effectively on the task without losing cohesion and without individual needs being overlooked that the designated leader cannot supply them all himself, and he must therefore delegate some of them to others.

Conclusion

In 1952 C. A. Gibb concluded an extensive survey of research into the subject by stating that 'any comprehensive theory of leadership must incorporate and integrate all of the major variables which are now known to be involved, namely (1) the personality of the leader, (2) the followers with their attitudes, needs and problems, (3) the group itself ... (4) the situations as determined by physical setting, nature of task etc ... No really satisfactory theoretical formulation is yet available.'[9] In this chapter the simple concept of 'functional leadership' has been outlined not so much to meet the academic need mentioned by Gibb but to serve as a basis for more effective leadership training.

Although 'theorising about' and 'analysing' a subject like leadership, which will always transcend even the most comprehensive description, may not appeal to many readers, it has been a necessary labour. For if we are not clear upon the meaning of leadership it is impossible to design an effective training programme.

2 Looking at leaders

This chapter is in fact a 'pocket anthology' mainly of descriptions of actual leaders in concrete historical situations. The reader is invited to study them, however, bearing in mind the *functional* concept of leadership described in Chapter 1. It is hoped that he will find that this theory illumines these practical examples, that it becomes easier to *see* leadership and to understand why a particular individual was successful as a leader. After he has completed this chapter, the reader may have been able to clothe with flesh-and-blood the rather abstract and analytical ideas of Chapter 1.

Not all the extracts are descriptions of leaders. Some have been chosen because they contain the thoughts of a proven leader upon the group or the situation in which he exercised his responsibility. The theme of the anthology is the relation of the leader to other members of his team in the context of a common task, and therefore general quotations about leadership, or the mere listing of 'qualities', have been omitted in favour of concrete examples of how leaders think and act in order to attain the task, build and foster team maintenance, and meet the needs of individual members.

The fact that more than half of the extracts refer to leaders in military situations is not significant. It is largely due to the fact that descriptions of military leadership tend to appear in print more often than, for example, those of individual industrial leaders at work. The *underlying* principles of leadership are the same. Indeed it could be argued that the crisis element of war serves to reveal the essential nature of leadership more clearly. This does not mean, of course, that the applied form or pattern of leadership necessary in a military situation will be transferable to any other setting. Here it is sufficient for the reader to identify the main areas of need present in a group as depicted in the three overlapping circles on page 12, and to distinguish the key functions performed by leaders to meet them effectively.

Gino Watkins

Gino Watkins led expeditions to Edge Island (near Spitzbergen), Labrador and Greenland. This extract from J. M. Scott's biography concerns his leadership in Greenland during 1930. The average age of the 14 members of the party was 25 years old, eighteen months more than Watkins. He died in 1933, drowned in a Greenland lake while out hunting in a kayak. Postumously he was awarded the Polar Medal with Arctic clasp.

As quietly as if it had been a Scottish shooting-party Gino had organised the greatest British expedition to the Arctic for half a century, and he was carrying it through in the same unofficial, unheroic spirit ... When he sailed for Edge Island he had no first-hand knowledge of the conditions. He was successful because he could sum up positions quickly and act without hesitation, and he was a tactful and popular leader because he asked the opinions of the members of the party who had each some special knowledge to impart. In Labrador it had been the same. Everyone he came in contact with was gratified by his respectful interest in all they said and, without fully realising it, they did what he wanted them to do and taught him all the useful knowledge they possessed. In England he had read widely and had asked pertinent questions whenever he met well-travelled men, so that by now he knew a great deal about polar technique; and although he was no scientist he understood clearly enough what the specialists were after ...

He did what he enjoyed and visited the places that he wanted to visit, but, being there, he used all the resources in his power to bring back everything he could. By knowledge he was best qualified to lead in Greenland quite apart from the fact that he had created the expedition. Most of the party had seen little of him before they sailed, and they were ready to treat him at least with the outward deference they were accustomed to show to a commander. If he had enjoyed that sort of thing he could very easily have kept it up. But his sense of humour made it absurd. He took trouble to climb down from this uncomfortable eminence by telling stories against himself, flirting with the Eskimos, posing as an utter Philistine or joining in every menial task ...

Besides, he gave himself no privileges at all. His bed was no more comfortable than ours; probably it was less so, judging by the dog harness and rifles which were piled on top of it. His clothes were no better and his private possessions far less numerous. His dogs I had given to him after selecting what I considered the best team for myself. Only his native hunting instruments were superior because he had taken great trouble in acquiring them. I was reminded that once in Labrador I heard a man call him Boss, and Gino had been a little embarrassed and very much amused. That was not his name, so why address him so? /

As unemotionally as one is conscious of a fact of life, he knew that he would lead in any circumstance. Neither familiarity nor conventional discipline could alter that, and he preferred familiarity because he had no wish to be lonely. He was a young man who set out to enjoy himself and to make others enjoy themselves as well, because he believed that people work better when they are happy.

All that was comparatively easy. Almost anybody with a sense of humour could have done as much if his sole object was to be accepted as a member of the party. But to one who was responsible for making people do unpleasant tasks it was a self-imposed handicap which could only be overcome by a very high type of personality. There could be no bluffing in such leadership; it would either prove magnetic by its inspiring originality or lead to chaos by its non-existence.

At first there was some argument as to Gino's wisdom in following the course which he had chosen. People like the Bedouin are used to such methods: they expect a leader to be one of themselves and recognise a strong character most easily in contrast to circumstances which they themselves experience ... One or two of the Service men in particular were upset by the apparently casual suggestions which passed for commands. Gino said it was absurd to write to a man you could talk to; but even so, they would have appreciated the comfortable definiteness of written orders, if only to assure them that they had done all that was expected. Others, although they could not have admitted it, had looked for something more in exploration: a consciousness of adventure and romance. All this was so straightforward and matter-of-fact that if one so much as grew a beard one felt theatrical. Gino's plans and his rebellious why-not? points of view were exciting enough if one could swallow them; but without experience we had no personal standard to judge by; and could anyone so casual have taken trouble to prepare the best equipment?

As time passed and experience brought knowledge, these doubts were laid one after another. It very soon became apparent that the equipment was extraordinarily good. The clothing was light and warm, while the sledging rations – Gino's most striking innovation – were excellent; no one had been really hungry on any journey and there had only been one serious case of frostbite. The sledging tents, lighter and easier to pitch than the older Antarctic models, had withstood considerable storms. The dome-shaped tent at the ice-cap station, which was designed somewhat on the lines of an Eskimo igloo with a tunnel entrance and small tube ventilator at the apex, had so far proved efficient, though it had not yet had to withstand the hardest test of all. The Base hut, with its double walls and central kitchen, was warm and well designed. These facts and a thousand little things bore proof of care and foresight.

The work of the first season proved remarkably successful. Luck played a part, as in the absence of heavy ice at Kangerdlugsuak, but luck is a valuable addition to a leader's reputation. In detail the journeys had not developed exactly as expected; but the acting leaders, unrestricted by precise directions yet understanding very clearly the general objective, had used their initiative to achieve a useful end. In the course of our work we had done things that we had never done before – we had driven dogs and navigated small boats through ice – and we had found these things remarkably easy. Knowing that so much had depended upon ourselves, our self-confidence increased and with it our confidence in Gino; for his plans were only alarming when we doubted our ability to fulfil our part in them. Having discovered the surprising fact that we were as good men as Gino thought we were, we accepted him as a splendid leader. He was exacting, he was ruthlessly indifferent to small discomforts like cold or unvaried fresh meat diets at the Base, he was disconcerting in his words and actions, but he would never be at a loss and would never blame. Once only Gino remarked that a man was beginning to behave badly and that he thought he would have to have a row with him. He had his row, in a roaring temper, so it seemed, and afterwards they were far stronger friends than they had been before.

If he told inexperienced men to do what they thought best, and if they made some fatal blunder, the responsibility would be his just as surely as if he had expressly ordered that disastrous action. The world would see it thus and so would he. It was a risky policy, but for his purpose the risk was unavoidable.

Briefly, his method of leadership was to train each man to be a leader: his ideal exploring party consisted of nothing else. These were young men and he was looking ahead towards other, more perplexing, quests.

In Gino's opinion, initiative and self-confidence were all-important and so he would keep nobody in leading-strings. The boy who stood on the burning deck seemed to him nothing but a fool. Once, too, he had gone to a film about the sinking of a great liner. When he saw the last brave men, who had put the women and children in the only boats, standing at attention to sing, 'Nearer, my God, to Thee,' he turned to his neighbour in the darkness and in an urgent whisper said, 'Why the hell don't they build rafts instead of wasting their time being heroic?' From the same coldly practical point of view he had told me on our last journey that if the food ran out and he himself should die he would naturally expect to be eaten; and, when I demurred, he added, 'Well, I'd eat you, but then, of course, you are much more fat and appetising.' ...

He did not preach this philosophy which I have attempted to explain. He followed the path which he had chosen, enjoying every step, quick to shock, slow to offend, but caring nothing how his words and actions were interpreted when he felt their aim was right, leading without looking back because he knew that we would follow him. Both as a friend and a leader he had always something in reserve, some depth which gave occasional proof of its existence, but which even he did not understand. The one aspect aroused interest and the other confidence.

Field Marshal Lord Slim

In this chapter from *Defeat into Victory* Lord Slim describes how he analysed his responsibilities as a leader in a given situation, and then carried them out. Of particular interest is the way in which his appreciation and action covers comprehensively the task, team maintenance and individual needs of a great army. Lord Slim saw from the outset that it was necessary for the leader to explain not only 'how' the aim is to be achieved, but also 'why', and this he did by relating objectives to larger purposes. The passage illustrates most clearly the interrelation of the three areas, and how the leader went about providing the necessary functions effectively.

So when I took command, I sat quietly down to work out this business of morale. I came to certain conclusions, based not on any theory that I had studied, but on some experience and a good deal of hard thinking. It was on these conclusions that I set out consciously to raise the fighting spirit of my army.

Morale is a state of mind. It is that intangible force which will move a whole group of men to give their last ounce to achieve something, without counting the cost to themselves; that makes them feel they are part of something greater than themselves. If they are to feel that, their morale must, if it is to endure – and the essence of morale is that it should endure – have certain foundations. These foundations are spiritual, intellectual, and material, and that is the order of their importance. Spiritual first, because only spiritual foundations can stand real strain. Next intellectual, because men are swayed by reason as well as feeling. Material last – important, but last – because the very highest kinds of morale are often met when material conditions are lowest.

I remember sitting in my office and tabulating these foundations of morale something like this:

1. *Spiritual*
   (a) There must be a great and noble object.
   (b) Its achievement must be vital.
   (c) The method of achievement must be active, aggressive.
   (d) The man must feel that what he is and what he does matters directly towards the attainment of the object.

2. *Intellectual*
   (a) He must be convinced that the object can be obtained; that it is not out of reach.
   (b) He must see, too, that the organisation to which he belongs and which is striving to attain the object is an efficient one.
   (c) He must have confidence in his leaders and know that whatever dangers and hardships he is called upon to suffer, his life will not be lightly flung away.

3. *Material*
   (a) The man must feel that he will get a fair deal from his commmanders and from the army generally.
   (b) He must, as far as humanly possible, be given the best weapons and equipment for his task.
   (c) His living and working conditions must be made as good as they can be.

It was one thing thus neatly to marshal my principles but quite another to develop them, apply them, and get them recognised by the whole army.

At any rate, our spiritual foundation was a firm one. I use the word spiritual, not in its strictly religious meaning, but as belief in a cause

...

We had this; and we had the advantage over our enemies that ours was based on real, not false, spiritual values. If ever an army fought in a just cause we did. We coveted no man's country; we wished to impose no form of government on any nation. We fought for the clean, the decent, the free things of life, for the right to live our lives in our own way as others could live theirs, to worship God in what faith we chose, to be free in body and mind, and for our children to be free. We fought only because the powers of evil had attacked these things. No matter what the religion or race of any man in the Fourteenth Army, he *must* feel this, feel that he had indeed a worthy cause, and that if he did not defend it life would not be worth living for him or for his children. Nor was it enough to have a worthy cause. It must be positive, aggressive, not a mere passive, defensive, anti-something feeling. So our object became not to defend India, to stop the Japanese advance, or even to occupy Burma, but to destroy the Japanese Army, to smash it as an evil thing.

The fighting soldier facing the enemy can see that what he does, whether he is brave or craven, matters to his comrades and directly influences the result of the battle. It is harder for the man working on the road far behind, the clerk checking stores in a dump, the headquarter's telephone operator monotonously plugging through his calls, the sweeper carrying out his menial tasks, the quartermaster's orderly issuing bootlaces in a reinforcement camp – it is hard for these and a thousand others to see that they too matter. Yet every one of the half-million in the army – and it was many more later – had to be made to see where his task fitted into the whole, to realise what depended on it, and to feel pride and satisfaction in doing it well.

Now these things, while the very basis of morale, because they were purely matters of feeling and emotion, were the most difficult to put over, especially to the British portion of the army. The problem was how to instil or revive their belief in the men of many races who made up the Fourteenth Army. I felt there was only one way to do it, by a direct approach to the individual men themselves. Not by written exhortations, by wireless speeches, but by informal talks and contacts between troops and commanders. There was nothing new in this; my corps and divisional commanders and others right down the scale were already doing it. It was the way we had held the troops together in the worst days of the 1942 retreat; we remained an army then only because the men saw and knew their commanders. All I did now was to encourage my commanders to increase these activities, unite them in a common approach to the problem, in the points that they would stress, and in the action they would take to see that principles became action, not merely words.

Yet they began, as most things do, as words. We, my commanders and I, talked to units, to collections of officers, to headquarters, to little groups of men, to individual soldiers casually met as we moved around ...

General Slim then described the reactions of different nationalities to these addresses.

I learnt, too, that one did not need to be an orator to be effective. Two things were necessary: first to know what you were talking about, and, second and most important, to believe it yourself. I found that if one kept the bulk of one's talk to the material things that men were interested in, food, pay, leave, beer, mails, and the progress of operations, it was safe to end on a higher note – the spiritual foundations – and I always did.

To convince the men in the less spectacular or less obviously important jobs that they were very much part of the army, my commanders and I made it our business to visit these units, to show an interest in them, and to tell them how we and the rest of the army depended upon them. There are in the army, and for that matter any big organisation, very large numbers of people whose existence is only remembered when something for which they are responsible goes wrong. Who thinks of the telephone operator until he fails to get his connection, of the cipher officer until he makes a mistake in his decoding, of the orderlies who carry papers about a big headquarters until they take them to the wrong people, of the cook until he makes a particularly foul mess of the interminable bully? Yet they *are* important. It was harder to get this over to the Indian subordinates. They were often drawn from the lower castes, quite illiterate, and used to being looked down upon by their higher-caste fellow-townsmen or villagers. With them, I found I had great success by using the simile of a clock. 'A clock is like an army,' I used to tell them. 'There's a main spring, that's the Army Commander, who makes it all go; then there are other springs, driving the wheels round, those are his generals. The wheels are the officers and men. Some are big wheels, very important, they are the chief staff officers and the colonel sahibs. Other wheels are little ones, that do not look at all important. They are like you. Yet stop one of those little wheels and see what happens to the rest of the clock! They *are* important!'

We played on this very human desire of every man to feel himself and his work important, until one of the most striking things about our army was the way the administrative, labour and non-combatant units acquired a morale which rivalled that of the fighting formations. They felt they shared directly in the triumphs of the Fourteenth Army and that its success and its honour were in their hands as much as anybody's. Another way in which we made every man feel he was part of the show was by keeping him, whatever his rank, as far as was practicable in the picture of what was going on around him. This, of course, was easy with staff officers and similar people by means of conferences held daily or weekly when each branch or department could explain what it had been doing and what it hoped to do. At these conferences they not only discussed things as a team, but what was equally important, actually *saw* themselves as a team. For the men, talks by their officers and visits to the information centres which were established in every unit took the place of those conferences.

It was in these ways we laid the spiritual foundations, but that was not enough; they would have crumbled without the others, the intellectual and the material. Here we had first to convince the doubters that our object, the destruction of the Japanese Army in battle, was practicable. We had to a great extent frightened ourselves by our stories of the superman. Defeated soldiers in their own defence have to protest that their adversary was something out of the ordinary, that he had all the advantages of preparation, equipment, and terrain, and that they themselves suffered from every corresponding handicap. The harder they have run away, the more they must exaggerate the unfair superiority of the enemy. Thus many of those who had scrambled out of Burma without waiting to get to grips with the invader, or who had been in the rear areas in 1943, had the most hair-raising stories of Japanese superefficiency. Those of us who had really fought him, believed that man for man our soldiers could beat him at his own jungle game, and that, in intelligence and skill, we could excel and outwit him.

We were helped, too, by a very cheering piece of news that now reached us, and of which, as a morale raiser, I made great use. In August and September 1942, Australian troops had, at Milne Bay in New Guinea, inflicted on the Japanese their first undoubted defeat on land ...

General Slim also ordered aggressive patrolling in the forward areas, and larger scale actions designed to build up unit and formation self-confidence.

We had laid the first of our intellectual foundations of morale; everyone knew we could defeat the Japanese; our object was attainable.

The next foundations, that the men should feel that they belonged to an efficient organisation, that the Fourteenth Army was well run and would get somewhere, followed partly from these minor successes. At the same time the gradual, but very noticeable, improvements that stemmed from General Giffard's re-organisation of the rear areas, and Snelling's and the line of communication staff's almost incredible achievements within the army itself, were making themselves felt. Rations did improve, though still far below what they should be; mail began to arrive more regularly; there were even signs of a welfare service ...

Other steps towards higher morale included the improvement of rest and training facilities, the reinforcement of disciplinary standards such as saluting, and the institution of a theatre newspaper. When Admiral Mountbatten arrived to take command of the newly-formed South East Asia Command, his presence and personal talks to the troops proved to be a 'final tonic' to morale. Meanwhile supplies or material gradually improved, but due to the priority of the war in Europe they remained small compared to the needs of the Fourteenth Army, a reason which General Slim was careful to explain to the soldiers.

These things were frankly put to the men by their commanders at all levels and, whatever their race, they responded. In my experience it is not so much asking men to fight or work with inadequate or obsolete equipment that lowers morale but the belief that those responsible are accepting such a state of affairs. If men realise that everyone above them and behind them is flat out to get the things required for them, they will do wonders, as my men did, with the meagre resources they have instead of sitting down moaning for better.

I do not say that the men of the Fourteenth Army welcomed difficulties, but they grew to take a fierce pride in overcoming them by determination and ingenuity. From start to finish they had only two items of equipment that were never in short supply: their brains and their courage. They lived up to the unofficial motto I gave them, 'God helps those who help themselves.' Anybody could do an easy job, we told them. It would take real men to overcome the shortages and difficulties we should be up against — the tough chap for the tough job! We had no *corps d'élite* which got preferential treatment; the only units who got that were the ones in front. Often, of course, they went short owing to the difficulties of transportation, but, if we had the stuff and could by hook or crook get it to them they had it in preference to those farther back. One of the most convincing evidences of morale was how those behind — staffs and units — accepted this, and deprived themselves to ensure it. I indulged in a little bit of theatricality in this myself. When any of the forward formations had to go on half rations, as throughout the campaign they often did, I used to put my headquarters on half rations too. It had little practical effect, but as a gesture it was rather valuable, and it did remind the young staff officers with healthy appetites that it was urgent to get the forward formations back to full rations as soon as possible.

The fair deal meant, too, no distinction between races or castes in treatment. The wants and needs of the Indian, African, and Gurkha soldier had to be looked after as keenly as those of his British comrade. This was not always easy as many of our staff officers, having come straight from home, were, with the best will in the world, ignorant of what these wants were. There were a few, too, who thought that all Indian or African troops required was a bush to lie under and a handful of rice to eat. The Indian soldier's needs are not so numerous or elaborate as the Britisher's, but his morale can be affected just as severely by lack of them.

In another respect we had no favourites. I was frequently asked as the campaign went on, 'Which is your crack division?' I always replied 'All my divisions are crack divisions!' This was true in the sense that at some time or other every division I ever had in the Fourteenth Army achieved some outstanding feat of arms, and it might be any division that at any given period was leading the pack. The men of each division believed that their division was the best in the whole army, and it was right they should, but it is very unwise to let any formation, however good, be publicly recognised as better than the others. The same thing applies to units, and this was especially important where we had fighting together battalions with tremendous names handed down from the past, newly raised ones with their traditions yet to make, men of recognised martial races and others drawn from sources that had up to now no military record. They all got the same treatment and they were all judged by results. Sometimes the results were by no means in accordance with accepted tables of precedence.

The individual, we took pains to ensure, too, was judged on his merits without any undue prejudice in favour of race, caste, or class. This is not always as easy as it sounds or as it ought to be, but I think, promotion, for instance, went by merit whether the officer was British or Indian, Regular or emergency commissioned. In an army of hundreds of thousands many injustices to individuals were bound to occur but, thanks mainly to officers commanding units, most of the Fourteenth Army would, I believe, say that on the whole they had as individuals, a reasonably fair deal. At any rate we did our best to give it to them.

In these and in many other ways we translated my rough notes on the foundations of moral, spiritual, intellectual, and material, into a fighting spirit for our men and a confidence in themselves and their leaders that was to impress our friends and surprise our enemies.

Lord Attlee

Lord Attlee served as Labour Prime Minister of Great Britain from 1945 to 1951. This extract is taken from 'In the Driver's Seat', an article which appeared in *The Observer Week-end Review* on 18 October 1964. It is printed here not to suggest that Lord Attlee was a better leader than any other prime minister, but because it contains the reflections of a leader on a group composed of other senior leaders. Again the leader's concerns with task, team maintenance and individual needs may be picked out in their distinctive form in this situation, and some of the functions by which they were met. Choosing members of the team is often a key function, and Lord Attlee's remarks upon this matter are full of interest.

In a way it [forming a Cabinet] is more difficult than winning the election, because in choosing his Cabinet the Prime Minister is on his own, and carries the can for his mistakes. Once the appointments have been made, he is going to be stuck with them for a considerable period. If some of the choices soon look unsatisfactory, he cannot start sacking them right away. However, he must give each man a chance, and stand the racket while he improves, grows to the job. If the Prime Minister starts pushing his departmental heads, the morale of the Cabinet as a whole will suffer.

The qualities of the ideal Cabinet Minister are: judgment, strength of character, experience of affairs, and an understanding of ordinary people.

Judgment is necessary because the Cabinet is the instrument by which decisions are reached with a view to action, and decisions stem from judgment. A Cabinet is not a place for eloquence – one reason why good politicians are not always good Cabinet Ministers. It is judgment which is needed to make important decisions on imperfect knowledge in a limited time. Men either have it, or they haven't. They can develop it, if they have it; but cannot acquire it if they haven't.

Strength of character is required to stand up to criticism from other Cabinet members, pressure from outside groups, and the advice of civil servants.

It is also necessary when policies, on which the Cabinet has agreed, are going through the doldrums, or are beginning to fail. A man of character will neither be, nor seem to be, bowed down by this. Nor will he be blown about by 'every wind of vain doctrine'.

Lord Attlee then discussed the value of a wide general experience in cabinet members.

It is more important that the Cabinet discussion should take place, so to speak, at a higher level than the information and opinions provided by the various departmental briefs. A collection of departmental Ministers does not make a Cabinet. A Cabinet consists only of responsible human beings. And it is their thinking and judgment in broad terms that make a Government tick, not arguments about the recommendations of civil servants. It is interesting to note that quite soon a Cabinet begins to develop a group personality. The rôle of the Prime Minister is to cultivate this, if it is efficient and right-minded; to do his best to modify it, if it is not.

While a collection of departmental heads mouthing their top civil servants' briefs is unsatisfactory, a collection of Ministers who are out of touch with administration tends to be unrealistic. And a Minister who has an itch to run everybody else's department as well as, or in preference to his own, is just a nuisance. Some men will be ready to express a view about everything. They should be discouraged. If necessary, I would shut them up. Once is enough. Ernie Bevin held forth on a variety of subjects, but Ernie had an extraordinary variety of practical knowledge.

It is a curious thing that nearly every Cabinet throws up at least one man, whether he is a departmental Minister or not, of whom a newcomer might ask, 'What is *he* doing here?' He is there because he is wise. You will hear a junior Cabinet Minister being told by the Prime Minister, perhaps, 'If you are going to do that, old boy, you would be well advised to have a talk with X.'

The ability to talk attractively in Cabinet is not essential. Being able to put a case clearly and succinctly and simply is what counts. The Cabinet is certainly not the place for rhetoric. Though an excellent head of department and a conciliator of genius, Nye Bevan used to talk a bit too much occasionally. Usually he was extremely good, often wise, and sometimes extremely wise; '75 per cent of political wisdom is a sense of priorities,' I remember him saying once – an admirable remark, and good advice for Cabinet Ministers.

The occasions when he talked too much were when he got excited because he felt that our policies were falling short of the pure milk of the word. This goes for most such interruptions, and a Prime Minister should try to avoid these time-consuming expressions of guilt – or electoral fear – by trying to reassure from time to time the pure in heart who feel the Government is backsliding.

However, you cannot choose people according to what makes an ideal Cabinet Minister. In the first place, you must choose people with regard to keeping balance within the party. This need not be overdone. It is a matter of democratic common-sense, not a craven below-the-scenes manipulation. It would not do to have all trade unionists in a Labour Cabinet, or all constituency members, or all middle-class intellectuals, or all ornaments of the Co-operative Party. Some working-class trade unionists are in fact honorary members of the intelligentsia – Nye again – while I have known upper-class intellectuals try desperately to behave like horny handed sons of toil
...

A Prime Minister must have his own view of a man's capacity to serve in the Cabinet. Nor can selected members always have the job they want. High qualifications are required for the most important posts in the Cabinet.

The Cabinet usually meets once a week. That should be enough for regular meetings, and should be if they grasp from the start what they are there for. They should be back at their work as soon as possible, and a Prime Minister should put as little as possible in their way. We started sharp at 11, and rose in time for lunch. Even in a crisis, another couple of meetings should be enough in the same week: if there is a crisis, the less talk the better.

The Prime Minister shouldn't speak too much himself in Cabinet. He should start the show or ask somebody else to do so, and then intervene only to bring out the more modest chaps who, despite their seniority, might say nothing if not asked. And the Prime Minister must sum up. Experienced Labour leaders should be pretty good at this; they have spent years attending debates at meetings of the Parliamentary Party and the National Executive, and have to sum *those* up. That takes some doing – good training for the Cabinet.

Particularly when a non-Cabinet Minister is asked to attend, especially if it is his first time, the Prime Minister may have to be cruel. The visitor may want to show how good he is, and go on too long. A good thing is to take no chance and ask him to send the Cabinet a paper in advance. The Prime Minister can then say, 'A very clear statement, Minister of—. Do you need to add anything?' in a firm tone of voice obviously expecting the answer, *No*. If somebody else looks like making a speech, it is sound to nip in with 'Has anybody any objection?' If somebody starts to ramble, a quick, 'Are you *objecting*? You're not? Right. Next business,' and the Cabinet can move on.

It is essential for the Cabinet to move on, leaving in its wake a trail of clear, crisp, uncompromising decisions. This is what government is about. And the challenge to democracy is how to get it done quickly.

An Unknown Worker

This description of leadership on the shop floor is taken from J. A. C. Brown's book 'The Social Psychology of Industry', pages 83 and 84.

Briefly, it was found that absenteeism and high labour turnover occurred predominantly amongst those workers who did not make a team, who had not managed to fit into any group (either because of personal peculiarities or, more usually, because they had not been given the opportunity to do so). Having no social background, they had no feelings of loyalty and took little interest in what went on around them in the factory. On the other hand, investigation of a work team which had a production record 25 per cent above the average for the firm, showed up some of the factors which lead to good morale in the workshop. This group of men was recognised by the other workers as being somewhat clannish in that its members felt themselves to be superior to other groups – that is to say, they showed loyalty and pride of membership. The foreman of the department where the group was employed was a busy man and rarely visited it, while his senior assistant visited it only once a day. All the work was in charge of a man who had no official standing whatever, but was the natural leader of the team. This man had both the time (in that he was not distracted by the necessity of dealing with technical problems) and the ability to concentrate on group solidarity. He handled this problem in the following manner: all new employees were introduced to the other members of the team and placed with those who seemed likely to make congenial associates; later, they were taken to the end of the assembly line to see where the part being made in the department fitted into the finished article. All complaints were dealt with at once by the leader, but if they were beyond his powers to handle he referred them to higher authority. The individual workers were in these ways given significance (they saw how their job fitted into the whole), comradeship (in being members of a team), and an awareness of being fairly treated.

R.S.M. John Lord

Brought up a Grenadier Guardsman, Mr Lord became a Company Sergeant Major at Sandhurst and then R.S.M. of the 3rd Battalion of The Parachute Regiment at its birth in October 1941. Captured at Arnhem he was incarcerated along with about 2,000 others from the British 1st Airborne Division in Stalag XI B. Gradually, hut by hut, his leadership spread until he finally gained control of the entire camp of 17,000 prisoners of all nationalities. These extracts are from a tape-recording made by Mr Lord for the author in 1966.

Eventually we moved into the huts which had been occupied by the Poles from Warsaw. It was a much better compound. There were, I think, six huts planned to hold about 200 men each in this one compound, and there was an open space which we could use as a football field nearby. At the same time as numbers grew each hut had to hold about 450 men, the winter was very severe, food was extremely short … There were no cleaning materials, the huts tended to get into a terrible state, but we managed to get some twigs from working parties that went out to get wood, and so we would keep the floors swept.

I insisted, gradually, that every man made his bed properly with his one blanket, and that the bed space was his responsibility and was clean, and his little box in which he kept his precious articles was tidy, and that all the rooms were swept out. And I also insisted, this was very important too, although it caused a lot of grumbles at times, that all the windows were opened in the morning and that every man jack who could walk at all went out for exercise round the compound in the morning. This was vital to their health. I was greatly assisted in this by the encouragement of the British doctors with whom I worked closely, and who did a wonderful job under most difficult circumstances.

Here I would like to say how interesting it was to see the individual behaviour of the men, and this deeply applied as time wore on and men from other units started coming in. You could pick out men who came from what I would call good battalions, well disciplined, happy battalions. They tended, almost straight away, to start to look after themselves, to keep themselves clean and as decent as possible and to muck in. To the other men – now of course these are generalisations, I know, but I think that they are true – who probably came from not quite such a good unit, the opposite applied in so many cases.

All this caused a lot of comment among the senior members of my team. Because, having mentioned that we had moved into this large compound, this gave me an opportunity to start some sort of military organisation going under our own steam. I built a set-up with each hut rather like a company, and when the time came for the majority of warrant and non-commissioned officers to go to a more suitable camp for them, I had had time to get to know a lot of them much better. I knew some of my own men, of course. I went round having hand picked six or seven senior leaders I wanted, all WOs whom I judged would be the ones to carry out the task ahead of us, and I am very glad and proud to say that every man I approached without fail volunteered to stay with me, although he had every right to think that had he moved on to another camp, a British camp, the conditions would have been much better for him. Everyone stayed and what a magnificent job they did. We set up this military organisation, rather similar to the one to which the men were accustomed, and in addition I sent one of my own Company Sergeant Majors from the Battalion up to the Hospital to do the administration there. He did a magnificent job. So that was a start.

Mr Lord then established his right to take the first part of the morning Roll Call parade before handing it over to the Germans. This meant that British soldiers heard words of command from their own Warrant Officer. To make sure that every man knew what Mr Lord's aims were he set up informal briefing groups in every hut. Meanwhile he made certain that his own personal turnout was as smart as possible in the circumstances. Daily bugle calls sounded on an old Belgian trumpet by a British prisoner served not only to maintain morale but also to impress the other nationalities, as did the simple military honours insisted upon by Mr Lord at the frequent funerals. Concerts and soccer matches also enhanced morale when the Germans would allow them. Most important of all, food rations, Red Cross parcels and firewood had to be seen to be justly distributed. In this situation the leader had to be ruthless in putting the group interest before that of any particular individual.

One of the worst offences one can commit in circumstances such as these is to steal another man's ration. Now several cases of this occurred and it was extremely difficult to detect and to prove. However, one day one of the CSMs came to me and told me he was quite convinced that a certain man, who had come into the camp recently, was responsible for one of these thefts. On the information I received I interviewed this man and questioned him for a couple of hours or more in the evening by the light of a small lamp, questioning and questioning until eventually this little man broke down and admitted that he had stolen this ration.

So here was a self-confessed thief, a very serious problem which could lead to the most terrible consequences of fighting and distrust and so on in the camp. What was I going to do about it? I never had any powers of punishment in those circumstances. I could tell him he would be court-martialled after the war, but what was the good of that? They couldn't care less. It had to be done by leadership and example. So, rightly or wrongly, I decided to take a drastic step. I ordered him to report to me next morning.

I went out on the morning roll call at 7 o'clock in the first light and I made him stand behind me. Having called the parade to attention, and stood the men easy, I got them all to look in my direction and produced this little man and said, 'Here you are, mark him well, this man is a thief'. I briefly and without elaboration told them what had happened. Now, some people nowadays would say, 'What a dreadful thing to brand a man like that.' But which is more important, the interests of the men as a whole, or this individual? I was very worried in myself afterwards whether or not I had gone too far, but I am quite sure I hadn't, because I don't think we had one more case of thieving after that. And, of course, it may have prevented a tremendous lot more thieving, and, what is worse, violence.

With the New Year of 1945 allied prisoners began to arrive in Stalag XI B, some captured during the initially successful German offensive in the Ardennes, and some from Poland, now threatened by the Russians.

It is of these men that I want to speak now because I had this responsibility completely upon my shoulders alone. The first lot who came in, after the New Year of course, were in good shape, they had come by train ... The next sight to greet my eyes was the first arrival of those who had had to march on foot for all those hundreds and hundreds of miles. I really never would have believed it possible. I saw some of them in the hospital, and saw those who succumbed, and I later saw the photographs of Belsen camp, and I can assure everybody that many of these men were in exactly the same state as those victims of Belsen. They were put into the huge marquees with only straw on the ground. Major Smith and his doctors went down. He came back and said, 'Mr Lord, I have segregated 300 of these men, and if these 300 do not receive, immediately, more food, and are not moved into better accommodation, they will die'. He was quite adamant about this.

What was I to do? First of all I put the word round our men what the position was. I shall never forget it. They quite voluntarily offered, each man, to give up a little, a very little, of their own food for these 300 men. Secondly, I went down to the first lot of British prisoners who had come by train, that I have just mentioned, in the good accommodation and I put the case to them. And 300 of the fittest came forward and volunteered to move out into the marquees, and remember it was jolly cold and it was very uncomfortable, but they volunteered without any pressure from me, after I had spoken to them collectively. These 300 men would at least have got more food and we could have managed a little bit of Red Cross stuff for them, and they would have moved into better accommodation. And this meant that, probably, the majority of those lives would be saved. So here we were. I went to the German Commandant and stated the case to him, quite simply, without embellishments. And to my horror he refused to allow the transfer. This was absolutely incredible and fantastic. I pressed the case; he lost his temper; I went away; and I must have gone up three more times to see him, so worried was I about this serious situation. But he would not allow the move.

I went down to the other two compounds, the one with the marquees with the very, very sick men in, and the one with the volunteers who had offered to change over the accommodation. And

I moved the fit men from their compound to the marquees without German permission. I had to do it. I was taking an awful chance, but what was this chance compared with the chance of saving some 300 men?

Of course the repercussions on the German Commandant's side were violent, absolutely violent. But I don't want to go into that. We succeeded, and the majority of those men came home fit, or reasonably fit and well. We lost, I suppose, of that 300 men about one tenth, about 30. So something was achieved. It was known, not only to my men, the actions that I had taken but also to every single man in that prison camp.

As time went on, it bore more and more upon me, particularly as it was obvious that the British and American armies were going to advance as the weather improved, what was going to happen in the camp when the time came, when the war, possibly suddenly, collapsed or came to an end? It could quite possibly do so before we were reached by our own allies. What was going to happen in the camp? What were the plans? There were several possibilities. One grave possibility was this. Opposite the camp, across the road were magnificent barracks in which were housed the SS Panzer Grenadiers, young Hitler fanatics. Now suppose Germany suddenly capitulated, what would the reactions of these young men be? Would they remember Hitler's words of dragging Europe down in flames with the Reich? This was not the realms of fancy; this was a distinct possibility and was not only my thought alone. It was the thought throughout the camp. Would they turn their weapons against the prisoners in this prison camp, all these different nationalities, in revenge and exterminate them? But what had been done about it? I could find out nothing. There had been no liaison between nationalities; I asked questions round about and literally nothing had been done. What were we going to do? Were we just going to sit there and hope for the best? This did not seem to me to be good enough. But who was going to do it? And how were we going to set about it? Well I was spoken to, talked to, by great friends of mine, Bill Kibble, Don Rice and others, and they impressed upon me, although I suppose secretly in myself I realised this, that I must be the man to get things organised. So I asked Sgt. Major Wickham, who knew so many of these other nationalities and whose great asset was that he knew who could be trusted. If we were going to lay plans for our actions when the camp was liberated or when the war finished, if that happened before, then those in our confidence must be absolutely reliable men. There must be no chance of one whisper, because if one whisper had got to the ears of the German authorities Heaven knows what their punishment of us would have been.

Sam Wickham sought out a representative from each of the nationalities whom he believed could be trusted. Let's see, there was the Frenchman (we knew we had a good representative there), a Russian, a Serbian doctor, a Belgian, a Dutchman and one or two others in the Committee. We didn't have on the Committee a member of the Polish community and I shouldn't like to be misunderstood about this, because I knew nothing about the Poles at all; I merely acted on the advice I'd received. But it should be realised how extremely dangerous this was.

So that was the Committee formed. Previous to this, I had had made a map of the camp in which every sentry post was plotted and everything from a security point of view I had worked out. So I set down on paper what I considered should be done ...

Mr Lord's careful preparations received an unexpected boost when the Commandant asked him to provide unarmed sentries to assist the Germans in keeping order in such matters as food distribution. Five days before the first British tanks arrived Mr Lord and his staff were in virtual control of the 17,000 men in the camp.

All the administration, the feeding and so on we controlled. From the warehouses opposite at the SS Barracks we brought out the food and the clothing, and we shared it out among the members of all nationalities of that camp. And there was no trouble at all that could not be controlled. These were very, very busy days. Five days.

In fact it was on the 16th April, early on, that the news had improved of the advance of the British Army. I received news very early that the British Army were just down the road. I went to the front gate, everything laid on, our sentries there, all nations in their own compounds under control of their own excellent men; in other words everything was in order. I waited. And up the road came a British tank. In the forelager our men were on duty, and the barbed wire inside the forelager was thronged with all these other nationalities. I shall never forget this tank arriving at the front gate with some others behind. The first figure out of that tank, begrimed and dusty, was a corporal of the 8th Hussars, old friends of my days in Egypt, and I was delighted. That corporal, having travelled, fought and campaigned and rushed through in the later stages, jumped out of his tank, spotted me at the gate, and he came up and he stood to attention to report himself. Now this was a wonderful thing for these other nationalities to see, this action by a begrimed corporal ... When these tanks arrived, we disarmed the German sentries who willingly gave up their arms, and our men took them over. That was the first thing. I took it upon myself to lower the swastika of the Reich and in its place to hoist up our own home-made Union Jack, which had been placed on the coffins of so many funerals. As I raised it and looked up the flagstaff towards the blue heavens I cannot describe my feelings, they were feelings of thankfulness and relief, and I hope I am not misunderstood if in myself I gave thanks to God for this moment ...

Thus with all the possibilities of what might have happened, of internal strife through the liquor which was obviously being brought into the camp, and a thousand and one things, we remained in control and until the day I left, of those 17,000 odd men of so many different nationalities and characters, not one man was injured by any offensive action, and not one man was killed. And when I look back on it I think, 'My word! how different it could have been'. And therefore we had cause to be thankful that things had worked out so well for our well-being in the long run.

Field Marshal Lord Montgomery

Lieut. General Sir Brian Horrocks commanded 13 Corps under Field Marshal Lord Montgomery (as he later became) at the battles of Alam Halfa andd Alamein. These passages from his autobiography *A Full Life* described the impact of Lord Montgomery's leadership upon both him and the Eighth Army. The first extract illustrates the way a senior leader met both the task and individual needs by developing the professional ability of a subordinate.

On the day after the battle [Alam Halfa] I was sitting in my headquarters purring with satisfaction. The battle had been won and I had not been mauled in the process. What could be better? Then in came a liaison officer from 8th Army headquarters bringing me a letter in Monty's even hand. This is what he said:

'Dear Jorrocks,

Well done — but you must remember that you are now a corps commander and not a divisional commander ...'

He went on to list four or five things which I had done wrong, mainly because I had interfered too much with the tasks of my subordinate commanders. The purring stopped abruptly. Perhaps I wasn't quite such a heaven-sent general after all. But the more I thought over the battle, the more I realised that Monty was right. So I rang him up and said, 'Thank you very much.'

I mention this because Montgomery was one of the few commanders who tried to train the people who worked under him. Who else, on the day after his first major victory, which had altered the whole complexion of the war in the Middle East, would have taken the trouble to write a letter like this in his own hand to one of his subordinate commanders?

The psychological effect of this victory was terrific, for nothing succeeds like success, particularly in war. Troops will always follow a successful general. Monty had unquestionably won the first round in his contest with the Desert Fox; what is more, he had won it in exactly the manner in which he had said beforehand he would win it. Everyone felt that new dynamic force had entered into the tired, rather stale old body of the 8th Army. I, of course, also benefited from the change of heart, and from now on things became much easier.

In Tripoli, after the successful 'break through' at Alamein, Horrocks witnessed an example of the army's affection for its commander — a standing ovation by all ranks before and after a concert-party's performance.

And here in the 8th Army was the same outward and visible sign of the greatest battle-winning factor of all — a spirit of complete trust, confidence and affection within a formation. This sort of happy family atmosphere is common enough in divisions which have lived, trained and grown up together, but it is comparatively rare in higher formations. I know of only two in our army where it existed strongly during the last war — Montgomery's 8th Army and Slim's 14th Army. And it is significant that both men took over their commands at a time when things were going badly and morale was low.

Monty had the harder passage of the two to start with. As we know, the old desert sweats did not welcome him with open arms — far from it. Yet only a few months later, here in Tripoli was this remarkable demonstration of personal affection.

How had it been done? Cynics will say that Montgomery was successful, and that soldiers will always follow a general who wins battles. Wellington's troops never loved him, yet they would have followed him anywhere. I would say that there were four main qualities of leadership which bound the 8th Army to Monty.

First. When all was confusion he had the supreme gift of reducing the most complex situation to simplicity. More than any other man I have ever met he was able to sit back and *think,* with the result that he was never deluded by 'the trees'.

Second. He took infinite pains to explain to every man in the Army exactly what was required of him.

Third. He was very tough mentally, both towards the enemy and, perhaps more important still, towards the political dictation from the United Kingdom. No amount of urging would ever induce him to launch his army into battle before it was ready.

Finally. He was obviously a complete master of his craft, the craft of war.

T. E. Lawrence

Field Marshal Viscount Allenby gave his fullest assessment of T. E. Lawrence in a broadcast which *The Times* reported on 20 May 1935. Despite criticism of the 'Lawrence legend', his leadership has never been doubted, a fact attested by Lord Allenby – no mean judge.

When first I met him, in the summer of 1917, he had just returned from a venturesome raid behind the Turkish front ... Lawrence was under my command, but, after acquainting him with my strategical plan, I gave him a free hand. His co-operation was marked by the utmost loyalty, and I never had anything but praise for his work, which, indeed, was invaluable throughout the campaign.

He was the mainspring of the Arab movement. He knew their language, their manners, their mentality; he understood and shared their merry, sly humour; in daring he led them, in endurance he equalled, if not surpassed, their strongest. Though in complete sympathy with his companions, and sharing to the full with them hardship and danger, he was careful to maintain the dignity of his position as Confidential Adviser to the Emir Feisal. Himself an Emir, he wore the robes of that rank, and kept up a suitable degree of state. His own bodyguard, men of wild and adventurous spirit, were all picked by Lawrence personally. Mounted on thoroughbred camels, they followed him in all his daring rides; and among those reckless desert rangers there was none who would not have willingly died for their chief. In fact, not a few lost their lives through devotion to him and in defence of his person. The shy and retiring scholar – archaeologist – philosopher was swept by the tide of war into a position undreamt of ... and there shone forth a brilliant tactician, with a genius for leadership. Such men win friends – such also find critics and detractors. But the highest reward for success is the inward knowledge that it has been rightly won. Praise or blame was rewarded with indifference by Lawrence. He did his duty as he saw it before him. He has left to us who knew and admired him, a beloved memory.

Lieut. Colonel W. F. Stirling served with T. E. Lawrence in the desert, and recorded his impression of him as a leader in *T. E. Lawrence By His Friends.* Lawrence not only saw the task more clearly than others and how it could be achieved, but also possessed a remarkable intuitive sense of what was happening in the minds of the group. Above all he led by example.

It was my great good fortune to be appointed General Staff Officer to the Arab Forces in the early part of 1918. From then throughout the final phase of the Arab revolt on till the capture of Damascus, I worked, travelled, and fought alongside Lawrence. Night after night we lay wrapped in our blankets under the cold stars of the desert.

At these times one learns much of a man. Lawrence took the limelight from those of us professional soldiers who were fortunate enough to serve with him, but never once have I heard even a whisper of jealousy. We sensed that we were serving with a man immeasurably our superior.

As I see it, his outstanding characteristic was his clarity of vision and his power of shedding all unessentials from his thoughts, added to his uncanny knowledge of what the other man was thinking and doing.

Think of it! A young second lieutenant of the Egyptian Expeditionary Force goes down the Arabian coast to where a sporadic revolt of the Western Arabs had broken out against their Turkish masters. Then, with the help of a few British officers, all senior to himself, and professional soldiers, who willingly placed themselves under his general guidance, he galvanises the Arab revolt into a coherent whole. By his daring courage, his strategy, his novel tactics, he welds the turbulent Arab tribes into a fighting machine of such value that he is able to immobilise two Turkish divisions and provide a flank force for Lord Allenby's final advance through Palestine and Syria, the value of which that great general acknowledged again and again.

No one, looking at Lawrence, would have considered him strong physically. The fact remains that this man was to break all the records of Arabia for speed and endurance. The great sagas sung throughout the desert of phenomenal rides carried out by dispatch riders and dating back to the days of Caliph Haroun Al-Raschid have been completely eclipsed by Lawrence's achievements. On one occasion he averaged 100 miles a day for three consecutive days. Such endurance as this is almost incredible. I myself have ridden 50 miles in a night, but never do I want to do it again. The difficulty is to keep awake. After the bitter glow of the desert night when the sun begins to rise and a warm glow envelops everything, the urge to sleep becomes a veritable torture. If you sleep you are apt to fall, and it is a long way from the top of a camel to the ground.

What was it that enabled Lawrence to seize and hold the imagination of the Arabs? It is a difficult question to answer. The Arabs were noted individualists, intractable to a degree, and without any sense of discipline. Yet it was sufficient for almost any one of us to say that Lawrence wanted something done, and forthwith it was done.

How did he gain this power? The answer may partly be that he represented the heart of the Arab movement for freedom, and the Arabs realised that he had vitalised their cause; that he could do everything and endure everything just a little better than the Arabs themselves; that by his investment with the gold dagger of Mecca he ranked with the Ashraf or the descendants of the Prophet, and the Emir Feisal treated him as a brother and an equal.

But chiefly, I think, we must look for the answer in Lawrence's uncanny ability to sense the feelings of any group of men in whose company he found himself; his power to probe behind their minds and to uncover the well-springs of their actions.

Lord Hunt

Lord Hunt led the first successful assault on Mount Everest in 1953. His views are drawn from 'The Top' in the *Observer Weekend Review* of 21 June 1965. This article took the form of a reported interview between Lord Hunt and Kenneth Harris.

Climbing with companions creates a wonderfully close relationship, of co-operation and sharing, which is rarely found in everyday life. To tackle a hard climb is a test of each individual's intellect, experience, will, guts and skill. But each is dependent on the other; not only for achievement, but for mutual security and survival.

This is the quintessence of team-work, in which each is playing an equal part, and all have complete confidence in one another. It is the very opposite of the gang idea ...

Other people come into your mountain picture both because you all enjoy doing it – because you are kindred spirits – and because with rare exceptions a man cannot safely and successfully achieve a big climb 'solo'.

On short rock-climbs it is somewhat different, but the principle and the spirit of the thing is, or should be, the same. I personally don't care for the competitive spirit which has crept in, with the increasing numbers of ever-rising standards of technical performance of our younger climbers. In the Soviet Union climbing is organised on a competitive basis even for the biggest mountains.

I have never seen mountaineering like that. The contest in mountaineering is between you and the mountain: or, better, between two sides within yourself. Not between you and your fellow men. Other human beings come into the relationship not as competitors, but as collaborators.

Lord Hunt was then asked if there was any 'fundamental difference' between tackling a mountain in Cumberland or Derbyshire and climbing Everest. Besides the physical contrasts Lord Hunt mentioned the psychological stress encountered at high altitudes.

The combined effect of the rarefied atmosphere, prolonged risk and discomfort, make people edgy and awkward. You're inclined to be intolerant, to see things out of proportion. You can become very selfish – get peevish if you don't think you have had your fair share of the food; get a 'fixture' about someone else's personal habits – things which you would laugh at anybody for noticing, let alone resenting, in normal conditions.

I would like to make another point about speed in climbing: it is a tremendously important aspect of safety. On a short rock climb in this country you can afford to be slow and careful in climbing a route on a cliff of 500–600 feet in height; there is time to take every possible precaution. In the Alps, you must learn to move faster, even on difficult ground, or you will be benighted. You may plan to do so, but the longer you are on a climb, under tension, with the ever-present chance of bad weather setting in, the greater the risk.

On a Himalayan climb you are physically slowed down and the climb becomes more like a siege: advancing with your shelter, food and equipment slowly upwards by stages. So the climb takes a long time and the chances are much smaller on this account. Hence the need for oxygen, to reduce the risks, increase the pace and thus the chance of success.

Physiological wastage and deterioration are very marked in a man at 25,000 feet and above. The sheer effort of getting out of a sleeping bag, of putting on boots, of cooking, require an immense effort of will – let alone the climbing.

Harris 'I'm interested in this point about will-power. Is it just that you need more of it, the higher you go?'

Yes, for all the reasons I've mentioned. But to get to the top of the highest mountains you need to apply your will-power to the achievement well in advance – not merely when you are there. In a sense you have to do the climb in your mind before you start. This is because of the many circumstances which combine to reduce your powers of determination at the time, and which limit your ability to think clearly. Predetermination is a most important aspect of a successful Himalayan climb.

Harris 'You mentioned exposure. Do you mean getting cold?'

No; not just that. Exposure on mountains has two distinct meanings. There is the sense of being out on a vast precipice, on small holds or on steep ice, with space beneath your feet and the nearest level ground several hundreds of thousands of feet below you. That's one meaning of exposure.

Then there is the physiological sense, of prolonged exposure to the elements, not only to cold, but even more to damp and wind and the exposure of the mind to loneliness and fear. This kind of exposure is the combination of physical strain and psychological anxiety; it varies with the degree of risk and the time you continue to run it.

Common to both types of exposure, I believe, is fear. And the answer to both aspects of exposure is training – or experience – and good technique. Knowing what you should be doing in any predicament. It not only increases your chances of survival and focuses your faculties on what you are doing; it also exorcises the hypnotic spell which the sense of exposure casts about you. A number of accidents in our own hills are due to exposure, due to lack of experience.

Harris 'Is mountaineering really all about the facing of fear?'

No. The facing of fear is involved, inevitably. But that isn't the only motive. Most men who climb mountains don't do so because they are driven by a neurotic obsession with the need to face their own fears. Though, as I said to you earlier on, they find they have to do so, time and again, in the process of climbing mountains. But as I also said, a very powerful motive is the comradeship which comes from sharing a risk, which reduces your fears.

I would say another one is the exercise of judgment in the face of danger – the opposite of foolhardiness. It may require more moral courage to abandon a climb than to go on. It is the fanatic, or the addict who lives on fear like a drug, who insists on going on, sometimes to his death. Most men who climb mountains do so because they enjoy it and because they want to go on doing so.

Some years ago in the Caucasus, near the summit of a 17,000foot peak and with most of the technical difficulties behind and below us, a climbing party of which I was a member decided that the objective dangers of continuing to the top were such that we should turn back – only 600 feet below our much-desired goal. It was a hard decision, but this happens frequently to every mountaineer.

We went back to base. Our Russian friends were amazed that we had turned back and, I think, because we freely admitted it. For me, accepting that a situation is too big for me, and deliberately acting on that decision to bow to it, is moral victory. It is the open-eyed acceptance of one's circumstances and shortcomings which is the essence of humility. And humility is one of the ingredients of leadership.

This brings me back to your first question: Why do men climb mountains? It is just as well to answer it, for yourself, sooner rather than later, because the wrong reasons can lead to the wrong decisions at moments of crisis.

You see, Kenneth, to my mind it is not getting to the top of Everest that matters in life – it is why and how you try to get there. And sometimes it is better not to get to the top of a mountain at all. The victor on a mountain is the man who can conquer his own ambitions if need be.

3 Leadership selection

The last chapter gave the reader an opportunity to look at concrete examples which illustrate one or more of the aspects of leadership discussed in Chapter 1. It is hoped that these 'case-studies' will have put some flesh-and-blood on what otherwise might have remained a skeleton of theory: a delight to the anatomist but to no one else. In this chapter, which is largely historical, the first major experiment in applying the functional approach to leadership on a large scale will be recounted. The successful results of that experiment should also serve to remind us throughout the rest of the book that in considering the functional approach we are no longer dealing with an unproven theory on the nature of leadership, but one that has been imaginatively tried and tested for over a quarter of a century.

In May 1942 a group of psychologists and psychiatrists who had individually been 'called up' into the British Army for the duration of the Second World War, came together to devise a new method of officer selection. The old approach whereby the candidate for a commission was interviewed by a committee of senior officers intent on spotting his leadership 'qualities' had turned out to be ineffective: a large number of cadets selected in this way had had to be subsequently returned to their units as unfit for promotion. In place of these interviews the team devised a series of three-day conferences which became known as War Office Selection Boards (popularly known as 'Wosbies' from their initials, WOSB) from 1942. Fortunately one of this pioneering team, Dr Henry Harris, who himself served on the staff of a number of the early conferences attended by some 6,000 potential officers, has left us in his *The Group Approach to Leadership Testing,* an invaluable 'individual reaction to a collective effort', from which the subsequent quotations are taken.[1]

Before considering the WOSB method in detail, it is both interesting and worthwhile to note how the Army as a whole came to be persuaded to embrace the new approach. In his foreword to Dr Harris' book General Sir Ronald Adam, who was Adjutant General of the Forces 1941—46, gave a short account of this important piece of reform:

> The Army, during the early days of the war, carried out its selection of candidates for training as officers by interview boards. It was clear that these were not being successful. The failure rate at OCTUs [Officer Cadet Training Units] was high, and I know one course at an OCTU when 50 per cent of the course failed to pass out. This was a waste of time and had unfortunate effects even on good candidates, for the knowledge of a high failure rate did not give confidence to those attending.
>
> The interview had a deterrent effect on potential officers too. The average candidate did not feel that he was being given a fair chance, and there was a completely mistaken impression that the questions asked favoured the public school boy at the expense of those not so educated.
>
> The decision to change the old methods was taken after a trial board, when groups of presidents interviewed candidates and recorded their opinions separately. This showed so marked a difference of the opinions expressed on the same candidate that a new method had to be found.
>
> Early experiments were based on the test which the German Army had employed from 1923 onwards, apparently to their satisfaction, but these were not a success.
>
> The experimental board, which tested its methods by judging the officers attending a Company Commanders' School, produced a system that showed promising results, and these were continually improved until the system described by the author evolved.
>
> The first board set up under the new system proved that the candidate considered that it was a great improvement on the old interview. In the Command in which it worked the number of volunteers for commissions went up by 25 per cent. It is to be remembered that no one could be forced to take a commission.

Great efforts were made to validate results, but the Army was working against time in producing the continual stream of officers required by units, and validation could not be complete. To my mind the best validation was that the candidates going before the boards were satisfied that they had been given a fair chance to show their mettle and there was no discrimination or favouritism.

In these sentences we may see the sequence of reform in any organisation. It may be summarised as follows:

1 A widespread feeling that present methods are inadequate. The reformer must convert this feeling into conviction by producing some concrete evidence to support it.
2 A period of 'trial and error' experimentation. (This may overlap with 1.)
3 The production and trial running of a possible new method. A comparison of it with the old methods by some form of evaluation.
4 A general introduction of the new method, and a confirmation of its value. (In the case of WOSB note the importance of the candidate's reactions as one of the criteria for assessing the relative merits of the methods.)

Having briefly mentioned the then recent work of Kurt Lewin and others on the 'dynamics of inter-personal relationships' Dr Harris moved to a description of the theories upon which the WOSB method of selection was based. Although his background as a psychotherapist who had come to selection *via* group-psychotherapy conditioned the author's discussion of the small group (as he readily admits) it is clear that the research team behind WOSB had seized upon the key ideas of the situational and functional approaches, as described above in Chapter 1. It was understood, for example, that groups with different 'characteristic working situations' might require dissimilar leaders. In particular, small military groups which would have to operate in the stress conditions of the battlefield needed a leader who could function efficiently under stress. The essential problem was how to select the right man for the right group:

WOSB's answer was to test and evaluate him in the context of the small experimental group submitted to considerable time and problem stress, i.e. required to execute a difficult task against time.

That which one sought to observe and evaluate one might call his group-effectiveness, the sum total of his contribution to the group and its task. In this book we will differentiate group-effectiveness into the following components:

1 the effective *level of his functioning:* of his ability to contribute towards the functional aspect of the common task by planning and organising the available abilities, materials, time, etc.

2 his *group-cohesiveness* or ability to bind the group in the direction of the common task: to relate its members emotionally to each other and to the task.

3 his *stability* or ability to stand up to resistance and frustrations without serious impairment of (1) or (2) and the results of their interplay. *[Cf. 'Stability' is not a very dynamic term for what is essentially a dynamic concept, i.e. the active and continuous capacity not only to resist the deteriorating effects of stress, but also to return to normal when these have passed off ... Mental stamina might do (as a better word).]*

In short, in the WOSB technique of officer selection, one observes a *man* in a group-task in order to determine his group-effectiveness (in a particular field): one selects and *tests* him *in* a group *for* a group.

Although emphasising that it was too early to attempt a definitive formulation on the nature of leadership Dr Harris tentatively suggested that the whole of it may be represented by the concept of 'group-effectiveness' as analysed above. Both 'general factors' (those which determine a man's level of general leadership in a group, regardless of task) and 'specific factors' (those which equip him to lead in relation to certain tasks) could be described as 'group-effectiveness'. As Dr Harris wrote in a thoughtful summary:

One may suggest provisionally that leadership is the measure and degree of an individual's ability to influence – and be influenced by – a group in the implementation of a common task. This circumscribes three important aspects of leadership function: the individual, the group and the task: and indicates leadership as a functional relationship between these three basic variables.

In respect of the first two, it can only be highly effective if based on a sensitive understanding of the group's needs and on the ability to be influenced by it. The leader who dominates and drives a group towards an end they do not seek is unlikely to retain his leadership: his domination is brittle and will stand little stress. In so far as he considers the needs and mobilises the initiative of every member in the group; in so far as he helps them towards the goal which will give the group its greatest satisfaction and provide every member of it with the profound gratification of effective participation on his own level, and at his own optimum tempo ... his leadership is more real, more flexible, more resistant to stress, and incidentally more democratic – in the best sense of the word – than any leadership which is insensitive to the group in which it is exercised.

The 'Leaderless Group' or 'Stress Group Task' formed the most characteristic and long-enduring technique of selection employed by WOSB. In essence the idea was simple: eight candidates in an experimental 'micro-community' were given a series of tasks to perform while one or more observers stood by to spot and record the task and team maintenance (or group-cohesive) functions which each member naturally performed. The tasks varied in character (e.g. outdoor physical, indoor planning, and group-discussion), and also in the amount of stress latent in each situation, but the size and composition of the group remained the same. It appeared to be unorganised (with no appointed leaders) but as regards its task it could be directed or undirected:

In the WOSB Group Discussion – an indoor task involving the management of men and ideas – the discussion is usually undirected, i.e. no topic is set but the conversation is allowed to follow its own spontaneous directions. The session can be considerably improved by directing the last part of it: if, after 45 minutes of undirected discussion, a highly provocative topic of general interest – an emotional bomb – is tossed into the group for 10–15 minutes vivid high-tempo discussion.

The WOSB Progressive Group Task – an outdoor task involving the management of men and materials – is unorganised but directed. The task includes several sub-tasks or obstacles of progressive difficulty and increasing frustration. Tasks will naturally be related to the field of activity for which men are being selected. If they are to be soldiers, the testing pattern may include physical outdoor tasks though these are not indispensable, or even necessary: if they are to be civil servants, group discussions or planning projects will be more relevant.

The Human Problems Session — where the candidates took it in turns to act the parts of officer and 'stooge' discussing the latter's problem in an interview — had a Leaderless Group background. Like another important variant, the outdoor task with a designated leader, the Human Problems Session gave the selectors an opportunity to gain a clearer impression of a particular individual. Indeed, Dr Harris believed that 'this was possibly the most valuable single technique in WOSB procedure. One which could give more useful information in a given time than any other: though, being but one item in the entire observational field, it must of course be related to the rest of the evidence.'

What did the Stress Group Task, in its various guises, reveal? The answer of course is that this depended on what the selectors were looking for. In the early WOSB there appears to have been a strong emphasis on the value of the Stress Group Task for revealing those who were naturally 'group-cohesive' or 'group-disruptive'. Stress, it was hoped, would bare the candidate's degree of stability, that 'mental stamina' without which he could not bind the group together to face the external or internal threats of disintegration, and without which he could not accept and use his own inner anxiety in the moments of *impasse* or crisis to both understand and act with sympathy towards his men.

At a distance of over 20 years, it is possible to criticise some of the points of emphasis in the early WOSB doctrine, and also some of the experimental techniques which enjoyed a brief summer of popularity in the late 1940s. Certainly many of the individual tests, questionnaires and interviews which made up the rest of the three day board have long since been improved out of all recognition. But the essential contribution of WOSB — the functional understanding of leadership and its use as a selection device of the small group with a task to perform — have proved enormously successful. Even by 1949 this method had been adopted by the Royal Air Force, and by the French and Belgian Armies. In 1962 I was shown a number of small group obstacles erected by the officer selection wing of the United States Marine Corps at Quantico, Virginia, and the colonel in command informed me that he had visited a WOSB in England some years earlier to make drawings for them. In this country the ending of National Service reduced the need for a number of WOSBs and only one has been retained, now known as the RCB (Regular Commissions Board), which is situated at Westbury in Wiltshire. In the non-military sphere, the Civil Service, many large firms such as Unilever Ltd., and the Church of England, have adopted the WOSB approach, and adapted it with varying degrees of success.

One important question remains. How far are psychiatrists and psychologists necessary in leadership selection boards? Dr Harris expressed the view more than once in his book that their help was essential at future WOSBs, and in designing tests; he clearly assumed that there would be scientists of both kinds available at future conferences. In favour of this opinion we may note that leadership selection boards may easily lose their character and revert to the old interviewing, or subjective 'talent-spotting' methods where there is no one present on the staff with a firm grasp of the essential theory and the principles of applying it for that purpose. Only a historian, for example, would today be able to trace much connection between the Church of England ACCM (Advisory Council for the Church's Ministry) selection week-ends, and the early WOSBs, or even the present RCB, and this is so even when full allowances have been made for the necessary changes in method. Secondly, the psychological testing of individuals for intelligence, interests, aptitudes and relevant personality factors must remain largely the preserve of the professional. If not actually administering the tests he must retain a close watch on the way they are used and the conclusions which are drawn from them. In both these fields when professional help is withdrawn there tends to be a gradual invasion of old assumptions about leadership which may be still luxuriant in the remaining 95 per cent of the sponsoring organisation, just as a clearing in a forest abandoned by the first pioneers will be slowly overgrown until it becomes indistinguishable from its surrounds.

There are, however, two factors against the continued employment of psychologists and psychiatrists by organisations to select leaders. In the first place, their long professional training makes them expensive to hire. Secondly, they tend to import other sectors of their professional interests into the work in hand. In the case of Dr Harris, a group psychotherapist, this is evident from the many pages in his book which reflect his academic and practical interest in his chosen specialisation, such as his attempts to relate the individual's behaviour in a small group to personality categories (schizoid, hysteric etc.) and his concern for giving therapeutic help at WOSBs where possible. The group psychologist, or psychotherapist may also consciously or unconsciously import into a board selecting leaders for an organisation, his own assumptions about the rôle of a leader (based perhaps on the rôle of the therapist in a discussion group of mentally maladjusted individuals) which are inappropriate to the characteristic working situation of the organisation or institution in question. For example, Dr Harris' composite description of a 'group-cohesive' individual does not correspond in several respects to that of a platoon commander on the battlefield.

Thus the leadership selection area requires a marriage of two kinds of knowledge: social psychological (A), and practical experience of the command in the characteristic working situation (B), making together AB. The professional psychotherapist can often only contribute AA, just as the practising leader can only offer BB. In fact, WOSB was the child of A and B, and it is a matter of regret that we still await the official history of this most exciting creation, a chronicle which would no doubt give the B elements their just place and enable us to see the experiment more in perspective. It is usually the A contributors who write the books!

In my own view, a leadership selection conference or training course may be likened to the design of an industrial machine, which must be constructed so that it meets the needs of the organisation and yet is simple enough to be operated by a person with less theoretical knowledge and technological know-how than the inventor. So the professional group psychologist and psychiatrist can evolve a selection or training scheme in dialogue with the organisation's practitioners which can be run by others in that particular field with a given level of training. This implies that there will be enough men in the organisation with sufficient natural aptitude and professional experience to act as selectors or trainers, and secondly, that the length of time necessary to train them in A knowledge and skills is acceptable to the organisation. The 'expert' can then simply keep a watching brief on the conference or course, just as a firm which sells a computer to an organisation might remain responsible for maintaining this complex piece of equipment. The fact that RCB today can be staffed by officers seconded from ordinary units without losing its overall effectiveness speaks much for the work of the early experimenters. In this case, however, a small number of professional psychologists at the Defence Operational Analysis Establishment in Surrey remain responsible for certain aspects of the RCB's design, such as the invention of new group task obstacles.

In the light of the successful application of the functional understanding of leadership to the problem of *selection* the reader may well wonder whether or not any attempts were made to apply the same group approach to the more difficult task of leadership *training*. In fact, one such experiment was made during the Second World War. This deserves consideration in this chapter, partly because it stands close in time to the early WOSB 'trial runs', and secondly because it never quite divested itself of a 'selection' flavour.

On 16 March 1943 General Sir Ronald Adam decided to open a special leadership training school for those who had gained (usually on the grounds of immaturity) a 'Not Yet' verdict from WOSB. Eleven weeks later the school opened at Poolewe in Wester Ross, with its purpose suitably disguised by the title 'Highland Fieldcraft Training Centre', and with Lord Rowallan as its first Commanding Officer.

The chief merit of the HFTC lay in the fact that during its ten week course it provided the participants with plenty of outdoor work in small groups, with specific tasks to perform. These were somewhat similar to natural primitive hunting groups, and they provided a concentrated dose of practical group experience which could, and did, develop latent leadership talent. An especially valuable feature was the re-arrangement of groups at regular intervals, which made the candidates go through the important process of adjusting themselves to others not once but several times. On average, rather more than two-thirds of the students passed WOSB after their ten weeks course (868 out of 1,286 in just over one year).

Perhaps the most serious limitation of the course as leadership training, was the apparent failure of the staff to appreciate the important new *theory* which lay behind the WOSB technique. They still thought of leadership in terms of inherent qualities and therefore offered no instruction on the nature of the small group and the functions needed within it. Only the sociometric technique of asking each member of the group to place the others in order of leadership-merit seems to have been borrowed from WOSB. In the tenth week selectors from WOSB would also attend the course, which must have reinforced its selection atmosphere.

Many ingredients went into the HFTC pudding, notably Scouting (derived from Lord Rowallan), Character Training on the lines of Kurt Hahn's school at Gordonstoun, and Battle Schools, which at this time were stimulating a more imaginative approach to field exercises. Perhaps because the staff were not conversant with the research developments in their subject, they tended (like the group psychotherapists at WOSB) to bring too much of their own 'luggage' with them. Hence the students received instruction in such subjects as botany, astronomy, arms-training, make and mend of clothing, first-aid, bayonet combat, boxing, rock climbing, and the use of explosives! As Chief Scout after the war, Lord Rowallan wrote to some old course members, 'Of course the great problem was to disguise from you the fact that it was Scouting...'[2]

Therefore only in a somewhat accidental sense could the HFTC be described as an application of the functional approach to the problem of leadership training. Rather the course should be regarded as a development of Boy Scouting, with more mature groups than the usual patrols, operating in situations fraught with some degrees of stress or danger. Membership of five working groups in ten weeks with an officer leader, whose example could be observed and then emulated by the candidates themselves in practice command appointments, could only stimulate leadership potential. But much of what passed as leadership training was, in fact, only an extended form of selection. This appreciation of both the good and weak points of the HFTC may also be held to apply to a much smaller extent to its linear descendants, the Outward Bound Trust Schools.[3] Certainly the achievement in leadership training was not in the same order as that in the field of selection, where WOSB represented a real 'break-through' which was achieved by the application of intelligence and research to the solution of a pressing practical problem.

4 Developing leadership

'In industry we are frequently faced, though rarely in such specific terms as in the Services, with the problem of defining what we mean by leadership, and why we need it.' So wrote the training manager of a large firm in a letter to the author. 'Although industry,' he added in a subsequent conversation, 'has tended to shy away from the word "leadership" the reality behind it has now come to be recognised as an ingredient in successful managers. Can it be developed?' In different words many other managers have made the same point and asked the same question. Can the methods of developing leadership potential first accepted and proved in the Services be applied to the training of managers?

Leadership and management

Before answering this question however, it is necessary to raise a further one: 'To what extent and in what ways is the manager a leader?' On the one hand some would want to make a sharp distinction between 'management' and 'leadership' while on the other hand others would virtually equate them. Are the terms inter-changeable?

In reply to these questions the author would refer the reader back to the conclusions of Chapter 1, that essentially leadership lies in the provision of the functions necessary for a group to achieve its task and be held together as a working team. Now this is basic, the raw 'silver' called leadership, which to some extent may be separated and analysed in functional terms. But in reality leadership always appears in a particular form or 'vessel' which can be distinguished from others. This shape is fashioned above all by the *characteristic working situation* of the group or its parent organisation. To some extent the degree of participation in decision making by group members may be used as a measure to contrast these different forms of leadership, but there are other variables as well. In the military *milieu* the shape which leadership assumes is best called 'Command'; in the industrial and commercial situation it is known as 'Management'. Two boughs from the same trunk, they can easily – but should not be – confused.[1]

In particular the modern industrial situation dictates a necessary technical knowledge for the leader. Besides the particular knowledge required for the firm or branch of business or industry in which he finds himself, the manager should also possess a general technical knowledge of the way in which scientific techniques can be systematically employed for the efficient use of resources. But management techniques do not qualify a man for leadership in industry. They are only effective as extensions of leadership functions. Far from occupying a remote corner in 'industrial sociology' or 'industrial relations', leadership is *the* integrating concept, relating and binding together those subjects which are loosely grouped together as 'Management Studies' in business schools and universities.

'It is the job of leaders in industry, as elsewhere, to get the best – the very best – out of everybody,' said Sir Basil Smallpiece, then Chairman of Cunard, in a lecture to the Institute of Directors. 'This needs two things. First, to see that everyone fully understands the purpose of the new thinking, that they appreciate the policy needed for the business to prosper, and how this will affect people and their jobs. This is why I have been meeting Cunard's staff in our ships, to see that every man jack of them understands what we are up against.'

'And secondly, it is the task of leaders so to organize the business that the people in it can work freely and effectively together. In these ways, untold resources of new energy will be released at all levels of a company. And so it should be surely, with our national affairs.'

Some managers assume that leadership is 'easier' in the armed services than in industry. 'We have no Queen's Regulations,' lamented one. But this is an unrealistic assessment. In fact there are advantages and disadvantages as far as leadership is concerned in both fields. For example, the serviceman rarely sees an 'end product' to his labours; it is often difficult for him to regard his tasks in tangible, worthwhile or profitable terms, a factor which may contribute to a lack of enthusiasm on the job.

One important and obvious difference between the general leadership situations of industry and Armed Forces (in the United Kingdom and America, but not – for example – in Germany or Norway) is the existence of trade unions in the former. They provide a 'third dimension' in industrial relations which render many comparisons between the Services and industry invalid.

Within the terms of this book the trade union movement could be understood in the following way. Although the three areas of *task, team maintenance* and *individual needs* overlap and can mutually influence each other for good (see pp. 12–14) it is also possible that the circles could be pulled out so that they no longer touch. In other words, the most effective pursuit of the group's 'task' can come into conflict with the satisfaction of some or all of the 'individual needs' of its members. The trade unions may be seen as bodies organised to protect and promote the 'individual needs' circle, in the context of – or over against if need be – the task and team maintenance of the organisation.

For historical, social and psychological reasons a degree of tension, and some would say potential – but not necessarily open – conflict, is unavoidable between the 'task' and the 'individual' areas of need in industry as in any other large organisation. This potential conflict of interests forms a challenge to the 'team maintenance' abilities of industrial and commercial leadership. And the way of meeting it lies in ensuring that the three areas of need always in fact overlap and are seen to do so. This may involve a re-definition and interpretation of the organisation's aims, and a better communication of their true nature.

One manager now responsible for industrial relations in a nationalised industry recently summed up the situation in these words: 'Although it is in the interests of both management and unions that industry should develop and grow, when it comes to deciding how the benefits of growth and development should be shared their interest are not the same, nor will they necessarily agree about the best method of promoting growth. Essentially the rôle of the unions is to look after the interests of their members (in the long term as well as the short term), while management has to judge what is in the best interests of shareholders and customers as well as employees. The fact that their interests are bound to clash when it comes to deciding who gets what share of the cake all too often obscures the point that management and unions need to co-operate together to increase the total size of the cake and must co-operate if the economic objectives of the company and all the people in it are to be achieved.'[2]

If the trade unions therefore solve many individual welfare problems for management they can also pose others of a 'team maintenance' nature. Because of them, leadership in industry may encounter different problems and opportunities from those in the Services, but it retains its essential nature as the functional response to – or responsibility for – the task, team maintenance and individual needs of the organisation concerned.

To a British Institute of Management audience of senior managers in 1962 Lord Slim underlined the issue at stake:

> There's more than opportunity for leadership, there's stark necessity for it. The men in the workshop and office today are the same, or of the same breed, as those who won the war. They are as ripe now as they were then for intelligent, understanding personal leadership – and they would rather be led than managed. 'Man management' is a horrible term and I'm ashamed that the army introduced it. Men like being led – not managed. This country has never failed to produce leadership when needed. It will not fail now to find the kind of leadership that puts life and meaning into management. There's a lot of it in this room now. There's more outside. Let's use it.[2]

Based upon the 'functional leadership' courses held at Sandhurst in the 1960s I have developed with the Industrial Society a programme known as Action-Centred Leadership (ACL). Here is an outline of that practical approach to developing leadership skills.

The ACL course

To some managers, whether in commerce, public service, or industry, the relevance of leadership to management is not immediately apparent. It may help to an understanding of the connection if we define that part of a manager's job concerned with getting the best contribution from those for whose work he is responsible as – *leadership.*

In the case of a 'leadered' group, such as inevitably exists in business, that which characterises the leader is by no means confined to his personality, his presence, his 'charisma'. What *actions* the leader performs *and how he performs them* is also a vital factor in the formula which represents the successful manager.

It is these actions, these functions of the leader, which are capable of being learned and developed to improve a manager's performance in maximising his human resource. Both the awareness and the skills which combine to produce this ability can be developed and, from time to time, need to be refreshed. The Action-Centred Leadership course concentrates on the actions and awareness necessary to improve leadership performance.

The aims of the course

To be efficient a manager needs:

- technical competence sufficient to manage the technology of the job
- sufficient knowledge to cover the 'technical' aspects of management
- ability to get the best work out of those for whose work he is responsible and accountable.

It can, and does, happen that a manager has a more than sufficient competence in the requisite technology and also in the techniques of management, yet, at the same time, is ineffective in the use of the human resources; that is, he is a poor leader.

This course arises directly from the urgent need to develop in those capable of benefiting – the potential leaders and many existing managers, untrained in leadership – their ability to lead.

More specifically, the course is designed to improve a manager's leadership back on the job:

- By awakening APPRECIATION of the essential FUNCTIONS of the leader.
- By developing RECOGNITION of the FUNCTIONS of the leader – when observing them in practice.
- By testing, in the case of a few members of the course, their ability to APPLY the new knowledge of the FUNCTIONS of the leader. For the rest, to encourage this APPLICATION on their return to the work situation.

The course method. The emphasis of the course is on observing and participating in practical exercises. Formal lectures are kept to the absolute minimum and every member of the course takes part in exercises, group discussion, and case studies.

Because of the importance of individual involvement the maximum number of course members should be 24, although a smaller group of not less than 10 is viable (five for an exercise and five to observe). It has been found that a minimum amount of pre-course work saves valuable programme time.

Tutor's rôle. The tutor's rôle is two-fold:

● To promote understanding of:
  (a) the concept of functional leadership,
  (b) the practical implications of functional leadership within the member's own practical situation.
● To ensure that:
  (a) everyone participates and that tasks are fairly distributed,
  (b) the lessons learnt at each session are relevant to the stated purpose of the session and that vital ones are not overlooked by stating the aim of each session at the start, and finally checking how well this has been achieved.

Leadership exercises. Vital to the success of this course are the leadership exercises. The purpose of these practical exercises is to give an individual member practice in leading, at the same time giving the rest of the team participating rôles in a leadership situation and the rest of the course the opportunity to observe the leaders' actions or omissions and to learn from his successes and failures. The leader is given as free a rôle as possible without allowing the exercise to deteriorate into collapse through bad leadership. Lessons can be learnt from the latter situation, but the experience is liable to be too traumatic to be practical in the training situation.

Since a manager is almost invariably a leader appointed by higher management and not elected by his subordinates, the course exercises are not designed for 'leaderless' groups, where the leader naturally emerges from the group. For each exercise, therefore, the leader should be chosen by the course tutor who, either explicitly, or implicitly, thereby invests him with sufficient authority to achieve the given task.

A crucial part of the leadership exercises is the assessment by both the team and the observers of the leadership during the operation. To aid recollection this is conducted immediately the exercise is finished, by which time the observers are required to have completed a Leadership Observation Sheet on which is recorded actual events, comments, and reactions as they occurred. The data must be factual – 'He did (not) tell the team what exactly they were supposed to be doing' is acceptable. 'He communicated well' or 'he was a powerful leader' is not.

The observers are looking for actual signs (or their absence) of leadership within the operation of the three areas – achieving the task, keeping group cohesion, and satisfying individual needs.

The tutor is not only responsible for seeing that the performance of the team leader is assessed accurately but also for ensuring that each observer has shown by the data he has produced that he is capable of recognising leadership functions in action. This he does by asking specific questions of the observers, insisting on evidence to back up their answers. Finally he summarises the lessons to be learned from the exercise and will continue to do this throughout the course. Thus the involvement of all those taking part is an essential feature of the course.

Course programme

The typical programme of a two-day course shows that the twelve sessions include periods involving tutor explanation, group discussion, group reporting, and several types of exercise.

Continuing the practical nature of the course and the stated objective to improve each manager's leadership back on the job the final session is one of personal commitment in which each delegate is encouraged to state the actions he intends to take back in the work situation resulting from the course.

Delegates are given handouts throughout the course to aid recollection of the principles and the functions of leadership covered. Each session starts with an explanation of its stated aim and ends with a summary of the items relevant to leadership which have been discovered. A more detailed explanation of the course, session by session, follows.

Session One. This starts with the tutor explaining the aims of the course (q.v.). He then explains the need for the manager in business, industry, or commerce to be a good leader, since he is

Table 4.1 A specimen course programme

SESSION		DAY 1	SESSION		DAY 2
1	9.30	INTRODUCTION Course objective Definition of need for leadership	7	9.45	– PART II
	9.55	GROUP DISCUSSION		10.45	ANALYSIS & DISCUSSION Practice in identifying & observing leadership
	10.30	REPORT BACK – Discuss			
	10.45	THE QUALITIES, SITUATIONAL & FUNCTIONAL APPROACH TO LEADERSHIP	8	11.30	LEADERSHIP EXERCISE III ANALYSIS & DISCUSSION Further practice in observing leadership
2	11.15	LEADERSHIP EXERCISE I	9	12.15	PRACTICAL IMPLICATIONS OF THE MODEL
	*12.00	OBSERVATIONS & DISCUSSION Practice in observing Leadership		12.45	(approx) Lunch
3	12.15	SHARING DECISIONS	10	2.00	AN ORGANISATIONAL STUDY Practical implications applied
	12.45	(approx) Lunch			
4	2.00	LEADERSHIP EXERCISE II OBSERVATION & DISCUSSION	11		REPORTING BACK ON ORGANISATIONAL CASE STUDY
5	2.45	MOTIVATION	12	3.45	DISCUSSION OF GROUP REPORTING BACK ACTION FOLLOWING THE COURSE
6	3.30	LEADERSHIP FILM – PART I ANALYSIS & DISCUSSION Practice in identifying and observing leadership			
				4.45	Course Conclusion

* Exact timing to depend on exercise selected

required to encourage the best performance from those for whose work he is responsible. Evidence is briefly adduced supporting the principle that this type of leadership is a function not solely of the personality of the manager, nor of the situation or the climate in which he operates but also of the actions he takes in achieving his objectives successfully. The awareness of the need for leadership training is thus aroused in the members of the course.

The course is then divided into groups of not more than eight and each instructed to discuss and report back their answers to some such questions as – 'What should a leader BE to lead effectively?' and 'What should a leader DO to lead effectively?' The purpose of this exercise is to get delegates, early in the course, digging for answers out of their own experience. This enables them the easier to identify with the purpose of the course.

The findings of the groups are analysed in plenary session which then leads directly into an explanation of the three approaches to leadership covered in the first chapter – the qualities, situational, and functional approaches.

Session Two. Through a practical exercise course members are given practice in the observation of leadership functions. A team of five is chosen from the course members and one of their number appointed leader. He is briefed out of earshot of the rest of the team but in the presence of the rest of the course who are observing. The observers are then briefed on the use of the Observation Sheet.

The exercise now starts and is allowed to proceed for the allotted time. The leader and team are then thanked for performing the task thus providing the opportunity for others to observe and for the tutor to test the observers' ability to recognise leadership in action. This testing of the ability of observers to recognise the leadership functions is a crucial part of all the exercises. It provides the opportunity for all to learn and is vital to the success of the course.

Going through the relevant functions the tutor requires the observers to produce evidence and to 'speak to data'.

'Was the task achieved?' 'If not, why not?'
'Which of the functions should have applied here?'
'Which were done? How well? Which omitted?'
'Were the needs of each of the three areas served adequately?'
'Were the needs of one area allowed to dominate to the

detriment of the task?'

Members of the participating team are asked whether they felt they were taking part as a team, or group or whether individuals were allowed to dominate.

The leader is asked to comment on his leadership in the light of the comments and his own analysis. 'What have you learned from the experience?' 'Repeating the exercise, what would you do differently, and why?' The tutor then summarises the lessons learned, drawing attention especially to those functions which were omitted or performed inadequately thus affecting the result adversely. The kind of analysis here described is performed after each exercise during the course.

The actual exercise used varies according to the background of the course members but at this stage only an uncomplicated one is required. Those proving successful have involved the piecing together of two different jig-saw puzzles whose pieces have been mixed; the reassembling of two copies of different issues of a magazine previously reduced to their separate sheets and reassembled as a pile of completely haphazard sheets; the transporting of a team over a marked area on the floor (a pirhana-infested river) via planks and oil drums (or their equivalent in plastic shapes). A leader is appointed by the tutor for all these exercises and all are set to a time limit.

Session Three. By means of a dialogue with course members the tutor elicits that the categorising of leadership styles into autocratic, bureaucratic, charismatic, democratic, and *laisser-faire* is inadequate since many variables are concerned.

Leadership style will be affected by such factors as the type of *organisation* (its traditions and attitudes to authority); the *situation* (does the time available allow consultation in depth?); the expectation of *subordinates* (does their background, history, degree of education demand their greater involvement?); the *personality* of the leader himself (is it 'natural' for him to expect instant obedience to his orders or does he believe that in order to get the best out of people they must be involved and consulted as much as possible?). The concept of the decision continuum is then introduced and discussed.

In summary, the tutor emphasises the point that in today's climate it is vital that whatever his natural leadership style the successful leader is one who has learned to be flexible and to suit his actions to the requirements of the often changing occasion.

Session Four. Through another exercise, this time more difficult, course members are given further practice in the observation of leadership functions and their awareness and skills as observers further developed.

An exercise calculated to give the right complexity at this stage of the course is one where the leader with a group of four others has, in twenty minutes, to produce a winning idea capable of persuading a rich Trust to award him £20,000 to be used for character training, educational, or social activities with young men of all levels under the age of twenty years. Unknown to the leader the individual members of his team are given rôles to play. The leader is the personnel manager and his team is composed of the planning manager, a senior works foreman, the production manager and a trade union representative. The aspirations of each are different and there is here inherently a conflict situation to which the leader must find an answer. The usual assessment is made at the end of the exercise, the observers having noted their evidence (on their observation sheets) of leadership functions during it.

In summary, the tutor brings out the essential need of the leader to recognise the differing individual needs of his team and that unless the conflict is resolved successful achievement of the project is in jeopardy. At worst, the situation deteriorates and either the leader fails, or he uses autocratic power or a compromise is reached which does not satisfy all individual needs and group cohesion is lost. If a solution can be found which unites or integrates the differing needs, individuals can adapt to it, group unity is maintained and the task is successfully achieved. With the aid of a Leadership Checklist he analyses five functions of leadership in terms of action within each area of need.

Session Five. The purpose of this short session is to enable each delegate to understand the nature and individual needs of man at work and to know how to provide maximum opportunity for challenge, achievement and satisfaction within the work situation. By examining human behaviour more closely insights into motivation are widened and deepened.

The tutor briefly explains the work and the thinking of such people as McGregor (theory X and theory Y), Maslow (the hierarchy of needs) and Herzberg (hygiene-motivator theory), all concerned with a deeper understanding of the reasons why man works and his expectations from his life at work. A simple exercise (which could be pre-course work) concerned with ranking various motivational factors for both themselves and a subordinate enables course members to come more quickly to an understanding of those matters which influence the actions of man both within and without the work situation.

After insights have been awakened or deepened the course then considers the practical implications for the leader in terms of what he needs to do if he is (as far as is practicable) to satisfy the needs of the individual members of his group. Recent examples are studied of how the jobs of a wide variety of people have been 'enriched' to the benefit both of the individual and the organisation for which they were working.

Although one of the shortest sessions of the course this one is often one of the most rewarding for course members. In such cases a sudden enlightenment arises from the realisation that feelings and conceptions they have vaguely felt, perhaps never expressed, have been shared by others and by some, actually translated into practical terms to the advantage of the individual, the group, the job, and the organisation.

Sessions Six and Seven. The change of medium to a film gives course members further practice in the observation of contrasting types of leadership and in identifying the actions which it is necessary to take in particular leadership situations.

The most successful film from the point of view of giving course members further practice in identifying leadership actions has been a commercial, box-office success *Twelve O'Clock High* concerning the US Air Force and the famous Flying Fortresses. Although the film pertains to a crisis situation in wartime, it is replete with examples of leadership actions in all three areas – task needs, group needs, and individual needs, and the great majority of managers are easily able to extrapolate from the crisis to the normal business, non-crisis situation.

During the first part of the film the leader of a bomb-group fails, is relieved of his post and another leader appointed. The film is stopped at this stage and the reasons for the failure of the first leader analysed. During the film the course members are making brief notes on observation sheets so that during the analysis they are required to give evidence for their assessments.

From answers to the question 'Why did the colonel fail?' the tutor elicits that 'he over-identified with the men'; he paid too much attention to individual needs at the expense of achieving the task and keeping the squadron together as a closely-knit group. The evidence in support of this thesis is collected, displayed, and analysed.

Before the second part of the film is shown the tutor gets from each individual course member an answer to his question 'What will this new leader do to recover the situation?' He gets each to judge whether the new leader will go first for task or team maintenance and asks for the grounds for such a decision. These decisions are then later compared against the actual ones as revealed in part two of the film and the implications of any discrepancies discussed.

After the second part is shown, from his question 'What has the new leader done?' the tutor elicits that he has concentrated on actions to satisfy team maintenance needs thereby successfully achieving the squadron's objectives. He further draws out that in doing so the leader improved discipline; set and maintained behaviour standards; insisted on training to raise standards; strengthened morale; achieved pride in the group; increased individual performance through getting identification and commitment and ensured the continued successful operation of the group after his departure or lapse from the group by ensuring continuity of leadership and succession.

Finally the actions or omissions of the two leaders are compared in their approaches to satisfying the individual needs of the main characters.

In summary, the tutor reiterates the lessons of a leader achieving his objectives through concentrating at various times on the task needs, the group needs, and the individual needs and also the necessity for a leader to decide on the priorities he must give to each area according to the situation. A leader must also have the skill and training to perform the functions to satisfy these needs.

Session Eight. Another practical group exercise enables one course member to practise leading four others and the rest of the course to observe leadership functions being performed.

A manager is responsible for producing certain results through providing and maximising certain resources. He does not normally have resource to unlimited funds, countless personnel, or endless time. These, and others, are among the usual constraints within which he is obliged to operate.

This exercise is designed to test leadership in a situation in which these constraints operate. Within a specified time and with a given group and material provided, the leader must produce a tower built of small building bricks (e.g. Lego). His success will be measured in terms of financial profitability and this will be measured by computation from three profit or incentive graphs. In these graphs, profit is correlated with the height of the tower reached (performance); with the number of building bricks used (use of material); with time taken to build the tower (use of time). It is possible to make losses in all three areas; thus an overall loss.

The exercise itself is divided into two phases – the planning phase (maximum 25 mins) and the construction phase (maximum 10 mins). During the planning phase the incentive graph should be studied and an optimum profit target selected. At the end of the planning phase the tutor is to be provided with the operating plan giving details of target profit, materials to be used, time to be taken, height to be attained, a rought sketch of the tower design, and a brief plan of construction. During the construction phase the tower is built by the team and the time taken noted. Throughout this exercise the tutor must be especially careful to see that the observers are concerned with observing the leader at work and not with the technical intricacies of the problem. At the conclusion of the exercise the relevant measurements are entered with the graphs, the overall profit or loss computed and the results displayed side by side with the stated targets.

For the majority of course members the main value of the exercise lies in the lessons learned during the leadership assessment session:

● Were the relevant skills within the group identified and used?
● When arriving at target plans were all the parameters taken into account?
● Was the group too eager to start experimenting with the building materials before a proper, viable plan had been made?
● Were one or two or more people virtually idle whilst the rest got involved in trial runs?
● Did the final results bear any relationship with the stated targets? If not, why not?
● Did the leader optimise his resources? Support your comments with evidence.

Session Nine. The purpose of this session is to translate into practical terms for the manager the day-to-day implications of each of the three areas of need: task, group and individual.

Although we have seen leaders in action in short-time exercises, if functional leadership is to have any relevance at all it must also have meaning outside the training situation into every-day working life. With the exception of the one-man business, with which we are not concerned here, a manager, by definition, is one who works with and through others – a group. Such a working group differs from a crowd or random selection of individuals in that

- its members share a common aim, a purpose,
- its members must use their powers to keep the group as an operating unit and to protect it from those forces which threaten it, while supporting those forces which give it cohesion,
- the individual needs of its members must be satisfied in the long term.

It is the leader's job to see that all these three areas of need are met, in order persistently to achieve his objectives. Checklists can be used to interpret the functions which arise out of each area of need into specific actions the leader must take to get the job done well. These checklists should be discussed, analysed, and illustrated in plenary session.

They should include, for instance:

1 *Achieving the task*
  The efficient leader,
  - is clear what his task is and understands how it fits into the long-term and short-term objectives of the organisation,
  - plans how to accomplish it,
  - defines and provides the resources needed,
  - ensures that each member of the group has clearly defined targets for improving performance,
  - plugs any gaps in the abilities of the group by training and development,
  - constantly evaluates results and monitors progress towards the goals.

2 *Getting the best out of each individual*
  He will see that each person,
  - gets a sense of personal achievement in his job,
  - feels he is making a worthwhile contribution,
  - if his performance is unsatisfactory is told in what way and given help to improve,

- feels that his job challenges him and his capabilities are matched by the responsibilities given him,
- receives adequate recognition for his achievements, etc., etc.

3 *Keeping high group morale*
The leader,
- provides regular opportunities for briefing the group,
- provides regular opportunities for genuine consultation before reaching decisions affecting them,
- accords the official representative of the group the facilities he needs to be its effective spokesman,
- ensures that there is a formal and fair grievance procedure understood by all, etc.

Actions of the leader in one area of need affect other areas. Defining and achieving objectives will not only help in getting the job done, it will also help ensure high group morale and get maximum commitment from individuals.

When the course is being run for the managers of a particular company or organisation, the tutor here may well wish to bring out the practical implications of ACL in the special situation of the organisation. For one, it may be the urgent need for each person to agree with his boss his main objectives, standards of performance, and targets for improvement. For another, it may be the need for briefing groups. For another, the right use of delegation or an exercise in job-enrichment, making the job more worthwhile.

To provide the right climate in which the opportunities for these needs can be met for each member of the group is probably the most difficult but certainly the most challenging and rewarding task of the leader.

Sessions Ten and Eleven. At this stage of the course the aim of these sessions is to give course members an opportunity to apply the practical implications of leadership, as studied in the last session, to a case study designed to simulate their normal job situation.

The case study is designed according to whether course members are from a commercial, industrial, or other background. A situation which has been found successful for those in industry or business concerns the trace-metal extraction division of a chemical company. The division has recently been engaging the attention of the group managing director on several counts: not the least being its steadily declining profits. A year or so ago the division was the subject of a study by consultants and a brief report of their findings and notes on the persons in the case are available.

Depending on the level of experience of course members a situation is contrived where groups of members are charged with being either the newly appointed general manager or the newly appointed production manager and briefed with the job of reporting to the group managing director on their plan of actions to be taken on taking up their new responsibilities.

The two groups of eight members are each observed by a team of two or three observers, who, without taking part in the discussion are observing and examining the findings of the team in the light of the three areas of leadership – the task, the group, and the individuals concerned.

During the reporting-back session each group explains the actions it will take on assuming office and, most important, the reasons for so doing. Immediately after each group report the associated observers give their analysis of the group's discussions and the management decisions recommended with special reference to the three areas of need. They are encouraged to probe along the lines:

'Will the group's recommended actions lead to achieving the desired task of bringing the division back into a viable state? Was this task clearly recognised and defined? Which actions should lead directly to meeting it? What steps have they suggested which should lead to improving morale in the division or department and to getting closer working among and within groups? Have the separate needs of the individuals in the case been met, as far as is possible in the present situation? How?'

In summary, the tutor comments on the groups' recommendations and also on the observers' analyses, drawing out the main lessons, revealing the opportunities missed by the groups, the matters undetected by both the groups and observers. A down-to-earth dialogue ensures that the practical actions which a leader must take in such a likely situation are recognised and understood.

'Is this new leader going to meet the needs in the situation, the group needs and the individual needs? Has he achieved the right balance between the needs to enable him not only to show immediate results but to achieve these consistently and in the long term? Has he got his priorities right? Has he ensured that in the urgency to re-organise, the importance of reducing costs and improving morale, housekeeping, and liaison within and between departments is not overlooked? Is he going to succeed?'

Session Twelve. The final session is one of personal commitment.

Course members are given further practical help in being effective leaders in the industrial, commercial, or service situation by summarising functional leadership in terms of the actions they will each take on return to their jobs arising from their course experience.

The course is divided into groups of not more than six members. These groups then spend 30 minutes discussing the individual actions each member intends to take on his return from the course. The chairman of each group ensures that each member is helped to an accurate solution of his problems and to seeing where lie the opportunities for his leadership in terms of actions he may take. Each group then chooses the three or four best 'actions' which are then displayed and discussed in plenary session.

In a final summary of the course the tutor points out that it would be quite wrong to imply however that simply going through the motions just listed will make a leader out of everyone. The 'person' of the leader, his 'humanity' as well as his actions, is an essential part of the formula which makes a man an effective leader. A better word for this is integrity, in the sense of the 'wholeness and wholesomeness' of the man.

This integrity is best seen reflected in the sort of comment made about a respected manager who is also a successful leader. For example:

● He is 'human' and treats us as human beings.
● Doesn't bear grudges; has no favourites; is fair to us as well as the company.
● He is easy to talk to and he listens – you can tell he listens.
● He is honest; keeps his word; doesn't dodge unpleasant issues.
● Drives himself hard – you don't mind him expecting the best of you.

The course is now finally summarised.
The job of the leader is:

● To ensure that the group works well together.
● To get the required results.

● To get each individual playing his maximum part.

These are the functions of the leader – the 'work' a manager has to perform to be a successful leader.

These are not inborn traits. They are skills which can be recognised, practised, and developed. A manager becomes a better leader when he improves his skills in these areas. How are YOU going to apply these ideas? What actions are YOU going to take back on the job?

PART TWO
DECISIONS

Introduction

Leaders are involved with others in making decisions, solving problems and generating new ideas. Behind them is the basic activity of productive thinking. The skills of thinking in these three applied forms are the themes of this section. The quality of your leadership will be a reflection of the quality of your thinking. It is no good having an inspirational personality if you cannot make the right decisions.

Chapter 5 looks at the way your mind works when it is thinking. For progress in thinking skills, as with leadership and communication, depends upon developing awareness and understanding of the underlying principles. Chapter 6 contains some case studies of effective thinkers.

The specific stages or steps in the decision-making process are reviewed in Chapter 7, while Chapter 8 concentrates more on problem solving. Both are areas of critical importance to managers. As Lord Thomson said 'If you want to be successful in management you have to think until it really hurts'.

Innovative or creative thinking, which is also essential, is explored in Chapter 7. Leadership and change seem to me to have a magnetic attraction for each other. While some managers merely react to change, seeing it as more a threat than a change, the true leader will welcome change, and modify or direct its course. For leadership means being out in front. At the very least a leader should always be on the look-out for ways of improving performance. Getting the best out of people, moreover, includes harvesting new ideas from individuals, groups and the organisation as a whole: ideas about how to achieve the task better, how to work together more effectively and how each person may develop his or her maximum contribution.

5 The nature of thinking

Thinking about thinking is naturally a difficult business, indeed some think it an impossible one, like trying to jump on your own shadow. It may also seem a rather distasteful occupation. For many people do not care to analyse such a living process as thought: they recoil from the necessary introversion. They fear that the whole movement and colour of their minds will be dissected and explained in psychological or chemical terms.

On the other hand, to be practical, all of us do have to spend much of our time thinking in the deliberate or conscious sense of that word. We have to formulate problems, consider alternatives, search for new ones and choose courses of action. Depending on the matter a decision may be almost instant or it may take years of reflection and inquiry. Increasingly we tend to be selected for our jobs, judged and paid by our capacity to make the right decision. Sometimes that decision may be only a careful choice between known possibilities. More often than not, however, in a rapidly changing society, it will require a creative dimension, the bringing in of the unexpected into a familiar situation.

For this reason among others I do not believe that one can divide thought into separate categories such as logical and creative thinking, or usefully maintain for long, distinctions between problem solving or decision making or creativity. The intellect is a whole, a unity which resists such division. Most deliberate thinking is walking around the base of a decision, or pushing on slowly up its lower slopes or going over the summit and then viewing it from the other side. A decision does not end the process of thinking – it is just one peak in a range of mountains that may show itself more clearly above the clouds.

Before getting involved with all the intellectual detail described and discussed in the 'how-to-do-it' books, articles and courses, let us therefore first take a step back, so to speak, and look at thinking itself. For it may well be that many of the confusions and contradictions evident in the writings and teachings on these interrelated subjects spring from treating them as separate or autonomous too early on.

Certainly if we look at these well-worn phrases the only concept common to all of them is thinking. 'Problem' comes from a Greek word meaning literally a thing thrown or put forward, and is mainly defined as 'a doubtful or difficult question; a matter of inquiry, discussion or thought', while 'solving' springs from the Latin *solvere,* to loosen or break, which came to mean: 'explaining, clearing up, resolving or answering'. The *Shorter Oxford English Dictionary* also defines 'to decide' as: 'to determine (a question, controversy or cause) by giving the victory to one side or other; to settle, resolve'. Thinking is obviously implied by the phrase creative thinking although the stress often seems to be placed on the first word, with its overtones of effortless inspiration, rather than the second.

However, when we turn for information to the psychologists about the more shadowy process of thinking behind the more definite or concrete terms mentioned above they have little to tell us, at least not in a form made coherent by any general theory. 'We know very little about the psychology of thinking', wrote Robert Thompson in *The Psychology of Thinking* (1959). 'The psychologist cannot claim to be able to offer a complete description or a well-evidenced general theory to explain how we come to think the way we do. This book gives an interim report on what the psychologists have had to say on the subject so far.'[1]

Evolution and thinking

The elaboration of a general theory concerning the origins of thinking, or 'how we have come to think the way we do', is beyond the scope of this chapter. Yet if the first step towards any advance in education or training is an increase in awareness and if one part of the latter springs from a knowledge of origins and development – in short the historical approach – then a brief introduction to a general theory about the beginnings and therefore (to some degree) the nature of thinking is certainly relevant.

Perhaps an understanding of how we have come to think the way we do can be gained best in the context of the general theory of evolution. If the process of evolution has become conscious in man, as many distinguished scientists have argued,[2] may not thinking have its roots in the unconscious and (gradually) conscious response of man to the challenges of his environment?

Essentially the theory of evolution rests on the assumption that life in all its forms is a precarious state of matter always striving to maintain its existence, and suggests that changes in a biological species take place as result of responses to the challenges posed to it by the environment. The method of evolutionary adaption is 'natural selection': a complex process by which information from the environment influences the ever-changing pattern of genetic mutations in the species to adapt it to the conditions in which it finds itself. Let us now explore what happens when this pattern of environment–information–change becomes conscious in the mind of man. The main suggestion in this chapter is that thinking in the deliberate or purposeful sense of the word takes three basic forms, all related to the evolutionary advance of man, namely: analysing, synthesising, and valuing.

Analysing

If the process of response was to become conscious it would imply some sort of analysis of the information received from the environment. 'Analysis' is a key word and to be used often in this book, and therefore it needs a definition. The *Shorter Oxford English Dictionary* derives it from the Greek verb 'to loosen', and gives the primary meaning as 'resolution into simple parts'. In other words, when I take my watch to pieces I can strictly be said to be analysing it. The word, however, has overtones of meaning beyond this simple physical act of taking things apart. Indeed, the concept of 'loosening' does not imply a complete separation of elements. The knot tying two pieces of rope may be untied, or merely loosened, so that the nature of the knot can be understood. Analysis implies the tracing of things to their sources, and the discovery of general principles underlying concrete phenomena.

In the context of evolution man's superior ability as an

analyst of his environment has clearly aided his continued survival. By separating and categorising sense data, by probing behind the surface of appearances to unseen or abstract general principles, man has increased his control over the environment. Curiosity, therefore, or man's inherent inquisitiveness, had a survival value: the roots of our present desire to learn or know may thus lie far back in the ancestral era of *Homo sapiens.* The child pulling a toy to pieces to find out how it works is father to the man.

We are, however, endowed with a much greater desire to analyse than is required for our physical survival. As in other spheres nature seems to strive for success by its sheer prodigality and tolerance for immense waste. Many of our intellectual analysing activities are no longer means, however far removed, towards survival ends; they have become exercises for their own sake. In other words we analyse because we have the capacity to do it, regardless of the environment's challenges. Our culture and civilisation are partly results of this 'over-plus' of analytical ability.

Reinforcing the exercise of our inherent analytical talent lies the fact that we like doing it: there is a pleasure in successful analysis. Despite the popular notion of a dichotomy between thinking and feeling, between cold reason and warm emotion, nature has reinforced the total activity of thinking by a whole range of emotions. We feel baffled before an apparently intractable problem, elated at its elucidation: witness the famous story of Archimedes leaping from his bath and running through the streets shouting, 'Eureka! Eureka!' There is a pleasure to be found in loosening or separating a whole into its constituent parts, tracing its origins or discerning an underlying theory or principle, the relation of the parts to the whole. The common experience of understanding can come to us as a relief from the pain of incomprehension, the delight of a conquest after a costly struggle. 'If you had two lives that would not be enough for you,' declared the Russian scientist Pavlov in his *Bequest to Academic Youth.* 'Be passionate in your work and your searchings.'[3]

Synthesising

A second strand or theme in thinking is 'synthesis'. Again this word comes from the Greek language, and it means the opposite of analysing, namely: 'the putting together of parts or elements so as to make up a complex whole'. Indeed the Latin verb *cogito,* 'I think', can be derived from roots meaning 'to shake together'. When the resulting whole is substantially original we can describe the synthetic process as creative. There is a sense in which all syntheses are new, and it is a pity to restrict the word creative to the outstandingly original human inventions. Besides implying the emergence of something new the word creative is often used, however, with a value-judgement hidden within it. The new is then only called creative if it reveals some form of social or personal worth.[4]

Within evolution itself there is a creative dimension. Genetic types that did not previously exist come into being through natural selection. Rather than any rigid pre-determined uniformity there appears to be a freedom or tolerance for novelty at the heart of evolution: there are no prescribed solutions to the problems of an environment. Men, animals and vegetables survive in waterless deserts or arctic wastes, for example, by a remarkable variety of adaptations to the geo-biological situation.

Indeed, natural selection has been compared to a cybernetic device. Mutations (genetic variations which arise by chance) are 'assessed, accepted or rejected' not in isolation nor solely in the light of information from the environment, but *in relation to the other genes* of the organism in question. Nature matches its colours! It sees parts always in relation to the whole, and the whole as more than the sum of its parts. Consequently, what is fittest for survival may be a strange combination of strengths and weaknesses, a balance of advantages and disadvantages, abilities and failings.

An internationally known geneticist, Professor Theodosius Dobzhansky, has described this evolutionary process:

> We have, then, not a sieve but a cybernetic device which transfers to the living species 'information' about the state of its environments. This device also makes the evolutionary changes that follow dependent upon those that preceded them. The genetic endowment of a living species contains, therefore, a record of its past environments, as well as an imprint of the present one. This genetic endowment is not a mosaic of genes with autonomous effects; it is an integrated system, the parts of which must fit together to be fit to survive.[5]

In man this natural synthesis, the method of both the 'strategy' of evolution and the 'tactics' of individual growth, has become conscious, in the sense that man knows what he is doing when he makes a tool out of wood and stone whereas a bird fashioning twigs, leaves and mud together into a nest is not aware of what it is doing in the same conscious way.

This does not mean, however, that all of man's synthesising is done on the conscious level, as when he is making a tool out of wood and metal. If evolution has gradually become aware of itself in man he would expect to find within the less conscious depths of his mind the process of synthesis taking place, namely the putting together of parts of elements so as to make a complex whole. In fact this is what he does find, for it is the witness of many creative people that the welding of apparently disparate or diverse 'parts' into a pattern which is new (in the sense that the resultant whole has not been known before) takes place in the unconscious mind. In many cases evolution is yet more closely matched in that the new 'whole' seems to live and grow with a life of its own, like a baby in the womb. Examples of this unconscious dimension of thinking are given in the following chapter and the reader may care to refer to them now.

Valuing

There is a third theme or mode of thinking which is not finally reducible by or to analysis, or to synthesis or any combination of them, and that is the intellectual activity which I have named *valuing*, or thinking in relation to values or standards. Certainly value-thinking, or valuing should take its place besides analysing and synthesising as a major form of thinking in its own right. There is a cluster of meanings and associations around this more obscure kind of thinking which to some extent we can separate.

We have seen, for example, that natural selection seems to have its own criteria or standard of values by which it evaluates the kaleidoscopic changes of genetic patterns, namely 'fitness' for survival in the environment. Species may be tested by sudden changes in the environment: those highly adapted to one specific condition may go to the wall, while those with high adaptability will tend to survive.

Man proved able to judge for himself the merit of certain changes as means towards the end of survival. He could appreciate for example the value of fire, or the advantages of metal weapons over stone ones. By extension this kind of valuing or assessing (means in relation to ends) covered all the other end-fulfilling activities of man: the part is judged or evaluated in relation to the whole, and the whole in relation to its purpose. When we judge a horse or dog, for example, we assess it in these interrelated ways. Here the words good or bad simply mean suitable or unsuitable. (Compare the use of the word 'good' in the New Testament phrase 'the good shepherd'. The Greek word for good here, *kalos,* means 'skilled in the craft of' rather than morally good, which would be *agathos.*)

The perception of parts-whole and means-end relations may have led to the more abstract idea of beauty: certainly we find ourselves with that particular idea or 'value', and discussion of its origins can only be speculation. Given the reception of this particular value, however, as part of the information from the cultural environment, it influences the way we see things and the way we make things. The capacity to entertain such abstract constructs is part of our genetic endowment: the actual values we learn or absorb depend largely upon our particular environment.

We may speculate on the evolutionary origins of values, but the fact is that we find them indisputably there in our minds, in varying strengths according to the individual. Moreover, beyond the evolutionary value family already described and their aesthetic town cousins, we find another group living under the same thatched roof: the moral values.

Moral values, the planets that resolve around goodness in the moral sense (the Greek *agathos* as opposed to *kalos*), resemble their town and country relations in that we can discuss them in relation to the *mores* or customs of societies, and how far those invisible rules of standards of behaviour aid or hinder corporate survival. But moral values, without losing their roots in human history, have established a life of their own as interior linings of the mind which may colour the activities both of analysing and synthesising but do not lend themselves to any dissection. As the philosopher Wittgenstein wrote: 'That which mirrors itself in language, language cannot represent. That which expresses *itself* in language, *we* cannot represent.'[6]

On the other hand it is not to be lightly assumed that moral values have nothing to do with evolution. If evolution is a continuous process and if we can dimly discern the main axis as the advance in the social and individual growth of humanity towards greater diversity combined with a corporate and personal harmony or unity, may it not be that moral values, and particularly the constellation of values around love, are the magnetic forces which bestow an order of meaning or significance to certain external phenomena? In other words, are they not the bearings by which we navigate ourselves towards the undiscovered end of our evolutionary journey? It may be, to change the metaphor, that their radio-activity stems from the fact that they are witnesses to the end of the journey somehow joining us in the middle of it. Values, therefore, may be concerned with a meaning, significance or purpose beyond that anchored so firmly in the instinctive drives of humans, namely the natural activities of surviving, marrying, bearing children and working, whose worth is taken for granted by almost everyone, and questioned only by a few.

The further discussion of the nature of values in the philosophical and theological senses lies outside the scope of this book. The riddle of the universe might well be resolved if we knew who gives value to values, or why values are valued. Here it is sufficient to note the presence of value thinking as being one distinctive mode of thought alongside analysis and synthesis.

Like analysis and creative thinking, the perception and response to values is associated with its own unique range of emotions and feelings. As already suggested, these may serve an evolutionary function, much as pleasure does in connection with eating, by reinforcing our inclination towards the activity.

The capacity for experiencing the range of emotions connected with values obviously varies enormously. Ugliness makes some sick; others care for beauty with a passionate longing. Truth perceived can exhilarate a man and ignorance can depress him. Goodness can delight some men or arouse hatred and scorn in others. We vary in our emotional response to values.

Some of the feelings concerned with values are so relatively mild as to be hardly noticeable: admiration of courage, integrity or selfless love, for example, can have a strangely warming effect upon us. Worship, or worth-ship, the perception of and response to value, which can be closely allied or to compounded of those tender and rare feelings of awe and reverence, is often associated with joy and rejoicing, but more often it is a quieter movement of the whole mind.

Those who experience values and the fine or rare emotions connected with them find them incapable of analysis. In the first place, the act of observation contributes to, influences or changes the situation. Kant spelt this out for philosophers; a child gazing down at a cloud of minnows soon discovers the same truth. It is difficult to see, let alone study, the shy denizens of our own minds. Professor C. S. Lewis found himself invaded on occasions by joy, but he found it almost impossible to surprise it in return:

> You cannot hope and also think about hoping at the same moment; for in hope we look to hope's object and we interrupt this by (so to speak) turning round to look at the hope itself. Of course the two activities can and do alternate with great rapidity; but they are distinct and incompatible. ... But if so, it followed that all introspection is in one respect misleading. In introspection we try to look 'inside ourselves' and see what is going on. But nearly everything that was going on a moment before is stopped by the very act of our turning to look at it. ... This discovery flashed a new light back on my whole life. I saw that all my waitings and watchings for Joy, all my vain hopes to find some mental content on which I could, so to speak, lay my finger and say, 'This is it,' had been a futile attempt to contemplate the enjoyed. ... I should never have to bother again about these images or sensations. I knew that they were merely the mental track left by the passage of Joy – not the wave but the wave's imprint on the sand.[7]

Or, as William Blake wrote:

> He who binds to himself a joy
> Doth the wingèd life destroy;
> But he who kisses the joy as it flies
> Lives in eternity's sun-rise.[8]

In the foregoing pages I have tried to separate the single reality of thinking into the three keys of analysis, synthesis and valuing which make up its music. The balance between them is changing from moment to moment: one minute we may be primarily analysing and the next valuing. They have not, however, been so loosened that they are seen as quite separate realities rather than complementary ones. Indeed we may often appreciate this unity more clearly when we contemplate the distortions which occur when one mode of thinking becomes dominant at the expense of the others in a particular individual or group of people.

The depth mind dimension

Thanks to the popularisation of the work of Freud and other

psycho-analysts it is well-known that our minds include a semi-conscious and an unconscious area. The dichotomising tendency in analytical thought has tended to make a sharp distinction between the 'conscious' and 'unconscious' mind. The first is seen often as the seat of reason and order, while the latter is by definition largely unknown, presumed to be peopled by the blind childish impulses and sub-human appetites or desires that we have repressed out of sight and bolted down under trap doors, denizens which come out to play at night in our dreams.

As soon as we start discussing the unconscious mind we naturally resort to images, or vivid graphic mental pictures drawn from everyday life which serve as counters for the indescribable: metaphors or similes pointing us to a reality which they can only partially disclose. Our language for communication with or about the unconscious mind, either internally within ourselves or from person to person, is the language of images, as artists and poets well understand. The closeness of images to the synthesis process is illustrated by the double meaning of imagination as both the 'mental faculty forming images of external objects not present to the senses' and the creative faculty of the mind.

Now the main image used about the mind in this book is borrowed from the work of Marion Miller: the analogy of the sea.[9] Instead of an apparent dichotomy between two compartments of the mind (conscious and unconscious) this image suggests a continuum between surface and depth minds. The picture of the sea allows us to see the light of consciousness penetrating much further from the surface into the 'caverns of the mind' and gradually becoming dimmer in the depths 'no man – fathomed'. In all of the three modes of thinking – analysing, synthesising and valuing – the depth mind may be involved. Thus we have two inter-related variables: the alternations and interactions of analysing, synthesising and value-thinking on the one hand and the constant changes and mergings of level between surface and depth minds on the other hand. These variables, taken together with the emotions, begin to give us a model or a general theory of thinking.

The part of the less conscious ranges of the mind in analysis is not often recognised, although, as we shall see later, the depth mind is capable of acting like a computer, unconsciously performing feats of analysis if it is correctly programmed and if certain conditions are present. People vary, however, in the capacity of their depth minds to work in this manner. Intuition, the apprehension of the mind without the intervention of any conscious reasoning process, may describe the instant and immediate eruption into the surface of the mind of some swift piece of depth mind analysis of a total phenomenon. Consequently intuition may be the form of analysis most practised by predominantly holistic minds. (The word holistic comes from the Greek *holas,* meaning whole, and was first coined in 1926 by J. C. Smuts to describe the tendency in nature to produce wholes from the ordered groupings of units. When applied to minds it suggests an intellectual and emotional bias towards seeing life in terms of wholes rather than parts.)

Clearly, if the depth mind can play a part in analysis it follows that a disordered or damaged unconscious dimension in the mind, or a conflict or disconnection between them, can seriously impair or distort the process of analysing. For we do not bring an empty mind to the work of analysis, but one stocked by memory with knowledge, experience and values at various levels of consciousness. Consequently the whole minds of experienced practitioners in a general intellectual situation – e.g. medical, scientific, historical or managerial – may often do their analytical work more speedily, and less consciously than beginners. They may have hunches about a problem which they then proceed to test with their conscious analytical tools.

Writing about the scientist and theologian Teilhard de Chardin, one of his companions on expeditions described the speed with which he invested with significance pre-historic finds in the field: 'In his company, one could always bank on a mental reflex which placed facts in a wider context. ... When scrutinizing fossils or artefacts, he gave the impression that he had somehow been involved in their formation, that he could grasp their underlying significance by means of a kind of inner eye. This unusual gift may account for his dislike of expert classification, a necessary task but one which he gladly left to others.'[10]

Even in the mathematical and physical sciences intuitive thinking is essential for work on the frontiers of knowledge. In writing about creativity among mathematicians Hadamard postulated 'scientific taste', which turns out to be often reliable. Some of his subjects, for example, showed flair for choosing profitable lines of work, and for divining intuitively where the work was leading.[11] Writing in 1933 about the nature of scientific discovery Einstein could state: 'There is no logical way to the discovery of these elemental laws. There is only the way of intuition, which is helped by a feeling for the order lying behind the appearance.'[12]

Establishing an effective dialogue between surface and depth minds is obviously important if a person's work requires him to make use of the synthetic attributes of his depth mind. For, out of sight of the conscious mind, apparently unrelated facts or ideas may sort themselves out into right relationships with each other, thereby often forming a new unity. This is a natural process of the depth mind, evident also in the paintings and dreams of primitive people and children.

Often this collision and cohesion may be a chance process, without rhyme or reason, like some of the creations in *Alice in Wonderland* in which the author simply allowed two ideas to collide and fuse for the entertainment of children. Other manifestations – in science, art and religion – suggest that the depth mind can grow these constructs like crystals. We shall consider some examples of this unconscious synthesising in Chapter 6.

Lastly, it remains to note the influence of the levels of consciousness on value-thinking. Although the conscious activity of our surface minds may influence our values in a thousand ways we may properly say that they lie or live in our depth minds 'too deep for words'. They are the *regulae veritatis* or norms of truth, as St Augustine called them, following the Greek philosophers: the norms of truth by which we know truth but which cannot themselves be directly studied or contemplated.[13] The act of turning to study a value cuts us off from the external object which alone brought the latent magnetic feeling into consciousness. Yet we can be aware and catch fleeting glimpses of these values in our depth minds as they colour our thinking, thereby coming to know dimly these roots of our intellectual being.

Thus the depth mind, far from being a zoo without bars, or a chaos of divisive and amoral forces, has the capacity of bringing a natural dimension to the work of sifting information and grasping the relation of parts within a whole presented to it by the senses. It can recapitulate the natural and mysterious life-growth, using ideas and pictorial imagery as the materials from which it fashions living creations. Thus our values are found in our depth minds, or rather in the constant dialogue between surface and depth minds.

Conclusion

To summarise, behind the more-or-less specific activities of problem solving, decision making and creative thinking there lies the more general stream of applied thinking. In its deliberate sense thinking may be compared to an unfinished symphony with three main themes: analysing, synthesising and valuing. Behind our conscious thinking in these respects there lie the changing depths of our minds. We cannot, for example, allocate analysis solely to the conscious mind, nor synthesis entirely to the unconscious. Perhaps the first step towards improving our every day thinking is to become more aware of the paradoxically simple and yet complex process described so far. Let us now look at and comment upon some examples.

6 Thinkers in action

This chapter contains four case studies of thinkers in different fields. The first two – T. E. Lawrence and General Eisenhower – are given primarily to illustrate decision making. Both are from the military field. This is largely fortuitous. It so happens that soldiers tend to write their autobiographies more often than managers or administrators. Yet there is the advantage that the crises of war tend to bring to the surface factors and influences which are usually more hidden in peacetime situations.

The other two case studies involve scientific discovery and artistic creation. The selection of the people concerned in no way implies that they are more important than anyone else or unique; their decisions or work simply serve as good examples of general principles. As far as creative thinking is concerned I have sought to avoid the better known examples. In the literature some mathematicians and scientists are quoted to the point of becoming almost clichés (Poincaré, Kekulé, Pasteur, etc.), while Sir Lawrence Bragg is virtually unmentioned elsewhere. Nor has C. S. Forester's account of his own creative process as a writer received wide attention.

The sources of the excerpts are given in the Notes at the back of his book. All the case studies should be read in the light of Chapters 5 and 7. Therefore the reader may wish to return to this chapter when he has finished the rest of the book.

T. E. Lawrence

Despite many recent literary attempts to understand the personality of 'Lawrence of Arabia' he still remains something of an enigma. It is clear, however, that in the Arab Revolt of the First World War he played an important part as military adviser to the Arab leaders. This extract is an account of the intellectual turning-point in that campaign. Within the larger context of twentieth-century history it describes a significant moment in the development of guerrilla fighting as a coherent modern philosophy of warfare. We join Lawrence and the Arab Army as plans were being made for them to attack the Turkish forces in Medina early in 1917. While Lawrence was seeking to co-ordinate the plans he fell ill and for eight days lay in his tent. As he tossed and turned he began to think about the campaign as a whole.

Now, in the field everything had been concrete, particularly the tiresome problem of Medina; and to distract myself from that I began to recall suitable maxims on the conduct of modern, scientific war. But they would not fit, and it worried me. Hitherto, Medina had been an obsession for us all; but now that I was ill, its image was not clear, whether it was that we were near to it (one seldom liked the attainable), or whether it was that my eyes were misty with too constant staring at the butt. One afternoon I woke from a hot sleep, running with sweat and pricking with flies, and wondered what on earth was the good of Medina to us? Its harmfulness had been patent when we were at Yenbo and the Turks in it were going to Mecca: but we had changed all that by our march to Wejh. Today we were blockading the railway, and they only defending it. The garrison of Medina, reduced to an inoffensive size, were sitting in trenches destroying their own power of movement by eating the transport they could no longer feed. We had taken away their power to harm us, and yet wanted to take away their town. It was not a base for us like Wejh, nor a threat like Wadi Ais. What on earth did we want it for?

The camp was bestirring itself after the torpor of the midday hours; and noises from the world outside began to filter in to me past the yellow lining of the tent-canvas, whose every hole and tear was stabbed through by a long dagger of sunlight. I heard the stamping and snorting of the horses plagued with flies where they stood in the shadow of the trees, the complaint of camels, the ringing of coffee mortars, distant shots. To their burden I began to drum out the aim in war. The books gave it pat – the destruction of the armed forces of the enemy by the one process – battle. Victory could be purchased only by blood. This was a hard saying for us. As the Arabs had no organized forces, a Turkish Foch would have no aim? The Arabs would not endure casualties. How would our Clausewitz buy his victory? Von der Goltz had seemed to go deeper, saying it was necessary not to annihilate the enemy, but to break his courage. Only we showed no prospect of ever breaking anybody's courage.

However, Goltz was a humbug, and these wise men must be talking metaphors; for we were indubitably winning our war; and as I pondered slowly, it dawned on me that we had won the Hejaz war. Out of every thousand square miles of Hejaz nine hundred and ninety-nine were now free. Did my provoked jape at Vickery, that rebellion was more like peace than like war, hold as much truth as haste? Perhaps in war the absolute did rule, but for peace a majority was good enough. If we held the rest, the Turks were welcome to the tiny fraction of which they stood, till peace or Doomsday showed them the futility of clinging to our window-pane.

I brushed off the same flies once more from my face patiently, content to know that the Hejaz War was won and finished with: won from the day we took Wejh, if we had had wit to see it. Then I broke the thread of my argument again to listen ...

When it grew too hot for dreamless dozing, I picked up my tangle again, and went on ravelling it out, considering now the whole house of war in its structural aspect, which was strategy, in its arrangements, which were tactics, and in the sentiment of its inhabitants, which was psychology; for my personal duty was command, and the commander, like the master architect, was responsible for all.

The first confusion was the false antithesis between strategy, the aim in war, the synoptic regard seeing each part relative to the whole, and tactics, the means towards a strategic end, the particular steps of its staircase. They seemed only points of view from which to ponder the elements of war, the Algebraical element of things, a Biological element of lives, and the Psychological element of ideas.

The algebraical element looked to me a pure science, subject to mathematical law, inhuman. It dealt with known variables, fixed conditions, space and time, inorganic things like hills and climates and railways, with mankind in type-masses too great for individual variety, with all artificial aids and the extensions given our faculties by mechanical invention. It was essentially formulable.

Here was a pompous, professorial beginning. My wits, hostile to the abstract, took refuge in Arabia again. Translated into Arabic, the algebraic factor would first take practical account of the area we wished to deliver, and I began idly to calculate how many square miles: sixty: eighty: one hundred: perhaps one hundred and forty thousand square miles. And how would the Turks defend all that? No doubt by a trench line across the bottom, if we came like an army with banners; but suppose we were (as we might be) an influence, an idea, a thing intangible, invulnerable, without front or back, drifting about like a gas? Armies were like plants, immobile, firm-rooted, nourished through long stems to the head. We might be a vapour, blowing where we listed. Our kingdoms lay in each man's mind; and as we wanted nothing material to live on, so we might offer nothing material to the killing. It seemed a regular soldier might be helpless without a target, owning only what he sat on, and subjugating only what, by order, he could poke his rifle at.

Then I figured out how many men they would need to sit on all this ground, to save it from our attack-in-depth, sedition putting up her head in every unoccupied one of those hundred thousand square miles. I knew the Turkish Army exactly, and even allowing for their recent extension of faculty by aeroplanes and guns and armoured trains (which made the earth a smaller battlefield) still it seemed they would have need of fortified posts every four square miles, and a post could not be less than twenty men. If so, they would need six hundred thousand men to meet the illwills of all the Arab peoples, combined with the active hostility of a few zealots.

How many zealots could we have? At present we had nearly fifty thousand: sufficient for the day. It seemed the assets in this element of war were ours. If we realized our raw materials and were apt with them, then climate, railway, desert, and technical weapons could also be attached to our interests. The Turks were stupid; the Germans behind them dogmatical. They would believe that rebellion was absolute like war, and deal with it on the analogy of war. Analogy in human things was fudge, anyhow; and war upon rebellion was messy and slow, like eating soup with a knife.

This was enough of the concrete; so I sheered off ἐπιστήμη, the mathematical element, and plunged into the nature of the biological factor in command. Its crisis seemed to be the breaking point, life and death, or less finally, wear and tear. The war-philosophers had properly made an art of it, and had elevated one item, 'effusion of blood', to the height of an essential, which became humanity in battle, an act touching every side of our corporal being, and very warm. A line of variability, Man, persisted like leaven through its estimates, making them irregular. The components were sensitive and illogical, and generals guarded themselves by the device of a reserve, the significant medium of their art. Goltz had said that if you knew the enemy's strength, and he was fully deployed, then you could dispense with a reserve: but this was never. The possibility of accident, of some flaw in materials was always in the general's mind, and the reserve unconsciously held to meet it.

The 'felt' element in troops, not expressible in figures, had to be guessed at by the equivalent of Plato's δόξα, and the greatest commander of men was he whose intuitions most nearly happened. Nine-tenths of tactics were certain enough to be teachable in schools; but the irrational tenth was like the kingfisher flashing across the pool, and in it lay the test of generals. It could be ensured only by instinct (sharpened by thought practising the stroke) until at the crisis it came naturally, a reflex. There had been men whose δόξα so nearly approached perfection that by its road they reached the certainty of ἐπιστήμη. The Greeks might have called such a genius for command νόησις had they bothered to rationalize revolt.

My mind see-sawed back to apply this to ourselves, and at once knew that it was not bounded by mankind, that it applied also to materials. In Turkey things were scarce and precious, men less esteemed than equipment. Our cue was to destroy, not the Turk's army, but his materials. The death of a Turkish bridge or rail, machine or gun or charge of high explosive, was more profitable to us than the death of a Turk. In the Arab Army at the moment we were chary both for materials and of men. Governments saw men only in mass; but our men, being irregulars, were not formations, but individuals. An individual death, like a pebble dropped in water, might make but a brief hole; yet rings of sorrow widened out therefrom. We could not afford casualties.

Materials were easier to replace. It was our obvious policy to be superior in some one tangible branch; gun-cotton or machine-guns or whatever could be made decisive. Orthodoxy had laid down the maxim, applied to men, of being superior at the critical point and moment of attack. We might be superior in equipment in one dominant moment or respect; and for both things and men we might give the doctrine a twisted negative side, for cheapness' sake, and be weaker than the enemy everywhere except in that one point or matter. The decision of what was critical would always be ours. Most wars were wars of contact, both forces striving into touch to avoid tactical surprise. Ours should be a war of detachment. We were to contain the enemy by the silent threat of a vast unknown desert, not disclosing ourselves till we attacked. The attack might be nominal, directed not against him, but against his stuff; so it would not seek either his strength or his weakness, but his most accessible material. In railway-cutting it would be usually an empty stretch of rail; and the more empty, the greater the tactical success. We might turn our average into a rule (not a law, since war was antinomian) and develop a habit of never engaging the enemy. This would chime with the numerical plea for never affording a target. Many Turks on our front had no chance all the war to fire on us, and we were never on the defensive except by accident and in error.

The corollary of such a rule was perfect 'intelligence', so that we could plan in certainty. The chief agent must be the general's head; and his understanding must be faultless, leaving no room for chance. Morale, if built on knowledge, was broken by ignorance. When we knew all about the enemy we should be comfortable. We must take more pains in the service of news than any regular staff.

I was getting through my subject. The algebraical factor had been translated into terms of Arabia, and fitted like a glove. It promised victory. The biological factor had dictated to us a development of the tactical line most in accord with the genius of our tribesmen. There remained the psychological element to build up into an apt shape. I went to Xenophon and stole, to name it, his word *diathetics*, which had been the art of Cyrus before he struck.

Of this our 'propaganda' was the stained and ignoble offspring. It was the pathic, almost the ethical, in war. Some of it concerned the crowd, an adjustment of its spirit to the point where it became useful to exploit in action, and pre-direction of this changing spirit to a certain end. Some of it concerned the individual, and then it became a rare art of human kindness transcending, by purposed emotion, the gradual logical sequence of the mind. It was more subtle than tactics, and better worth doing, because it dealt with uncontrollables, with subjects incapable of direct command. It considered the capacity for mood of our men, their complexities and mutability, and the cultivation of whatever in them promised to profit our intention. We had to arrange their minds in order of battle just as carefully and as formally as other officers would arrange their bodies. And not only our own men's minds, though naturally they came first. We must also arrange the minds of the enemy, so far as we could reach them; then those other minds of the nation supporting us behind the firing line, since more than half the battle passed there in the back; then the minds of the enemy nation waiting the verdict; and of the neutrals looking on; circle beyond circle.

There were many humiliating material limits, but no moral impossibilities; so that the scope of our diathetical activities was unbounded. On it we should mainly depend for the means of victory on the Arab front: and the novelty of it was our advantage. The printing press, and each newly-discovered method of communication favoured the intellectual above the physical, civilization paying the mind always from the body's funds. We kindergarten soldiers were beginning our art of war in the atmosphere of the twentieth century, receiving our weapons without prejudice. To the regular officer, with the tradition of forty generations of service behind him, the antique arms were the most honoured. As we had seldom to concern ourselves with what our men did, but always with what they thought, the diathetic for us would be more than half the command. In Europe it was set a little aside, and entrusted to men outside the General

Staff. In Asia the regular elements were so weak that irregulars could not let the metaphysical weapon rust unused.

Battles in Arabia were a mistake, since we profited in them only by the ammunition the enemy fired off. Napoleon had said it was rare to find generals willing to fight battles; but the curse of this war was that so few would do anything else. Saxe had told us that irrational battles were the refuges of fools: rather they seemed to me impositions on the side which believed itself weaker, hazards made unavoidable either by lack of land room or by the need to defend a material property dearer than the lives of soldiers. We had nothing material to lose, so our best line was to defend nothing and to shoot nothing. Our cards were speed and time, not hitting power. The invention of bully beef had profited us more than the invention of gunpowder, but gave us strategical rather than tactical strength, since in Arabia range was more than force, space greater than the power of armies.

I had now been eight days lying in this remote tent, keeping my ideas general,* till my brain, sick of unsupported thinking, had to be dragged to its work by an effort of will, and went off into a doze whenever that effort was relaxed. The fever passed: my dysentery ceased; and with restored strength the present again became actual to me. Facts concrete and pertinent thrust themselves into my reveries; and my inconstant wit bore aside towards all these roads of escape. So I hurried into line my shadowy principles, to have them once precise before my power to evoke them faded.

It seemed to me proven that our rebellion had an unassailable base, guarded not only from attack, but from the fear of attack. It had a sophisticated alien enemy, disposed as an army of occupation in an area greater than could be dominated effectively from fortified posts. It had a friendly population, of which some two in the hundred were active, and the rest quietly sympathetic to the point of not betraying the movements of the minority. The active rebels had the virtues of secrecy and self-control, and the qualities of speed, endurance and independence of arteries of supply. They had technical equipment enough to paralyse the enemy's communications. A province would be won when we had taught the civilians in it to die for our ideal of freedom. The presence of the enemy was secondary. Final victory seemed certain, if the war lasted long enough for us to work it out.

General Dwight D. Eisenhower

As Supreme Allied Commander Eisenhower had presided over the final planning stages for the largest seaborne military operation of all time: the invasion of Europe

---

* Not perhaps as successfully as here. I thought out my problems mainly in terms of Hejaz, illustrated by what I knew of its men and its geography. These would have been too long if written down; and the argument has been compressed into an abstract form in which it smells more of the lamp than of the field. All military writing does, worse luck.

in 1944. In the week prior to D-Day Eisenhower's powers as a decision maker came under test.

By the time the operational staffs had moved to Portsmouth, I felt that the only remaining great decision to be faced before D-Day was that of fixing, definitely, the day and hour of the assault. However, the old question of the wisdom of the airborne operation into the Cherbourg peninsula was not yet fully settled in Air Chief Marshal Leigh-Mallory's mind. Later, on May 30 he came to me to protest once more against what he termed the 'futile slaughter' of two fine divisions. He believed that the combination of unsuitable landing grounds and anticipated resistance was too great a hazard to overcome. This dangerous combination was not present in the area on the left where the British airborne division would be dropped and casualties there were not expected to be abnormally severe, but he estimated that among the American outfits we would suffer some seventy per cent losses in glider strength and at least fifty per cent in paratroop strength before the airborne troops could land. Consequently the divisions would have no remaining tactical power and the attack would not only result in the sacrifice of many thousand men but would be helpless to affect the outcome of the general assault.

Leigh-Mallory was, of course, earnestly sincere. He was noted for personal courage and was merely giving me, as was his duty, his frank convictions.

It would be difficult to conceive of a more soul-racking problem. If my technical expert was correct, then the planned operation was worse than stubborn folly, because even at the enormous cost predicted we could not gain the principal object of the drop. Moreover, if he was right, it appeared that the attack on Utah Beach was probably hopeless, and this meant that the whole operation suddenly acquired a degree of risk, even foolhardiness, that presaged a gigantic failure, possibly Allied defeat in Europe.

To protect him in case his advice was disregarded, I instructed the air commander to put his recommendations in a letter and informed him he would have my answer within a few hours. I took the problem to no one else. Professional advice and counsel could do no more.

I went to my tent alone and sat down to think. Over and over I reviewed each step, somewhat in the sequence set down here, but more thoroughly and exhaustively. I realized, of course, that if I deliberately disregarded the advice of my technical expert on the subject, and his predictions should prove accurate, then I would carry to my grave the unbearable burden of a conscience justly accusing me of the stupid, blind sacrifice of thousands of the flowers of our youth. Outweighing any personal burden, however, was the possibility that if he were right the effect of the disaster would be far more than local: it would be likely to spread to the entire force.

Nevertheless my review of the matter finally narrowed the critical points to these:

If I should cancel the airborne operation, then I had either to cancel the attack on Utah Beach or I would condemn the assaulting forces there to even greater probability of disaster than was predicted for the airborne divisions.

If I should cancel the Utah attack I would so badly disarrange elaborate plans as to diminish chances for success elsewhere and to make later maintenances perhaps impossible. Moreover, in long and calm consideration of the whole great scheme we had agreed that the Utah attack was an essential factor in prospects for success. To abandon it really meant to abandon a plan in which I had held implicit confidence for more than two years.

Finally, Leigh-Mallory's estimate was just an estimate, nothing more, and our experience of Sicily and Italy did not, by any means, support his degree of pessimism. Bradley, with Ridgway and other airborne commanders, had always supported me and the staff in the matter, and I was encouraged to persist in the belief that Leigh-Mallory was wrong!

I telephoned him that the attack would go as planned and that I would confirm this at once in writing. When, later, the attack was successful he was the first to call me to voice his delight and to express his regret that he had found it necessary to add to my personal burdens during the final tense days before D-Day ...

We met with the Meteorologic Committee twice daily, once at 9.30 in the evening and once at 4 in the morning. The committee, comprising both British and American personnel, was headed by a dour but canny Scot, Group Captain J. M. Stagg. At these meetings every bit of evidence was carefully presented, carefully analysed by the experts, and carefully studied by the assembled commanders. With the approach of the critical period the tension continued to mount as prospects for decent weather became worse and worse.

The final conference for determining the feasibility of attacking on the tentatively selected day, June 5, was scheduled for 4 a.m. on June 4. However, some of the attacking contingents had already been ordered to sea, because if the entire force was to land on June 5, then some of the important elements stationed in northern parts of the United Kingdom could not wait for final decision on the morning of June 4.

When the commanders assembled on the morning of June 4 the report we received was discouraging. Low clouds, high winds, and formidable wave action were predicted to make landing a most hazardous affair. The meteorologists said that air support would be impossible, naval gunfire would be inefficient, and even the handling of small boats would be rendered difficult. Admiral Ramsay thought that the mechanics of landing could be handled, but agreed with the estimate of the difficulty in adjusting gunfire. His position was mainly neutral. General Montgomery, properly concerned with the great disadvantages of delay, believed that we should go. Tedder disagreed.

Weighing all factors, I decided that the attack would have to be postponed. This decision necessitated the immediate dispatch of orders to the vessels and troops already at sea and created some doubt as to whether they could be ready twenty-four hours later in case the next day should prove favourable for the assault. Actually the manoeuvre of the ships in the Irish Sea proved most difficult by reason of the storm. That they succeeded in gaining ports, refuelling, and readying themselves to resume the movement a day later represented the utmost in seamanship and in brilliant command and staff work.

The conference on the evening of June 4 presented little, if any, added brightness to the picture of the morning, and tension mounted even higher because the inescapable consequences of postponement were almost too bitter to contemplate.

At 3.30 the next morning our little camp was shaking and shuddering under a wind of almost hurricane proportions and the accompanying rain seemed to be travelling in horizontal streaks. The mile-long trip through muddy roads to the naval headquarters was anything but a cheerful one, since it seemed impossible that in such conditions there was any reason for even discussing the situation.

When the conference started the first report given us by Group Captain Stagg and the meteorologic staff was that the bad conditions predicted the day before for the coast of France were actually prevailing there and that if we had persisted in the attempt to land on June 5 a major disaster would almost surely have resulted. This they probably told us to inspire more confidence in their next astonishing declaration, which was that by the following morning a period of relatively good weather, heretofore completely unexpected, would ensue, lasting probably thirty-six hours. The long-term prediction was not good but they did give us assurance that this short period of good weather would intervene between the exhaustion of the storm we were then experiencing and the beginning of the next spell of really bad weather.

The prospect was not bright because of the possibility that we might land the first several waves successfully and then find later build-up impracticable, and so have to leave the isolated original attacking forces easy prey to German counteraction. However, the consequences of the delay justified great risk and I quickly announced the decision to go ahead with the attack on June 6. The time was then 4.15 a.m., June 5. No one present disagreed and there was a definite brightening of faces as, without a further word, each went off to his respective post of duty to flash out to his command the messages that would set the whole host in motion.

Later a President of the United States, Eisenhower died in 1969. In his memorial speech to Congress, President Nixon cited as a key to Eisenhower's character an undelivered statement prepared in case the Normandy landings during the war ended in disaster. The message read: 'Our landings in the Cherbourg-Havre area have failed to gain a satisfactory foothold and I have withdrawn the troops. My decision to attack at this time and place was based upon the best information available. The troops, the air and navy, did all that bravery and devotion to duty could do. If any blame or fault attaches to the attempt it is mine alone.' Although the message was filed away because the landing was successful: 'That was a man ready to take the consequences of decision,' Mr Nixon concluded. 'That was Eisenhower.'

C. S. Forester

As a novelist C. S. Forester is perhaps best known for his sequence of stories about Horatio Hornblower, a British naval officer in the era of the Napoleonic wars. In this extract from an autobiographical account of his early years the author reflects upon the part played in creation by the unconscious or depth mind:

There are jellyfish that drift about in the ocean. They do nothing to seek out their daily food; chance carries them hither and thither, and chance brings them nourishment. Small living things come into contact with their tentacles, and are seized, devoured and digested. Think of me as the jellyfish, and the captured victims become the plots, the stories, the outlines, the motifs – use whatever term you may consider best to describe the framework of a novel. In the ocean there are much higher forms of life than the jellyfish, and every human being in the ocean of humanity has much the same experience as every other human being, but some human beings are jellyfish and some are sharks. The tiny little food particles, the minute suggestive experiences, are recognized and seized by the jellyfish writer and are employed by him for his own specialized use.

We can go on with the analogy; once the captured victim is inside the jellyfish's stomach the digestive juices start pouring out and the material is transformed into a different protoplasm, without the jellyfish consciously doing anything about it until his existence ends with an abrupt change of analogy.

In my own case it happens that, generally speaking, the initial stimulus is recognized for what it is. The casual phrase dropped by a friend in conversation, the paragraph in a book, the incident observed by the roadside, has some special quality, and is accorded a special welcome. But, having been welcomed, it is forgotten or at least ignored. It sinks into the horrid depths of my subconscious like a waterlogged timber into the slime at the bottom of a harbour, where it lies alongside others which have preceded it. Then, periodically – but by no means systematically – it is hauled up for examination along with its fellows, and, sooner or later, some timber is found with barnacles growing on it. Some morning when I am shaving, some evening when I am wondering whether my dinner calls for white wine or red, the original immature idea reappears in my mind, and it has grown. Nearly always it has something to do with what eventually will be the mid-point of a novel or a short story, and sometimes the growth is towards the end and sometimes towards the beginning. The casualty rate is high – some timbers grow no barnacles at all – but enough of them have progressed to keep me actively employed for more than forty years.

Examination completed, the timber is dropped back again into the slime, to be fished out every now and then until the barnacles are found to be quite numerous. That is when the plot is really beginning to take shape; that is when the ideas relating to it recur to me more and more often, so that they demand a greater and greater proportion of my attention as the days go by, until, in the end, the story might almost be described as an obsession, colouring my thoughts and influencing my actions and my behaviour. Generally some real work is called for at this stage, to clear up some mechanical difficulty. At some point in the plot it may be essential for the *Lydia* and the *Natividad* to be at the same place at the same time – what forces (other than pure coincidence) can bring this about? What has happened earlier that makes it quite inevitable? A different kind of inventiveness has to be employed here.

This sort of difficulty is sometimes cleared up in a peculiar and often gratifying fashion – I have known it to happen half a dozen times. I have been developing two different plots, both of them vaguely unsatisfactory, and then suddenly they have dovetailed together, like two separate halves of a jigsaw puzzle – the difficulties have vanished, the story is complete, and I am experiencing a special, intense pleasure, a glow of satisfaction – entirely undeserved – which is perhaps the greatest reward known to my profession …

It was odd how that story haunted me. Then it began, the old familiar stirring of the emotions, the feeling of recognition, the knowledge that something was about to take shape. And so it did – with everything coming at once. That had happened before, and would happen again. I do not understand why it is, that when I am constructing a story which is quite episodic, the episodes should all take form at once, or as nearly as my capacity allows. One day all the episodes are chaotic, formless, and then on a later day, not so long afterwards, they have all taken shape and are arranging themselves in order – I had had the same experience with the *Midshipman* as well as with other books.

There have been occasions when psychologists have questioned me to discover the mechanisms of these processes. They call them 'creative', but that is a misnomer; the eventual result is creation, if such a self-satisfied word can be tolerated, but the processes are to a large extent – are almost entirely – involuntary. Does a chicken lay an egg because she wants to or because she has to? Just possibly the writer may assist, or speed up, his processes by making himself receptive, by offering hospitality to the wandering idea, but I not only do not believe it but I am inclined to think the opposite is true. Certainly there is a danger point at which there is a sharp transition between being receptive and trying to force the process; if ideas are forced the result is nearly always – let us say invariably – hackneyed or unnatural or pedantic. The average Hollywood story conference is a deliberate attempt to force the formation of ideas.

So far in my life I have flinched from going more deeply into this question; when the psychologists have started to probe I have always remembered how easy it is to take a watch to pieces and how hard it is to make it go again. Maybe my ideas come because, deeply rooted, there is something wrong with me, which analysis might cure. If this is so I cannot think of a better example of the remedy being worse than the disease. I have no desire whatever to be cured of something which has piled interest into my life from boyhood until now, and I hardly expect to grow so old that I shall decide that there is sufficiently little in the future to lose, and submit to analysis to discover the cause of the flow.

Sir Lawrence Bragg

Sir Lawrence Bragg is one of the foremost scientists in the world. He is the only one who has ever lived to celebrate the fiftieth anniversary of winning his Nobel Prize. His work was X-ray crystallography – the interpretation of peculiar patterns obtained by shining beams of X-rays through a crystal. In 1912 Bragg suddenly realised that they contained the vital clue to the way atoms were arranged in different substances. The most famous of these substances – the DNA molecule – is the blueprint of heredity. Its structure was solved in 1953 by Francis Crick and James Watson while working under Bragg. On this account many scientists have put Bragg's discovery on a level of importance with that of nuclear fission. What kind of mind did he possess? In order to illustrate some of the general statements about creative and inventive people in Chapter 9 here are some excerpts from a programme about Sir Lawrence Bragg televised by the BBC in 1965.

FRANCIS CRICK: I think the great quality that attracts one about Bragg is his enthusiasm, almost his boyish enthusiasm. There was a time when I was being rather critical about the work going on in the lab. and he said to me: 'Crick, you're rocking the boat.' By which he meant, you're destroying the confidence of the people who were working. And it was because of this enthusiasm that he attracted exceptionally good people to work for him. He made research exciting and I think basically it was because he enjoyed the aesthetic appeal of good science – it was simple and it was beautiful.

COMMENTARY: As well as being one of the most distinguished living scientists, Bragg is an extremely capable artist, a brilliant lecturer – especially to children – and a highly talented and popular grandfather. And he is perhaps unique among great scientists for the warmth and affection he inspires in his colleagues and even his rivals. Although he is seventy-five, Bragg is still very much on top of his subject. He founded X-ray crystallography fifty years ago, and he has led it and presided over it ever since – he's seen it grow from a single idea into a subject studied all over the world.

BARRY WESTWOOD: Sir Lawrence, you were as I know, born and brought up in Australia because your father had gone out there to be Professor of Physics and Mathematics at Adelaide University. How far were you influenced towards being a scientist by the fact that your father was one?

BRAGG: A great deal. I think that's bound to happen in a family. It was not only my father's interests, things he used to tell me about when I was quite young, six or seven (my favourite bedtime story was my father telling me all about atoms, hydrogen, oxygen and so on), but as well as that there's the general atmosphere, the fact that he had a laboratory, the fact that he had a head of the laboratory who used to make scientific toys for us to play with, little electrical things that worked and so on. All that influences a boy's hobbies very much. And then of course my grandfather was a scientist too. My mother's father – he was Postmaster General and Astronomer Royal of South Australia, two posts which I always thought inevitably went together. But that meant that he had all the Government stores out of the Observatory. I'm afraid my brother Bob and I used to raid those and beg all sorts of bits of wire and so on and make things with it, and so I naturally began to take a great interest in anything that worked scientifically.

WESTWOOD: You were really something of an infant prodigy, weren't you? You went to Adelaide University I think at the extraordinarily early age of fifteen, took a First Class Honours degree in maths at the age of eighteen and also by that young age made an original contribution towards scientific knowledge. Remember this?

BRAGG: Oh! I should think so! Yes indeed. Of course I was very unevenly developed. I think perhaps I was rather forward with the intellectual side but very backward indeed on the games and that kind of thing, and so I rather took to somewhat lonely hobbies and one of the great ones was shell collecting. I had quite a good collection of South Australian shells, but this really I am proud of because it was given my name and still bears it. Nobody's challenged the species. It's a little bone of a cuttlefish, very dainty little cuttlefish called *Sepia braggi*. It was named by Dr Virco who was the great authority in Australia and I remember very well indeed, I took it to him and he verified it was new; he said, I think I shall call it '*Sepia gondola*' because it looks so like a Venetian gondola, and then, I must have been about twelve or thirteen at the time – I think he saw my face fall and he said, 'No, we'll call it *Sepia braggi*.' And there it is ...

WESTWOOD: Then in 1912 this historic picture was published by the German scientist von Laue, and it was really the correct interpretation of the spots on this picture which led you on to your Nobel Prize work. I believe that it was whilst you were walking along the Backs in St John's College in Cambridge that you had this idea of the correct solution. Can you remember how you felt?

BRAGG: Very vividly indeed. I remember it almost as if it were yesterday, I'd been thinking a great deal about this picture of von Laue's – studying it and wondering what it meant – and as always in science, it was the putting of several things together that led to the answer. C. T. R. Wilson's brilliant lectures on optics and the relation of pulses to spectral light, J. J. Thomson on X-rays, and talk about crystals (we had a little society) and I suppose one's unconscious mind works on these things – but I do remember so vividly walking along the Backs and suddenly seeing that there was a much simpler way of looking at phenomenon than the rather complex one which Laue had developed. And that was it, that's what started me ...

PROFESSOR DOROTHY HODKIN: Sir Lawrence Bragg was already a legend when I first began X-ray analysis in the early 1930s. I remember Bernal telling us that when he was working with Sir Lawrence's father at the Royal Institution, they always sent any structures that proved too difficult for them to tackle to Manchester to be solved by Sir Lawrence Bragg. It was at Manchester that I first saw him when I casually visited the laboratory there, never expecting to see him. I was most proud and delighted that he spoke to me and tremendously impressed by his great kindness and his interest in one so young and unknown. Later I remember again at a meeting in Manchester that he was discussing the problem of the structure of proteins, and added 'the solution of which we shall all live to see'. I had a sense of immediate concern – did he really realize how very difficult this problem was? And this concern was followed by a wave of hopefulness that he might prove to be correct, as indeed he has done.

WESTWOOD: Sir Lawrence, do you remember that remark about proteins – 'The solution we shall live to see' – made thirty or more years ago.

BRAGG: I remember my enthusiasm and my hope at the time – I don't know that I remember the exact remark. People seem to remember a number of wonderful remarks I made which I've quite forgotten.

WESTWOOD: You say you had hope at the time – was it hope, or were you confident even that far back that this would ultimately be done?

BRAGG: Well, you know, it's a strange thing but I do feel in science that if you're absolutely determined to get a thing out you generally get it out. It's wonderful in that way how often that does happen. Science is very much a matter of sticking to it.

WESTWOOD: You've always got on remarkably well with children, haven't you?

BRAGG: Yes ...

WESTWOOD: And it seems ...

BRAGG: And I think I can say that, partly because I'm rather a case of arrested development and find it easy to understand them.

WESTWOOD: It seems also that they find it easy to understand and like you, at least according to your wife that's so.

LADY BRAGG: My husband has a magnetic attraction for children. Part of his mind, I think, is still a child's mind. I remember once when we were crossing the Atlantic a small boy attached himself to him. His mother was seasick and he was all alone. He came up to my husband and said, 'Could you show me a whale?' My husband said, 'Well it's very rare to see a whale at this time of year, but come along, we'll walk round the ship'. They walked round the ship and there was no whale. But suddenly, just at the end, my husband said, 'Look!' and there was a whale really doing its stuff and spouting. The little boy just looked at my husband and said, 'Can I stay with you always.'

FRANCIS CRICK: When Jim Watson and I were working on the structure of DNA we were doing it by building models in Bragg's lab. And I think it's an interesting question to ask: What did we learn from Bragg that helped us to solve that structure? Well, of course, through being in the Cavendish we had a lot of technical know-how – how you actually went about building models, all about lengths and angles and distances and the details of crystallography and helical differentials and in some ways, one of them was a little unexpected. That was, we learned not to put too much trust in the experimental evidence. Now when you're a student you're always taught you must of course observe the facts and that's what science is about. When you come to do research you find that this can be very misleading. Sometimes the facts aren't right – sometimes they just put you off the scent, even though they're correct, as they did in the case of the alpha helix which Bragg didn't solve and Pauling did, partly because of one experimental fact to which they paid too much attention. The other thing we learned, I think, was something a little more intangible, it was the style of attack, the way of looking at a problem, not getting involved in the detail too much, making a simple hypothesis, working it out, seeing how it fitted the broad run of the evidence and if it led to something interesting and unexpected. People are taught this but you actually learn it by seeing somebody do it. Of course, the real skill comes in telling actually *when* a problem is simple. And I suppose we must have learned a bit of that too, because Bragg has this particular power and that's why he's often been so successful in his work.

WESTWOOD: Now the solution of the structure of DNA is undoubtedly one of the great scientific highlights of the century and many people would say, the equivalent to splitting the atom.

BRAGG: I think eventually it will prove to be so.

WESTWOOD: And then it went on, this work on protein structures, to solve some incredibly complex structures, notably the work of Perutz and Kendrew who themselves in the same year, 1962, got the Nobel Prize for Chemistry.

BRAGG: Yes.

MAX PERUTZ: I have always been tremendously impressed by the speed and clarity of Bragg's mind and by his power of scientific judgment. While others doubt and hesitate, Bragg will see the importance of a scientific discovery in a flash. If he conceives a scientific idea of his own he goes home in the evening to write it up and comes back next morning with the finished paper ready for the typist – rather like Mozart writing the Overture to 'The Marriage of Figaro' in a single night. Not a word needs changing. His mind leaps like a prima ballerina, with perfect ease. What is so unique about it – and this is what made his lectures so marvellous – is the combination of penetrating logic and visual imagery. Many of his successes in crystal structure analysis are due to this power of visualizing the aesthetically and physically most satisfying way of arranging a complicated set of atoms in space and then having found it, with a triumphant smile, he would prove the beauty and essential simplicity of the final solution.

WESTWOOD: And in a sense it's true isn't it that all the things which we've mentioned, sound ranging, radio astronomy, crystallography, all are concerned with spatial relationships?

BRAGG: Yes. Of course that's so. My wife always puts that rather clearly I think – she always asks why we're making models. It's one of the few, perhaps the only advantage of science, where the essence of what you discover is a model. A number of things in the right – the relative – positions to each other.

WESTWOOD: One of your friends raises this point quite clearly.

SIR GEORGE THOMSON: I sometimes wondered what would have happened if Willie had ever run out of crystals. Was it luck? After all, he came into crystallography at the ideal time for it and him and he had the ideal equipment. Now just suppose there hadn't been any more crystals – would he have been a great scientist for the rest of his life? I am sure he would. He is not a one-idea man.

WESTWOOD: Do you think of yourself as a one-idea man?

BRAGG: I often think of myself as a no-idea man. When I think back in the history of all this work, to try and trace where the beginning of where any of it came from, I always remember some student, some friend who tipped me off with a remark of some kind that set me thinking.

WESTWOOD: Now this positive spate of Nobel Prizes in 1962, all arising basically out of the work for which you yourself had got the Nobel Prize nearly fifty years earlier, must have been very exciting for you. In fact your wife remembers quite clearly when the news came through.

LADY BRAGG: He was pretty ill at the time. I rushed round to the hospital with the news. He was terribly thrilled. He spent the night explaining protein structures in detail to the little Irish night nurse who listened very patiently but didn't understand a word. Next day the doctor said to me: 'Well he's over the worst, but now I think he may die of excitement ...'

WESTWOOD: You really love lecturing, don't you?

BRAGG: Yes, I do. I really enjoy it, and I think there really is a great artistic pleasure in making an experiment not only work, but work so that it looks aesthetically attractive, and with the maximum of simplicity.

WESTWOOD: Well, I know that this imagination that you have leads you not only to the study of crystal structures, but also to express yourself very well indeed, in paint and pencil and crayon, but you draw and paint a great deal. I know, for instance, that you've sketched most of your family; and now as a grandfather you combine, obviously with great joy, the artistic gift which you have with the love which you have for children ...

WESTWOOD: Sir Lawrence, your wife just said that you're really a very private character, so let me ask you only with reference to your scientific life, what have been the highlights?

BRAGG: They have, as I suppose with all scientists, been the times when one has suddenly seen the answer. It always comes – it's a curious feeling, it's a revelation rather that one's discovered something oneself as if one had been told the answer. I remember it in the very early work with the Laue photograph; I remember it in our work on silicates; I remember it, perhaps very vividly indeed, in the protein. Of course, it was Perutz who made the great tactical advance that made it possible – we ran into difficulties with his crystal – Kendrew it was who got out the first one, he sent me some of his results, and I played with them, he was doing the real work, but, I just saw for the first time, suddenly, the answer is there! It's going to go! I think that was perhaps the greatest moment of a scientific discovery in my life.

And then I suppose what gave me the deepest pleasure was when I heard about the four Nobel Prizes. I'm sure that ranked much higher than my hearing about my own in World War One. But as I look back, I can't help thinking the whole time of the young researchers. It's hard to think of any one of the great discoveries in which I don't have the feeling – well that, really, that idea was put to me by so-and-so or so-and-so and perhaps to sum it up, that very few of them indeed can I say stemmed from me – they rather happened where I was.

In order to complete the picture it is relevant to quote Sir Lawrence Bragg's views on the relation of science to moral values, for they further illustrate the qualitative differences between analysis, synthesis and value thinking. In a reply printed in *The Times* to a newspaper article by Dr Edmund Leach, Provost of King's College, Cambridge, which made large claims for the rôle of science in life, Sir Lawrence had this to say:

May I comment as a scientist on Dr Leach's article (November 16, 1968) on the responsibilities of scientists? The word 'science' is often loosely used to cover two quite different forms of human endeavour.

There is on the one hand the search for a deeper understanding of Nature. In this search one cannot distinguish between knowledge which could be put to good uses and that which could be turned to bad ends. The distinction is meaningless, and in any case it is hardly ever possible to guess to what use a new and fundamental advance can be put, at the time it is made; the future holds so many surprises.

This knowledge goes into a store from which industry draws the many items of information it wants in order to achieve its technical ends. The word 'science' is used in this latter case to stand for the technical achievements which are made possible by this deeper knowledge, and the vastly greater powers over Nature which they provide. Science has greatly amplified the powers of invention which man always employed to effect his purposes. Scientists have a deep responsibility not only for suggesting 'how it can be done' but also for foreseeing as best they can the possible dangers of exploiting these powers rashly. But the decision as to the ends to be achieved involves moral questions on which science as such has no authority to dictate, as others of your correspondents have stressed, and I am sure that responsible scientists would not wish to claim any such authority.

Not so long ago, science could point with some complacency to the advantage it had brought in comfort and health, ease of travel and communication, and opportunities to share in culture. Now it is not on so good a wicket. The advances in technology have been so embarrassingly rapid, and have raised so many new and difficult problems, that it is natural to wonder if the losses outweigh the gains from the Pandora's Box which we have opened.

But is not this taking too short a view? The portents show that we are entering on one of those times when the way of life profoundly changes. The last great change was the introduction of agriculture which made it possible for men to live in communities and so changed savagery into civilization. Civilization was based on a greater control of Nature. We can only dimly guess about this new 'X', based on technical achievements which bind the whole world so closely, but cannot it be foreseen that 'X' will be some higher form of social integration which bears the same relation to civilization as the latter did to savagery?

This is the challenge we are facing and man must try to guide his course by the 'Wisdom whose price is above rubies' which exists in a dimension for which science has no measuring scale.

7 Decision making

In Chapter 5 we looked at the intellectual themes which the mind weaves into the music of thought. In the last pages we have seen some examples of thinking drawn from a range of human experience and selected to illustrate the part played by the depth mind. Many managers or supervisors reading the book may have wondered in what ways the experience of generals, writers and scientists can be relevant to their own decision making and problem solving. The object of this chapter is to show how the universal mental abilities of analysing, synthesising and valuing combine or interlock together in ever-changïng kaleidoscopic patterns when we set about making a decision, and that the depth mind is necessarily involved at all stages, not just during the phase often labelled 'incubation' by many writers on creative thinking. Understanding this process should help us later on to improve our performance, both in learning to make better decisions ourselves and also in helping others to do the same.

What is a decision?

First, let us be clear upon what we mean by a 'decision'. By one extreme definition almost everything we do involves making decisions; by another, at the other end of the scale, we make only a few real decisions in our lives. The first school of opinion would hold that a manager spends almost all his time decision making; the second school declares that he makes few real decisions, but that they are highly significant events.

The *Shorter Oxford English Dictionary* gives us three current meanings for the word: (1) the action of deciding (a contest, question etc.); settlement, determination; a conclusion, judgement; especially one formally pronounced in a court of law: (2) the making up of one's mind; a resolution; (3) as a quality: determination, firmness, decidedness of character. The word itself comes from Latin and means 'to cut off'. By giving the victory to one side or the other, you 'cut off' the mental process of weighing both sides — or all angles — of a question, controversy or cause.

Note that the word implies some form of preliminary confusion or hesitation. Where there is no choice involved we do not have the experience of making a decision, or (because 'to do nothing' is usually a viable alternative in most situations) we experience it only in a mild form. If you want to get work and you are offered only one job, there is hardly a decision to be made. But if there are two equally inviting offers then you are in the decision-making situation.

Leadership decisions

The broad definition given above excludes the large areas which are 'programmed' by the computer of our depth minds, for example, the now almost unconscious repetitions of previous decisions we call 'habits'. On the other hand, the range of situations in which we make decisions in the defined sense is as wide as life itself. Nor can our decisions be kept in tidy compartments in our lives: we may have to choose the curtains in the office as well as at home, and ethical choices can pose themselves for decision by any way-side.

Yet there are decisions which we may describe as distinctly managerial, or, to widen the field to include all groups, organisations and societies, decisions which are the characteristic responsibility of leaders. These are decisions which involve selecting the best means of achieving the common goal.

On the whole people associate together in groups or organisations because there is a task to be done which one person cannot do on his own. Leadership is needed if the common task is to be achieved, not only to maintain the unity or cohesiveness of the group but to ensure that the necessary choices or decisions are made which will lead to the attainment of the objective. As we can say that management is the form that leadership assumes in the industrial or commercial environment, it follows that managerial decisions are those which concern selecting and implementing that course of action in a given situation which will lead to maximum results in terms of the aims of the company.

At the highest level of industry these can – and indeed will – almost invariably involve major policy decisions. The Chairman of Unilever, Dr Ernest Woodroofe, recently gave an example of such a decision, which could of course be matched by the chairmen or directors of any other company:

> A couple of years ago, one section of our business proposed that we should expand into yoghurt and dairy products. There was a natural link up with our existing cheese business and it was brand marketing of the kind in which we have some expertise. Much was in our favour. We knew a lot about the scientific and technological aspects of milk in our ice-cream and margarine businesses, about the distribution of chilled and frozen products. Our crystal ball seemed to indicate that more and more food products would be sold from the chilled cabinets in the shops. However, there were some very strongly entrenched competitors with well-known brand names and, of course, some of the supermarkets sell under their own names. We weighed the pros and cons and decided to back the proposal. We are well satisfied with our decision because, although we have had to withdraw in this country, we are making good progress on the continent of Europe.[1]

Five steps in decision making

Among writers on decision making there is broad agreement on the main phases or steps of the process. It should be emphasised, however, that the following summary of those steps is not designed to be a rigid and inflexible framework. One can have trained and disciplined thought without a fastidious concern for mental tidiness. Indeed, the 'scientific method' often held up as an example for the manager is not capable of being codified into a mental drill or procedure, except by hindsight.

Thus the five stages or steps outlined below might be compared to musical notes which can be arranged by the mind in any order. In analysing and presenting them it is convenient to use a logical sequence, but the reader should remember that this pattern is really a temporary and artificial one. For a variety of good reasons, one step may be missed out altogether. The five can be arranged like dance steps into any number of sequences – minuets, waltzes, sambas – according to individual idiosyncrasy and the prevailing circumstances. The music which both accompanies and invades the steps is made up of the three main themes of analysis, synthesis and valuing. We cannot arrange the latter into sequence and allocate them separately to one or more of the steps. In each of the overlapping and ever-changing set of five phases the three major forms of deliberate thinking may well be present in differing proportions.

Similarly, we cannot exclude the depth mind from each of the phases. This is particularly true when the time-span for a decision encompasses more than a few minutes or hours. But it leads us on to the central point that the mind can do a lot of work in the five areas when it is 'off-line' (to use a computer term). Indeed, there may be a close relation between this kind of background preparatory (but nevertheless directed) thinking and the ease with which a person makes decisions when he finds himself in a situation which demands a choice. Paradoxically, many decisions are decided before we make them: we come into situations with our minds made up in the sense that some possible courses are ruled out and certain values deeply seated in our minds. The relation of decisions to thinking is rather like that of battles to war: battles are only high peaks in a mountain range of military activity in which such 'depth' realities as economics and morale are much more important in the long run than any single encounter, won or lost.

With these considerations in mind the five steps or phases of decision making will be discussed in turn.

Specify the aim

Almost all books and articles on decision making highlight the cardinal importance of being sure that you know what you want to do. The first principle of war is 'select and maintain your aim', and all military 'appreciations' (or written decision-making exercises) begin with a consideration of the aim. Similarly the literature on management and organisational leadership generally stresses the need to determine or specify what is one's task.

For the sake of clarity useful distinctions can be drawn between purpose, aims and objectives both for organisations and individuals. The *purpose* is the ultimate end that the organisation is there to serve. Inevitably this will be stated in very general or abstract language, if it is put into words at all. By asking the question 'why?' for long enough we can reach the realm of purpose – the overall direction of an enterprise or a society – but our minds are not made to linger for long in a landscape of unrelieved abstract words. We may catch glimpses or insights, however, that in these higher reaches of purpose there is ultimately a fusion of action (or purposeful living) with values. The ability to think at the level of purpose or make decisions in the terms of values is certainly a characteristic displayed by leaders, especially those at a senior level.

In order to make decisions at this level the manager needs both a sense of responsibility and a set of values to which he adheres with integrity. Dr Ernest Woodroofe, from the viewpoint of being chairman of a company which employs 320,000 people in seventy countries and is the tenth largest company in the world, offered this definition of integrity:

> Most decisions in business are based on uncertainties because you don't have all the information you would theoretically like to have, but having what you have, you must use your judgement and decide. But, and this is what I mean by the overriding importance of integrity, the decision must be made within the framework of the responsibilities the business man carries. He has responsibilities to the shareholders, the employees, the consumer, even the Government of the day. He has to balance these responsibilities thoroughly, justly and without bias. You could, for instance, make a decision which was to the benefit of your shareholders, but to the detriment of the community as a whole. *Not* doing that, and knowing why you are not going to do it, and what not doing it is going to cost you, is what I mean by integrity.[2]

The exploration of the purpose of industry and commerce as a whole (from which individual companies and firms derive their purpose) leads one to see it in the wider concentric contexts of the given society and political situation, humanity and natural resources and the fulfilment of individual needs, both material and personal. The really hard managerial decisions at the top level are those which involve apparent or real conflicts between these responsibilities which taken together combine to constitute the single purpose of industry and commerce. The capacity to see clearly at the level of purpose, which implies seeing long-term consequences of decisions, is perhaps what is meant by vision.

We tend to speak of purpose in the singular: it has an integrating unity about it, like a broad river flowing towards an undiscovered sea. The tributaries which feed the river (and are fed by it) we might call the *aims* of an organisation. They are more specific and defined than purpose. Statements of aims begin with an infinitive such as 'to manufacture such-and-such goods'. Obviously an organisation can and almost certainly must have several aims which hinge together in a common purpose.

Lastly, we come to *objectives*, which are aims broken down into specific goals or targets, two concrete metaphors from the football field and the archery butts which imply an objective clearly seen within a limited time-and-space context. An objective or aim is often given to the decision maker, and all that he has to do is state it and check it. But the higher he climbs in any organisation the less he can take for granted the apparently 'given' objective or aim and the more the first step in decision making assumes importance. It is sometimes said that a problem stated is a problem half-solved. It is equally true that an aim correctly stated is a decision half-made. When they are not in the situation of having a decision to make leaders often ask themselves: 'What business are we in? What are we trying to do or achieve in the next five years?'

Consequently the purpose, aims and objectives which are implicit in an organisation (or explicit in the decision maker's brief) must be subjected to analysis. This means that their complexities should be unravelled and explored, so that the relation between them becomes apparent. Analysis, however short, should serve to confirm or replace the given objective or aim.

Synthetic thinking comes into play in the mental creation of aims and objectives. The ability to 'put together' the abstract and ideal with the concrete and the practical is necessary for the construction or definition of the kind of aims or objectives to which people will respond in the industry of the future. Even objectives do not just happen: someone has to put together or combine certain elements, just as an archery target is made up of straw, wood, paint, cord and canvas, sewn into an identifiable whole.

The ability to see ideas, people and things as parts of an

integrated whole clearly serves the middle or senior manager
well, and it should complement his analytical powers. Often he
may be a holistic thinker as well in the sense that consciously
or unconsciously he sees the purpose of the organisation as
growth. The tendency of nature to produce a whole from the
ordered groupings of units seems also to work in organisations,
often heedless of other factors, as Parkinson's Law humorously
proclaims. Growth can (consciously or unconsciously) become
a criterion of success, as the ardent 'empire-builder' has
recognised. The manager sees himself more as a farmer or
gardener: feeding and watering here, cutting and pruning there,
and justly enjoying the fruits of his labours. Growth, despite all
the problems it brings, is seen to be closer to the purpose than
profit making, yet it is a growth which the managerial gardener
must carefully regulate so that the organisation expands neither
too quickly nor too slowly.

Whether or not size is an end in itself and a value to be
pursued is a question which requires much more attention.
Perhaps we have uncritically accepted a hidden value-
judgement in the exciting (to holistic minds) idea of 'growth'.
Sometimes a decrease in size might also be a measure of
success.

Yet in the step of decision making which clusters round
consideration of the aim, the intellectual activities of analysing
and synthesising are not alone. Perhaps at no other point does
that deliberate thinking we have called here valuing so much
need to come into play. In the case of a given objective or aim
there should be some sort of scanning device which checks it
against deeply held values. What used to be called a bad
conscience (in reality a good conscience doing its work) may be
compared to a radar screen that illuminates some identified or
unrecognised object. An objective is not held to be morally or
legally defensible because someone told you to attain it, as a
generation of Nazi leaders discovered.

The conscience, however, is an emergency signal. Value
thinking is best done out of the decision-making situation; in
the quiet and calmness of the depth mind our values take
shapes only partly known to us. Purpose, if not aims, implies
values, for they are the directional compass bearings by which
we guide ourselves in the choices of our lives. Like a sports
player, the effective decision maker has done much of his work
off the field: often the race is won or lost before it has begun.
Similarly, those with a clear and usable frame of reference, or
hierarchy of values, will avoid perhaps the worst fate of any

decision maker – not knowing what he really wants to do.

Reviewing the factors

The hardest part of decision making is being certain about your objective or aim in the teeth of possible contenders for its position. The next lot of untidy or irregular bursts of analysing, synthesising and valuing cluster round the factors, the major elements or synthetic constructs of the facts which shape or shadow the situation. Facts come to us ready made in constellations that we call factors: they may have to be unpacked and re-assembled. We may of course be aware of the factors long before we define the aim or objective, but once we sense that a decision has to be made it is a good idea to take a fresh look at the factors and to see them in relation to the decision.

Factor analysis has received much attention, and we can summarise the advice which the text-books offer us:

1 List and name (or identify) all the major factors which are self-evidently important, and those minor ones which could have some influence on the achievement of the aim. For example, a general may have to consider: relative strengths, ground, time and space, climatic conditions, security and courses open to enemy.

2 Continually ask yourself when weighing a factor: 'So what?' If the answer does not add up to much then the factor is not worth considering. The answer to the question 'So what?' is the deduction. Vague and indecisive deductions are not of much use: deductions must be clear, definite and relevant. In other words, each factor must be 'squeezed dry' until it has yielded all it has to give.

3 Search for the critical factor, the one upon which the making of the decision really hinges. It is not always there, but seeking for it is a valuable way of turning over the ground.

4 Look at all the factors taken together. Here synthetic thinking comes into play to balance undue concentration on one factor or set of factors. The combined influence of all the factors, the mysterious sum of the situation which is more than all its parts, needs to be sensed or felt. Whereas the analyst may be competent at dissecting the factors in a situation, his judgement will be impaired if he lacks a sense of the whole picture.

Again, both value-thinking and the depth mind can be heavily involved in the consideration of factors. Obviously our own values and the values of other individuals, the organisation, or society, can be factors in their own right, and may well turn out to be the critical factor. The depth mind, providing we do not disturb its work with worry or anxiety, is adept at the holistic work of seeing factors as a whole.

Courses open

Having examined and turned over all the relevant factors it should become clear that there are a number of courses of action or possible decisions open to us. These again have to be listed, either mentally or on paper.

Through lack of imagination or circumspection we may easily miss possible courses of action. Our minds have a tendency to dichotomise, i.e. to see reality in terms of either/or, and we carry this bias with us into the decision-making situation. In particular it manifests itself in the mirage of there being only two mutually-exclusive courses open to us, whereas in fact there may be many more if we think hard. This tendency is reflected in the way that the word 'alternative' (which means literally one or other of two things, the choice of one implying the rejection of the other) has come to be used instead of 'possibility' (of which there can be many). We see life in terms of alternatives rather than possibilities, and are not aware that we are doing so.

Visualising or recognising a dichotomy because one is wearing mental blinkers must not be confused with the scanning process whereby many courses of action or possible decisions are steadily reduced to a short list of two runners. The either/or approach, especially when it becomes a mental habit, is dangerous because it over-simplifies reality. This may have been the fundamental flaw in the decision making of Adolf Hitler (after his abysmal set of values). Albert Speer, one of the Fuehrer's intimates, noted this trait. 'His close associates even openly made fun of Hitler, without his taking offence.' Thus his standard phrase, 'There are two possibilities', would be used by one of his secretaries, in his presence, often in the most banal of contexts. She would say: 'There are two possibilities. Either it is going to rain or it is not going to rain.'[3]

Experienced decision makers learn to be suspicious of premature consensus and either/or thinking. Peter Drucker declared provocatively: 'The first rule in decision making is that one does not make a decision unless there is disagreement,' and he illustrated his point with this story:

Albert P. Sloan [former head of General Motors] is reported to have said at a meeting of one of his top committees: 'Gentlemen, I take it we are all in complete agreement on the decision here.' Everyone around the table nodded assent. 'Then,' continued Mr Sloan, 'I propose we postpone further discussion of this matter until our next meeting to give ourselves time to develop disagreement and perhaps gain some understanding of what the decision is all about.'[4]

Von Moltke, the famous German strategist, once remarked: 'If you think your enemy has two courses open to him, be sure that he will choose the third.' Wise leaders seek to proliferate courses of action. They keep the span of their attention at wide focus, so that they receive most light from the situation, before narrowing down the focus of their minds. Other people on committees can be useful here, for every individual has a slightly different viewpoint. Some people can see round the 'hill of difficulty' which closes or restricts our own field of vision, and suggest courses of action that would not have occurred to us.

Peter Drucker also made the useful point that one possible course almost always involves taking no decision at all:

> To take no decision is a decision as fully as to take specific action. The danger is that we may simply drift into that possibility in the hopes of avoiding all unpleasant consequences. Only by judging the consequences of doing nothing can we transform it into a possible course of action. Decisions are like surgery, carrying with them all the setting up of all kinds of chain reactions in the living organisms of relationships, organizations and societies. Even if the decision is a minor one it can always cause a mild degree of shock. Sometimes the organism might survive the shock and benefit from the surgical operation; at other times a decision might finish it off. In the latter case the remedy can be worse than the disease.[5]

Making the decision

The analytical, synthetic and valuing (or critical) methods of thinking then get to work exploring and weighing the different courses of action. The facets of doing this are: listing the advantages and disadvantages; examining the consequences of each course; measuring against standards, criteria and values; testing beside the yardstick of the aim or objective; weighing the risks against the expected gains.

Obviously these considerations overlap, and the differences between them are partly semantic. But the major intellectual activity at this point is valuing. Sometimes, where the only relevant criteria are quantifiable, the decision may be easily reached. A decision is a course of action which is chosen in such a way that the thinking process is 'cut off' and we stop seriously considering the other possibilities. If the background and foreground intellectual work has been done properly, the mind should move through this phase as simply and smoothly as a turning wheel passing its zenith.

Clearly it helps if the criteria or ground rules for the decision are thought out in advance. Generally speaking there is rarely one single criterion against which a possible course can be measured: we have to rely upon a number of criteria. Management is the art of maximising a number of variables, not just one or two. Even an apparently simple criterion like 'profit' needs careful analysis.

Sir Arnold Weinstock, Chairman of General Electric, has been reported as employing seven key business ratios as a guide to management (which could also be used for assessing courses of action for the future with the word 'expected' placed in front of them). These ratios are: profits/capital employed; profits/sales; sales/capital employed; sales/fixed assets; sales/stocks; sales per employee; profits per employee.

Needless to say such terms as 'stocks' would require careful definition. It could also be argued that the concept of 'profitability' is not exhausted by this list. For instance, we would need to consider the ratio between output and capacity. Useful tools though they are, such ratios and formulas cannot ever replace the need for managerial judgement.[6]

Again the depth mind can be most important in this phase of the decision-making process. We all know the benefits of 'sleeping on it', thereby allowing the depth mind to do its work. The depth mind sometimes seems to be able to take account of the missing information, the gaps in our knowledge, the interrelations of factors and courses of action matched against deep moral and personal values, and then to suggest to us the right decision. Many people find that the practice of setting a date or time limit for the decision concentrates the depth mind for the final phase of its work.

When the depth mind has carried out its computer-like

calculations in the 10,000 million cells of the brain, it offers the decision: not neatly typed on a piece of paper, but by giving more weight to one course of action over the others. This requires a certain sensitivity to the workings of the depth mind. The relevant attitude or posture of the surface to the depth mind at this stage has been well described by the philosopher Simone Weil:

> Attention consists of suspending our thought, leaving it detached, empty and ready to be penetrated by the object, it means holding in our minds, within reach of this thought, but on a lower level and not in contact with it, the diverse knowledge we have acquired which we are forced to make use of. Our thoughts should be in relation to all particular and already formulated thoughts, as a man on a mountain who, as he looks forward, sees also below him, without actually looking at them, a great many forests and plains. Above all our thought should be empty, waiting, not seeking anything, but ready to receive in its naked truth the object which is to penetrate it.
>
> All wrong translations, all absurdities in geometry problems, all clumsiness of style and all faulty connection of ideas in compositions and essays, all such things are due to the fact that thought has seized upon some idea too hastily and being thus prematurely blocked, is not open to the truth. The cause is always that we have wanted to be too active; we have wanted to carry out a search. This can be proved every time, for every fault, if we trace it to its root. There is no better exercise than such a tracing down of our faults, for this truth is one of those which we can only believe when we have experienced it hundreds and thousands of times. This is the way with all essential truths.[7]

Implementing the decision

The act of decision may take place anywhere in the continuum of the surface and depth minds, but the process is not complete until it is implemented and we have learnt to live with the consequences. Decisions are often lost at this point and resolute choice gives way to wavering indecision. The reason for this phenomenon is that all decisions are a 'cutting off' or amputation of the thinking process. Sometimes the wound is clean and painless, the scars heal and the decision bears fruit.

In other cases the cutting off takes place effectively only in the surface mind: the rejected possibilities linger on in the depth mind, waiting their chance to appeal again in a higher court when occasion allows.

The re-emergence of a rejected possibility often coincides with vigorous criticism of the decision that has actually been made. This can be a testing experience for a leader, for he must tread the tightrope between inflexibility and rigidity on the one hand, and indecisiveness on the other hand. Once he entertains a serious doubt about his decision the leader falls into a dilemma. 'A foolish consistency is the hobgoblin of little minds,' wrote Emerson. Every leader hopes that he is flexible enough to change his mind if necessary or that he has sufficient humility to admit that he is mistaken or wrong. On the other hand, most managers fear being thought weak or indecisive and this may close their minds as tight as a Chinese puzzle.

In the Eisenhower case study there is a possible solution to the dilemma. The leader should indeed be prepared to reconsider his decision, but only if he weighs the proposed change against the consequences of changing his mind. 'Changing horses in mid-stream', as the well-worn phrase has it, is a hazardous manoeuvre, quite different from judging the suitability of the two mounts when they stand meekly upon the river bank. Among the consequences, besides the syndrome of 'order–counter-order–disorder', there may be a fall in the leader's popularity. Moreover, trust is linked to consistency and respect to firmness in maintaining a decision. But there are cases where a wrong decision has been reached through a miscalculation, and if there is still time the leader has to change course and face the consequences, both corporate and personal.

Therefore there is a point of no return between the time when the decision has been made and the moment when the commitment to it is judged to be irrevocable in terms of consequences. Before this important moment the decision maker can to a certain extent experience the feel of the decision as an actuality, knowing at the back of his mind that he has leeway to change to another decision, if new evidence demands it, before he has passed the point of no return.

Deciding where the point of no return lies can be an important decision in its own right. Unlike air flights, it does not necessarily occur at a middle point. A working definition of it would be: 'the last point when you can make a change without causing confusion in terms of the completion of the aim and the people involved'. Responsibility for a decision includes responsibility for changing it up to the point of no return. This does not mean, however, that a decision which is adequate and able to achieve the aim should be abandoned because a better course of action suddenly presents itself. Only if new factors weigh heavily against the feasibility of the adopted decision should another course be seriously considered. Once one is committed, beyond the no return point, new factors or proposals cannot by definition result in any change of course.

A corollary is that one should not commit oneself prematurely to a statement or position, as Alice found to her cost in *Through the Looking Glass.*

> 'The cause of lightning,' said Alice very decidedly, for she felt sure about this, 'is thunder – no, no!' she hastily corrected herself, 'I meant the other way.'
> 'It's too late to correct it,' said the Red Queen. 'When you've once said a thing, that fixes it, and you must take the consequences.'[8]

Most textbooks advocate that we should weigh the consequences of our decision in advance, but they ignore the fact that not all the consequences can be foreseen. We may conveniently distinguish between manifest and latent consequences, the former being those evident upon examination, and the latter unforeseen. For example, it was not evident that the building of the Aswan Dam in Egypt would lead to the death of a certain species of fish in the Mediterranean (by cutting down the flow of fresh water into the sea). Most decisions need corrective decisions to deal with such unforeseen or latent consequences, just as a car driver who corners to the right soon has to turn the steering wheel over to the left to come on course again.

The pressures which the decision maker can be subjected to (both from within and without) in the time between the act or moment of decision and the point of no return mount in ratio with the importance or gravity of the decision. The more costly an error the more potential pressure the decision maker may experience, and the more he will need to be clear and firm in his judgement. Often a leader's calmness and confidence, his ability to keep his head while others about him are 'losing theirs and blaming it on him', will help to create the climate in which the decision, possibly not the best one, can yet be effectively implemented.

Decision-making models

Observations of actual decision-making and problem-solving behaviour support the above theoretical contention that the human mind does not naturally follow the neat, logical and sequential analysis usually recommended in the textbooks. Rather our thinking tends to be often untidy and illogical, with the phases being tried in turns which vary like musical notes in a scale.[9]

In an American attempt to study how decisions are made in real life as opposed to the psychologists' laboratories, Nicholas Nicolaidis analysed 332 administrative decisions made by public officials.[10] Far from decisions being based purely on rational reasons, he found strong admixtures of emotions, power politics, the influences of other people and the individual decision maker's own values. Instead of following classic steps in which ends and means are distinguished, all the possible facts and factors gathered and weighed, alternative courses or solutions advanced and the most rational one (in terms of such criteria as expected consequences) chosen, he found that facts, values, ends and means were confused. Owing to the limitations of the human mind, shortage of time, defective or inadequate communications systems and the confusion of facts and values, many decisions rested upon very incomplete information and the course selected was only one of a limited and incomplete number available. Finally, though decision makers applied reason to their decisions, they also introduced their own values and often some organisational politics, and then, to make the decision seem objective and rational, they claimed it was for the good of the organisation!

Moreover, the decision makers rarely settled for the best or optimum solution as recommended by the management textbooks, but tended to look for a satisfactory compromise among two or more of the courses or solutions, i.e. one that:

1 agreed, at least to some extent, with their own personal interests, values and needs;
2 met the value standards of their supervisors;
3 was acceptable to both those who would be affected by the decision and those who had to carry it out;
4 looked reasonable in its context;
5 contained a built-in justification which would furnish an excuse, and possibly an avenue of retreat, in case the actual results of the decision turned out to be quite different from those anticipated.

Nicolaidis concluded that the 'real' decision makers tended to reach decisions by muddling through with a concern for deciding promptly and with the least uncertainty. In almost all cases other people were consulted or involved, and the resulting decision was a compromise which would be acceptable to as wide a spectrum of the people concerned as possible.

Peter Drucker graphically and simply distinguished between two different kinds of compromise:

> One kind is expressed in the old proverb; 'Half a loaf is better than no bread.' The other kind is expressed in the story of the Judgement of Solomon, which was clearly based on the realization that 'half a baby is worse than no baby at all.' In the first instance, the boundary conditions are still being satisfied. The purpose of bread is to provide food, and half a loaf is still food. Half a baby, however, does not satisfy the boundary conditions. For half a baby is not half of a living and growing child. It is a corpse in two pieces.[11]

The foregoing summary of the study by Nicolaidis may have first suggested to the reader that leaders in industry, commerce and the public services could do with some improvements in their decisionmaking approaches; and, secondly, that the sequential, rational or logical methods of deciding or solving problems so tirelessly recommended to them in management literature could also do with a great deal of attention. As models they bear too little relation to what actually happens in working situations.

One theme of this book is that such a classification is unnecessary if we go back to the nature of thinking. Here, analysis, synthesis and value-thinking co-exist naturally together. The everchanging colour patterns or musical harmonies of these three themes make up the observable part of applied thinking. Below the surface mind we have postulated a depth mind which plays perhaps the largest part in all our thinking. Moreover, we have early recognised that there is no final dichotomy between reason and emotion: even rigorous analytical thinking has its pleasures and pains, although it may take a sensitive palate to taste them.

We must now turn to the social dimension of decision making. For so far we have looked upon the decision maker as an individual, like Rodin's statue *The Thinker*; now we must set him in the context of the people in an organisation or society with whom and for whom he is deciding. For other people play an important part in the thinking process, both indirectly and directly, as we shall see in the next chapter.

8 Problem solving

The word 'problem' is sufficiently general in its meaning to lend itself to a wide interpretation. We talk, for example, about a 'problem child', the problem of world peace, problems in science, mathematics and the arts, and the daily problems facing a manager. Obviously a word that is used so widely needs careful definition by anyone bold enough to employ it.

As mentioned earlier in Chapter 5, 'problem' derives from the Greek word *problema*, literally 'a thing thrown or put forward'. The second part of the word comes from a root that gives us also 'ball' and 'ballistics'. Probably the earliest 'thing' thrown or put forward was a question for academic discussion or scholarly disputation, and the word has never quite lost an academic flavour owing to this parentage, as its frequent and specialised uses in the field of logic, geometry, physics, mathematics and chess testify.

This linguistic history has tended – consciously or unconsciously – to make managers and other practically-minded decision makers rather suspicious of problem solving. Their hesitation often arises from an awareness that problem solving and decision making, although superficially they overlap so much both in subject matter and in methods of approach, in fact require different orders of mind, heart and soul. Academic problems, for example, tend to be presented in a theoretical way in a limited environment. In other words, the problem is put to you in such a way that it is capable of solution in terms of given (or easily acquired) information; there are clear limits around the problem, like a fence round a house. The word problem also has academic overtones in that its existence or solution does not really affect the environment in which it is presented. The solution of the problem is an end in itself, and not a means towards some other end.

The contrast between problems of everyday personal or professional life and academic ones is at once obvious. Indeed, in the strict sense of the term, often the only problems a manager solves are those contained in the crossword puzzle that he might tackle on the train going to work! The problems that really concern us are open in that we often do not have all the information needed to find the best solution. Moreover, the problems are alive in that the way we handle them can influence both us and our environment. Very few of us seek out or invent such problems in order to solve them for the intellectual fun of it (which is not the same as saying that people do not enjoy – secretly or openly – having problems, and the challenging stimulus they bring to their lives).

However, the difference between academic problem solving and practical decision making is always in danger of yawning into yet another false dichotomy. One only has to reflect upon the exasperated comments of many senior managers upon the academic teachers of management in the universities and business schools, or the equally annoying air of Olympian condescension adopted by some academics, to see the force of this point.

What is the relation between problem solving and decision making, if we reject the view that they are totally distinct in every way?

Take the case of Napoleon. The biographer of the fallen emperor's last years on St Helena informs us that Napoleon invariably lost when he played chess: he made his moves too fast and he cheated shamelessly.[1] Now chess has the marks of being an ancient Chinese war game in origin, and so we have the interesting spectacle of perhaps the greatest battle-winner in history consistently failing to perform winning manoeuvres on the chessboard.

Confronted with this piece of evidence, it would be easy to jump to the conclusion that Napoleon's failure proves that problem solving has nothing whatsoever to do with decision making; that in the heat and confusion of battle, Napoleon excelled in the arts of summing up situations, making swift decisions on inadequate evidence and managing the movements of corps and divisions which he had previously successfully organised into armies. In the 'open' situation of real life, where speed of decision might matter more than a slow laborious computation of all the possibilities, surely

Napoleon had proved his worth. On the other hand, while freely admitting that chess may not reveal certain qualities of the true decision maker, it is quite possible that there was a relation or an overlap between the way in which Napoleon played chess against his aides and his battles with opposing generals. Many of his early victories, for example, were won by getting there 'firstest with the mostest', combined with the high morale of his armies. He excelled also at battles on the move, the highly mobile march-and-fight campaigns. At Waterloo, however, where he was much more in the chessboard situation, it could be argued that his defeat — so often blamed on illness, incompetent subordinates or bad luck — sprang from moving his pieces swiftly but thoughtlessly, relying on *panache* rather than a cool assessment of the possibilities. So much so that when he came to play his queen, the Old Guard, the game was already lost.

Only the existence of this kind of relationship between problem solving and decision making can justify the use of case-studies and practical exercises in management education. For a case-study is a linear descendant of the problems posed to the Greek philosophers. Like modern war games, it has been couched in a conceptual framework more relevant to the decision-making life of the student than the chessboard. Yet it remains a theoretical problem in a limited environment, however much real life is simulated in time/space terms. An army on training manoeuvres is still problem solving; real war is somewhere else on the almost completely different scale of decision making. Yet if there was no possible 'transfer' from one to the other situation, there would be no point in problem, case-study or manoeuvre.

We must therefore firmly reject the idea that problem solving and decision making are so far apart that ne'er the twain shall meet. The two are alike and different at the same time. Having explored the obvious differences, it is now time to look at the similarities, and to delineate the position that I believe that problem solving should occupy in relation to the decision making described in the last chapter.

Problem solving and decision making

Psychologically it could be said that 'a thing thrown or put forward' becomes a problem to me only if I am aware of the 'thing' as an obstacle between myself and the end I want to gain. In other words, I become aware of a problem only when I have a prior awareness of some objective, aim or purpose that I am seeking to accomplish. If I want to get from London to New York urgently by a certain time, I have no problem if I can get there by some simple method. But I soon become aware of a problem if my flight is cancelled or there is a dock strike. Now most problems in the conventional or academic sense either assume and expect you to accept some implicit or explicit aim and then tease you by creating an artificial problem state (e.g. games such as chess); or else they are really questions which become problems only in the psychological sense because they are obstacles to some external end the subject is seeking. For example, a riddle becomes a problem only to those who have some ulterior motive for wanting to answer it; hence the diligence of suitors in fairy stories at answering conundrums in order to gain the hand of beautiful princesses. Problems therefore concern the choice of a best means towards an end.

We should not create too rigid a dichotomy between ends and means, because every end turns out to be a means towards another end. In addition, any given means may be infused by those values which convey, like a magnetic quality, the flavour of the ultimate end of all things and people. Consequently we cannot distinguish too closely between decision making and problem solving: what may appear to be a strategic judgement about ends turns out to be the problem of deciding upon the best of several courses in order to achieve the next higher level of aim or purpose. Thus one's mental frames of reference are constantly tilting and shifting, as if one were using navigating instruments at sea and not on secure land.

Alternatively, what seems to be a problem may therefore reveal the need for a decision, that the problem cannot be solved until we know what we want to do. As noted above, these end decisions become more abstract the higher up the continuum one moves, and therefore are both more deceptively simple and more challenging. Problems, as defined here, therefore focus attention upon the means rather than upon the choice of ends, although it may be reiterated that problems can – and frequently do – lead to a redefinition of objectives, aims or purposes.

Research into problem solving

The American psychologist A. Ruger carried out some of the

earliest experiments in human problem solving. Published in 1910 in the *Archives of Psychology* (New York), his article describes the response of subjects to fairly simple mechanical puzzles, such as interlaced metal rings. Ruger noted that:

1 most people tried to identify the significant area ('it must slip through this space') and the right order in time ('but first I must get it loosened here');
2 many found that the solution just happened, and they then analysed the process retrospectively ('How did I do it? I had the two pieces like this, then ...');
3 finding the general or key principle comes first, and then the subject reconstructs the process step-by-step.

Karl Duncker, a German psychologist and pupil of Max Wertheimer, the founder of Gestalt psychology, set his subjects more complex tasks.[2] Like Ruger he made the subjects talk aloud during their attempts at problem solving. One celebrated example is the ray problem. Given a human being with an inoperable stomach tumour, and rays which destroy organic tissue at sufficient intensity, by what procedure can one free him from the tumour by these rays and at the same time avoid destroying the healthy tissue which surrounds it? Talking aloud, one subject groped his way towards a solution in the following manner:

send the rays through the oesophagus (the gullet);
desensitise the healthy tissues by chemical injections;
expose the tissue by operating.
[At this point the subject was given the reasons why all these possibilities were impractical.]
decrease the intensity of the rays so that they do not destroy healthy tissue and yet destroy the tumour;
swallow something opaque to the rays to protect the stomach walls;
alter the location of the tumour ... how?;
introduce a drainage tube;
move the tissue towards the exterior;
vary the intensity of the rays;
adapt the healthy tissues by previous weak use of the rays;
somehow use diffuse rays ... dispersed rays ... stop ...;
send broad and weak bundle of rays through a lens adjusted so that the tumour lies at the focal point;
send weak rays from different directions to converge on the tumour.

Duncker emphasises the need to keep reformulating or restructuring the problem. The start of a new hypothesis is the rearrangement of all the factors which make up the problem situation. In the language of Chapter 5, the subject tries out new syntheses of the given data. Duncker called it 'restructuration', or 'more precisely, this transformation of function within a system'. This led him to experiment with subjects in order to see how far they were able to perceive new functions for familiar objects.

Most solutions come about by the dialogue between previous experience and the present situation, or 'resonance' in Duncker's terminology. Success happens more or less by chance as the subject restructures (actually or mentally) the presented data, guided both by what he sees in the present and what he remembers from the past. Thus the problem solver may exhibit either the trial-and-error approach or a more analytical examination of the end (the goal) and means, before the 'resonance effects' provide the solution.

'Inspection may not have the last word, but at any rate it has the first,' he wrote. 'Its function is essentially heuristic', a searching for the decisive point of attack.[3] The preliminary stage includes analysis of the goal: 'what do I really want?' and perhaps the supplementary question, 'what can I do without?' According to Duncker, the heuristic method asks 'How shall I find the solution?', not 'How shall I attain the goal?' A solution is the way to a goal; a heuristic method, on the other hand, is the type of way to a solution.[4] Guided by heuristic methods the subject then reformulates the problem until 'the resonance effect of a signal' gives the solution.

Many of Duncker's problems are known today as 'functional fixedness' problems, and they all involve using a familiar object in a novel way. We tend to associate a particular object, person or word, with its customary function: the step of seeing a novel use may also be called dislocation of function. A hammer, for example, could serve as a doorknocker, bellclapper, or pendulum weight, instead of being used for driving in nails. The inhibition against novel use decreases with the lapse of time following normal use and the more time that passes since the object was used in its usual way the less likely you are to be a victim of functional fixedness.[5] There is some evidence that English schoolboys specialising in arts subjects are less prone to functional fixedness than science specialists.[6]

The easiest solution to a problem, declared Duncker, turns out to be, simply, if *a* then *b*. If one can reduce problems to these terms this will favour a speedy solution. Such a reduction happens when *a* has been so restructured that *b* can be read from it. Duncker also shows the value of having clues (or 'signals', as he called them). The more specific and definite they are the more they cut down the search for a solution. Models, signals, clues or hints – call them what you will – cut down the time spent in blind seeking or groping.

This latter aspect of Duncker's work has continued to interest both academics and practical managers. Take, for example, his word 'heuristics', which has appeared frequently in contemporary literature on problem solving, such as a *Harvard Business Review* article in October 1966 entitled 'Heuristic Programs for Decision Making'. What does it mean? Derived from the Greek and coined by 1860, 'heuristic' is defined in the *Shorter Oxford English Dictionary* as 'serving to find out; specifically applies to a system of education under which the pupil is trained to find out things for himself'. In current usage it has come to mean an operational maxim or rule of thumb for finding a solution. It serves as an umbrella term for more familiar concepts, such as rules of thumb, laws, strategies, policies, maxims and proverbs: i.e. general ways of going about things as opposed to specific clues or answers.

Duncker's long, difficult and often dull monograph *On Problem Solving* is far from clear either in structure or language, but its groping pioneer experiments and ideas have had a seminal influence. Several of his experiments are still used in management training today. Moreover, he has highlighted the distinction between 'organic' and 'mechanical' procedures, the former being the way it actually happens as the mind works in a new productive performance, while the latter is the shorter hindsight version. In teaching he suggests that the organic way of explanation should be followed, at the cost of the elegant brevity of the mechanical descriptions.

Phases of problem solving

There are hundreds of books and articles which attempt to outline the principle and techniques of problem solving. There is a wide measure of agreement on the main outline, which corresponds to the so-called 'scientific' method of investigation.[7]

Becoming aware of a problem and defining it

General unease does not constitute a problem. There is
something 'thrown forward' in one's path – a difficulty,
obstruction or frustration – which has to be identified. Once
known, the problem may be tackled or avoided, but until it has
been defined it is not a problem as such.

Surveying the data

Besides observation of the data this phase might also include
an inspection of the materials involved or an exploration of the
elements of the problem which have to be restructured.
Sometimes the 'hidden factor', the key to the problem, will leap
into significance at this stage, just as an important clue does to
an alert detective. Mostly, however, the subject is busy
analysing the components of the problem and their present
structure as a synthetic whole.

Advancing hypotheses

The synthesising capacity of the mind is already at work, and
now possible hypotheses for rearrangement or solution are
suggested and elaborated. If none fit, the problem has to be
analysed again, and possibly restated in terms of a fresh
analysis of the goal and other hypotheses advanced.

Moving towards a solution

Some partial solutions – getting sub-problems solved first –
might be a necessary preliminary to a final assault on the
problem. Emotion may accompany this phase – relief from
tension, anger and disappointment, satisfaction or despair. The
conclusions which stem from the chosen hypothesis are tested
against known factors, or by experiment and the gathering of
new facts, to see if they are valid and the hypothesis supported.
    In the case of simple problems these stages may occur very
quickly. Moreover, individual differences of approach, what
could almost be called problem-solving styles, make
themselves plain. These are not fixed, because people vary
their approaches according to the nature of the problem. Yet
there is a broad distinction, for example, between those who
prefer the so-called 'analytical approach' (the slow step-by-step
method of logical thinking), and those who tend to adopt the

more indefinite and groping pattern of trial-and-error and the sudden intuitive restructuring of the whole problem that is characteristic of insight.

Background factors

The results of factual experiments in psychological laboratories have given us a general idea of what human beings do when confronted with a problem. Now we must look at the background factors or conditions which influence performance in problem-solving situations:

Experience

This may be present in the problem solver's mind in varying degrees of specificity. At one end of the scale he may have encountered this precise problem before, and therefore know the solution at once. Secondly, he may have a general experience of this *genre* or family of problems. Thirdly, he may have some theories in his mind, and theories might be defined as abstract distillations of past experience. Writers on problem solving use a variety of words to describe this 'luggage' which the mind brings with it to a given problem, e.g. theory, model, set, direction and schema. All we can say is that problem-solving time is cut down when these relevant ideas are present.

Sometimes, however, the gap between these general ideas and the problem in hand is too wide, and some sort of clue or signal is necessary. Without such guidelines we can become entirely helpless when faced with a problem. The more specific and definite the clue the more likely we are to decode the problem into a solution.

Of course the ideas or ready-made constructs we bring with us may not fit the present situation. So deep is our need for some kind of theory, model or schema, that we too easily apply our past experience to the problem we perceive before us. Often the signals or clues which trigger off this mental reaction are the same as in a previous situation, and yet the repeated application of pre-conceived notions leads to the wrong solution. The mind's readiness to jump to conclusions by identifying a situation with others already experienced, through misreading accidental or deliberately false clues, leads to a large proportion of the errors in problem solving, as any detective story reader or writer knows. There is an optimum here between the past and the present: loyalty to past knowledge and experience balanced against an open and free-thinking capacity of being surprised by the uniqueness and never-before quality of the present.

Motivation

Earlier in this book we noted the false dichotomy between thinking and feeling. The idea that effective problem solvers have to be cold calculating machines is far from the truth; as we have seen, emotion may accompany both the main intellectual activities of analysing, synthesising and valuing, and also the phases or stages through which a decision maker or problem solver may move.

From the experimental evidence there seems to be an optimum for motivation in problem solving. Too much desire to solve a problem can impede one. High motivation can increase the tendency to persist in wrong or inappropriate directions. Too much emotional involvement is a handicap. This is one reason why boxers and wrestlers hope that their opponents will lose their tempers: over-anxiety, fury, tantrums, annoyance and intense distaste for the problem, all these can heighten the possibility that the subject will make mistakes. On the other hand, lack of interest, concern and involvement are equally a handicap. A certain degree of excitement and tension is necessary to get the best out of a person, and the human mind working at its best seems to have some sort of thermostat for maintaining the right motivational temperature.

At this point the significance of value-thinking comes out again. Values ought to give us a sense of proportion so that we rate or weigh the amount of emotion and time which we are prepared to devote to a given problem. The person with a sound sense of values and the capacity to use or apply them will tend to hit the right optimum on the motivational scales. Clearly this will depend upon the nature of the problem and the value of the solution.

Concepts

The language or concepts used in problem solving are important. If one talks aloud while problem solving (as Duncker and Wertheimer suggest) or writes down the problem (as the British Army 'appreciation' method dictates) then there is a good chance that any unconsciously fixed idea or preconception will come to the surface. Often we are held up in problem solving because some pet assumption is blocking the way forwards (see page 128). As we shall see, one of the advantages of problem solving in groups is that others are more likely to challenge faulty premises or inappropriate concepts.

Conceptual thinking is closely linked with the useful but often misleading ability to categorise, or place things into classes. For example, the pencil that writes this sentence could be variously classified as tool, writing implement and finally pencil. Accepting the definition 'pencil' saves me a lot of time in responding to this particular long thin hard object: I know, for example, that it won't bite me. People like to have things, ideas and people in mental pigeon-holes according to concept, class or category: if they cannot do so they often show signs of anxiety.

Summary

For the leader, problems are essentially obstacles in the common path of himself and his team. His field of vision is as open as nature itself: it is not bounded by the artificial picture-frames of academic problems and questions. Yet he can learn from research into problem solving the need to sharpen his analytical faculties while retaining a flexibility in his powers of restructuring and synthesising parts into new wholes. So far research has not thrown up any gold rules that can legitimately be transferred to the world of the manager, but it has enlarged our understanding and stimulated our imagination. Moreover, the steps or phases of problem solving (like those of decision making) provide a useful framework for training our mental faculties, particularly when the discipline involved has sunk deep into our depth minds.

9 Creative thinking

It is a major contention in this book that there is no sharp (or blunt) dichotomy between different types of thinking. In that aspect of thinking and doing called here synthesising, the assembly of parts into a whole which is more than the sum of them, we have an elementary form of creation. In this respect we may say that the vast majority of people are creative. A little further up the scale or continuum we find the less common ability to combine or unite in an unexpected way apparently dissimilar parts for a given object. This capacity for invention or construction, contrivance or design, we might best call ingenuity.

We rightly reserve the extreme right of the continuum or scale for original productions of human intelligence or powers: for example, great scientific discoveries or works of art. It is the quality of outstanding originality – a value-judgement by universal consensus – which sets creativity at this level apart from other points on the scale of making, forming, producing or bringing into existence.

Creativity in any stretch of this continuum should not be confused with productivity, the bringing forth of goods in quantity. Sometimes quantity and quality go together, but this is not always so. One novelist may write two or three hundred novels and be forgotten; another may write one book which is truly original and which will live. It is not true, of course, that if a writer or inventor is exceptionally fertile or creative in the productivity sense, his work is necessarily inferior in creative quality: among playwrights, for example, the name of Shakespeare at once refutes the false but not uncommon inference that more means worse.

As we have seen, creative thinking at the level of synthesising and resynthesising (sometimes called restructuring) plays a part in both decision making and problem solving because it is one of the fundamental elements of deliberate thinking. Needless to say, ingenuity frequently comes into both processes as well. Occasionally highly original solutions or courses of action are thought up as well. But when we come to the higher reaches of the creativity continuum we see some significant differences, which are worth considering in a book primarily on decision making because of the light which they throw upon thinking in general, the raw material or stuff of all decisions.

We may explore the contrast by certain propositions which, if not always true, are generally so. In comparison to decision making, where the goal is either given or deducible from aims, the creative thinker (at this level) may accept or choose not to start from the stated or assumed objective. Creativity of a high order may throw up a whole new range of aims and objectives.

To the eyes of the predominantly decision-orientated manager the creative thinker may also show signs of what appears to be a lack of decisiveness. In his summary of research into the creative personality, after noting the persistence into maturity of childlike (but not childish) attributes such as a spirit of wonder, a capacity for rapture and a certain openness closely akin to gullibility, Dr Haefele noted that growth into adulthood brought the creative person, along with such fruits as confidence and sensitivity to oblique thoughts, 'deferment of judgement, and its other face, ability to see others' viewpoints; [which] may lead to apparent vacillation or indecision. This is partly true, but partly comes from insistence on keeping as many avenues of choice open as long as possible.'[1]

Therefore the creative thinker may have to free himself or herself from the goal-orientation which is necessary in other major shapes or patterns of thinking (and, incidentally, heavily rewarded socially and financially). In the 1930s the psychologist Marion Miller writing under the pseudonym 'Joanna Field' gave a valuable introspective account of her own depth mind at work, in which she described how she began to wonder whether:

> ... Life might be too complex a thing to be kept within the bounds of a single formulated purpose, whether it would not burst its way out, or if the purpose were too strong, perhaps grow distorted like an oak whose trunk had been

encircled with an iron band ... (I began to guess that my self's need was for equilibrium, for sun, but not too much, for rain, but not always. I felt that it was as easily surfeited with one kind of experience as the body with one kind of food, and that it had a wisdom of its own, if only I could interpret it.) So I began to have an idea of my life, *not as the slow shaping of achievement to fit my preconceived purposes, but as the gradual discovery and growth of a purpose which I did not know.*[2]

Marion Miller contrasted her 'discovery' with the handbooks which told her to define the main purpose and the subordinate purposes. But introspection revealed that her mind was always wandering. It took time for her to accept this tendency 'but I had at least begun to guess that my greatest need might be to let go and be free from the drive after achievement – if only I dared. Then I might be free to become aware of some other purpose that was more fundamental ... something which grew out of the essence of one's own nature.'[3]

From this tentative conclusion there developed a different attitude to thought. 'It seemed as if I had been used to treating thought as a wayward child which must be bullied into sitting in one place and doing one thing continuously, against its natural inclination to go wandering, to pick one flower here and another there, to chase a butterfly or climb a tree. So progress in concentration had at first meant strengthening my bullying capacity.'[4] In other words, the mind could be set at 'wide focus' as well as narrow.

As a result Marion Miller had a sharpened awareness of the 'whole' in paintings, for example. This vision could be hindered by too much desire and expectancy. She found that emotion formed a dimension in thinking: 'Moods also had an absolute quality.' Happiness or despair presented themselves as absolutes, colouring the future as well as the present. Tiredness could allow a really unimportant worry to dominate her mind. The part played by feelings was much larger than she had supposed. This feeling-laden thinking which ignored or patronised the facts she called 'blind thinking'. She noted that 'blind thinking' desired extremes, either/or choice; it could swing with disconcerting suddenness, from superiority to inferiority, success to failure, present to past. Studying the facts could check this sudden tilting, especially the facts of time.

Not least, as others have confirmed, fear inhibits the wandering of thought. Marion Miller referred to 'those continually present fears which had so often prevented me from emerging into the fresh air of wide, purposeless attention.'[5] She knew the desire to hide a painful thought from oneself as much as from others, and the flood of panic impulses 'which tried to rush me to greater effort at the first hint of difficulty'. Anxiety could also stem from the unexamined values by which the self (or one's thinking) was judged: 'In face of the hard facts of my own imperfections, it set me all sorts of impossible standards without knowing it.'

Eventually Marion Miller struck upon the concept: 'Think backwards, not forwards.' The clue to thinking (or living, as she would put it) lay in the right relation between the surface and the depth minds. 'What I had to do, in the conscious phase of my thinking, was not to strain forward after new ideas, but deliberately to look back over the unconscious phase and see what bearing the ideas there thrown up had upon the matter in hand ...'

From the above quotations it is clear that despite some fundamental links which show that by origins they belong to the same family or kind of thinking, creative or original thinking takes a markedly different shape from decision making or problem solving. In particular it cannot be classified as a sub-division or branch of the latter, although there are close or tenuous connections between them, depending on a given situation. Creative thinking can go on when there is no problem presented to the mind; as with aims and objectives it can throw up new problems and questions. On the other hand, the creative faculty of the depth mind can be harnessed to problem solving.

The study of creative thinking at the point of unusual originality confirms that in these cases there is frequently a flash of significance. This may be like a blinding flash of lightning or a tiny crackle as a spark leaps from one idea to another. Perhaps more often it is the sudden realisation that two or more parts have been welded (in the unconscious mind) into a whole, plus the more-or-less instant *instinctive* judgement that the new combination is right. But there is an element of surprise and perhaps delight, although this may be foreshadowed by a sense of expectancy, a feeling of being on the right track. These experiences do not necessarily guarantee the originality of the creation; this depends upon a much wider judgement of its quality in the context of its concentric frames of reference.

Individuals clearly vary in their originality, and some

psychologists have tried to distinguish the traits of the more creative thinkers. They come up with long lists of such qualities as intelligence, general knowledge, fluency, flexibility, originality, independence, scepticism, awareness, orientation to achievement, humour, psychological health, persistence, self-confidence, nonconformity, less-than-normal anxiety, dynamism and integration. Such lists share the same disadvantages as those listing the traits of leaders: they do not agree with each other and tell us little that is peculiar to creative people, for there are many people who have some of the above qualities but are not particularly original. To say that creative people have 'originality' does not get us very far.

There is agreement, however, that certain conditions favour original or inventive thought. From a careful reading of the C. S. Forester, Sir Lawrence Bragg and 'Joanna Field' quotations above, the diligent reader may note the following characteristics:

1 Thinking is allowed to play upon the materials at hand. The mind is set in wide focus, and thus it observes or takes in what others would eliminate as irrelevant or accidental. Goals or problems, although of interest, do not dominate the foreground of the mind. There is a willingness to scrap the present goal or problem altogether if something more interesting (within the overall purpose) crops up. Here the mind is like a hanging sticky paper with which ideas collide like flies.

2 Besides the present data the depth mind is well-stocked by background experience or reading in a variety of fields rather than any one speciality. As Pasteur wrote: 'Chance only favours invention for minds which are prepared for discoveries by patient study and persevering efforts.'

3 There are periods of conscious work when the relationships between the material is analysed as well as the question or problem being carefully formulated and perhaps reformulated several times.

4 There is a friendly and often humorous interest in the depth mind and its vagaries. This may be traced in the metaphors or images which writers use about it. R. L. Stevenson, for example, wrote about 'the little people ... my Brownies ... who do one-half my work for me while I am fast asleep, and in all human likelihood do the rest for me as well, when I am wide awake and fondly suppose I do it for myself'.

5 There is a definite organic or holistic dimension in their

minds, revealed by the frequent use of the word growth and also a marked preference for organic metaphors and analogies. But this holistic attitude (to life as well as thinking) is complemented by rigorous analytical skills and the ability to judge one's own work.

Inventions and scientific discovery

The first of the above characteristics can be swiftly illustrated by the many examples of famous inventions or discoveries hit upon by chance, from the days of Archimedes to our own:

In 1822, the Danish physicist Oersted, at the end of a lecture, chanced to put a wire conducting an electric current near a magnet, which eventually led to Faraday's invention of the electric dynamo.

In 1889, Professors von Mering and Minowski were operating on a dog when an assistant noticed a swarm of flies being attracted to the dog's urine. He mentioned it to Minowski, who found that the urine contained sugar. This was the first step towards the control of diabetes.

In 1929, Sir Alexander Fleming noticed that a culture of bacteria had been accidentally contaminated by a mould. This led to his discovery of penicillin.

This attribute of original creative thinking in itself creates some administrative problems. Managers and administrators tend to be goal-orientated in the sense discussed in Chapter 7. If they employ a scientist or creative man they usually want to define with him the goal of the research, the plan for it, the criteria of evaluation and so on. But a high proportion of original inventions will be accidents, unplanned fusions suddenly flashing into consciousness, while the alert mind is pursuing some other line, or perhaps working with no clear idea where it would lead. This fact has an important bearing on government and industrial policies in the provision of funds for various types of research, and particularly for research which seems to have no immediate practical application.

In a study prepared for the National Science Foundation of America, a group of scientists at the Illinois Institute of Technology made this point in a telling way by listing five important modern inventions which resulted from such 'pure research':

The video tape recorder was made possible by the

development of magnetic recording techniques originally intended for sound recording alone, in combination with the principle of frequency modulation – which was patented in the United States as long ago as 1902. Electronic control theory, dating back to 1920, was also an important factor in the development of video tape. Thus, much of the essential work had been done long before the first television station went on the air.

The contraceptive pill was a product of hormone research begun in the nineteenth century and later fertilized by the development of steroid chemistry. An important stage was the extraction of sapogenins – substances resembling cholesterol – from the Mexican wild yam. The oral contraceptive has wide biological implications which still remain to be investigated – so that it, in its turn, may produce unexpected yields of knowledge in other fields.

In the case of the electron microscope, there was a convergence of different streams of research on the wave nature of light and electrons, electron sources and optics. But it was a product developed for different purposes, the cathode ray tube, which supplied the high vacuum technology that made electron-microscopy feasible.

For non-scientists, the least familiar of the five inventions is probably matrix isolation, a technique for arresting and observing chemical reactions, which has wide uses in the study of high energy propellants, petroleum refining and synthetic materials. Many different lines of chemical and cryogenic research contributed to the first definitive description of a matrix isolation procedure at the University of California in 1956. The future of space flight with solid fuels, cheaper petroleum refining and other essential technologies will depend on this discovery. Of all the research work which the scientists found to have contributed to the discovery of matrix isolation none was listed as devoted to the development of a particular product for a practical purpose defined in advance; yet the implications for the future of industrial chemistry now seem almost limitless.[6]

The Illinois group came to the conclusion that in the case of the pill, videotape and the electron microscope, three-quarters of the research necessary had been completed before its practical application was understood and purposeful development was begun. In all five discoveries, the conscious development took place over quite a short period compared with the time it took for the essential pure research.

In a perceptive review of *The Double Helix*, the account by the scientist James Watson of how he and Francis Crick discovered the structure of DNA, Professor C. H. Waddington comments upon the difference of emphasis between decision making (with a goal in mind) and problem solving on the one hand, and the more characteristic method of scientific discovery on the other:

> Not only was the situation Watson describes, of a highly competitive race for a well-defined goal, rather unlike the conditions in which most science is done, but also the type of thinking he used is not typical of most science. Watson approached DNA as though it were a super-complex jigsaw puzzle; a puzzle in three dimensions and with slightly flexible pieces.
>
> Solving a puzzle like that demands very high intelligence, and Watson gives a vivid blow-by-blow account of how he did it. But this is not the sort of operation that was involved in such major scientific advances as Darwin's theory of evolution, Einstein's relativity or Planck's quantum theory. And one is struck by how little Watson used a faculty which usually plays a large part in scientific discovery, namely intuitive understanding of the material.
>
> I will mention two examples, one more technical, one concerned with more abstract logic. When Watson was trying to fit together certain molecules, known as thymine and guanine, known to occur in two alternative forms, he just copied the shapes out of a chemical textbook and had not a trace of technical intuition as to which shape was more probable.
>
> Again, on the more abstract level, the whole of genetics is concerned with one thing turning into two, or occasionally two turning into one; the number three never comes into the picture. Yet Watson spent a lot of time trying to work out a three-stranded structure for DNA. The very idea of threes would make all one's biological intuition shudder. Of course, intuition can be drastically wrong; but it is usually a strong guide in innovative thinking.[7]

What *The Double Helix* does bring out, however, in a very

vivid way is how emotion accompanies the various phases of thinking, and how even in first-class scientific work competition can be a stimulus to more general motivations.[8]

Despite the inevitable presence of mixed motives there is a strong tradition in science attesting to the greater value of the relatively purer or less self-infected forms of interest and curiosity. In the greater creative minds this apparently simple or unmixed desire can take on an attractive childlike quality. Einstein once told a friend:

> When I asked myself how it happened that I in particular discovered the Relativity Theory, it seemed to lie in the following circumstance. The normal adult never bothers his head about space-time problems. Everything there to be thought about, in his opinion, had already been done in early childhood. I, on the contrary, developed so slowly that I only began to wonder about space and time when I was already grown up. In consequence I probed deeper into the problem than an ordinary child would have done.[9]

The analogy with childhood and the attitude to work akin to a boy's love of playing appeared much earlier in a celebrated and profound remark attributed to Newton shortly before his death: 'I know not what I may appear to the world, but to myself I appear to have been only like a boy playing on the seashore, and diverting myself in now and then finding a smoother pebble or a prettier shell than ordinary, whilst the great ocean of truth lay all undiscovered before me.'[10]

Turning from scientific invention and discovery to art, the same characteristics of 'wide focus' attention and a willingness to abandon apparently fundamental preconceptions hold good. The British sculptor Reg Butler, for example, could declare in a lecture to art students:

> I have often myself recognized the fact that however exciting the ideas appear to be which I take to the studio in the morning, if I have not forgotten about them within half-an-hour, then that working day is a bad one. One of the first things one learns about being a working artist as opposed to a theoretician, is that the work comes from a level far below the top of one's head, and that, for all one knows, one's life is largely determined by the seemingly spontaneous behaviour of one's hands.[11]

Both the examples of C. S. Forester and Sir Lawrence Bragg illustrate the critical part played by preparation before any discovery or invention. The materials that will be broken down and fused together in new combinations in the depth mind can find their way to 'the bottom of the sea' only through the surface mind. Reading, talking to interesting people, visits and travel may all contribute to this end. Without the voyage of HMS *Beagle,* for example, Darwin might well have never 'discovered' the origin of the species. In a similar way experiences drawn from Somerset Maugham's travels coloured his stories and novels.

Yet there does seem to be an optimum, a 'not too little, not too much.' The avaricious reader, compulsive globe-trotter or party-goer does not seem to be among the more creative people. Indeed Einstein is said to have told his students not to read too many books. Certainly the shape or formulation of other people's ideas can play tricks with the development of one's own thoughts. C. S. Forester clearly preferred fact-filled manuals, the dry tinder upon which the creative spark could fall. One might perhaps distinguish between these larder-stocking readings and experiences, and the few paragraphs, incidents or personal encounters — supercharged with interest or emotion — which find their way still struggling and alive to the lowest fathoms of the depth mind.

In this context we should note the importance of the creative thinker finding his appropriate field. There are few people who show outstanding originality or discovery in more than one field. Besides being a sphere which engages their interest and curiosity at a deep level, it must lend itself to their particular imaginative abilities. We might group the main types of these as follows, stressing that although they are not mutually exclusive one tends to predominate over the others in any one person. They are all concerned with patterns or relationships:

Verbal: easily perceived relationships between words; concepts or ideas which can be verbalised in the chosen medium; good memory for written or spoken words. (Writers, poets, sociologists, philosophers, theologians, etc.)

Spatial: spatial relationships easily perceived; imaginative ability to think in three dimensions; can remember spatial arrangements. (Artists, architects, some scientists, town planners, engineers.)

Numerate: relationships between figures easily perceived; capable of working out complex mathematical calculations mentally; good memory for numbers. (Pure mathematicians, some scientists, etc.)

Colour: relationships between colours easily perceived; colour schemes can be swiftly visualised; good memory for colours. (Artists, dress designers, interior decorators, etc.)

Musical: relationships between sounds easily perceived; music can be composed mentally; good memory for tunes. (Composers, singers, jazz musicians, etc.)

In the case of genius the memory can become 'photographic' in any of the above aspects: Mozart, for instance, could remember precisely every piece of music he ever heard. But this sort of photographic memory does not guarantee genius (as quiz winners demonstrate); it is only one card in the winning hand the genius holds and in isolation has relatively little value.

Consequently the problem solver and above all the creative thinker must find the right *milieu* for their particular intellectual talents, like a wrestler who cannot demonstrate his individual skill to the full unless he is matched with an opponent whose style allows him to do so.

Lastly, the literature on scientific discovery and creative thinking bears out the close relation between thinking and feeling. Emotions precede, accompany and crown creative achievement. It may be that a well-balanced emotional life and a sensitive awareness of the movements of feelings 'too deep for words' are pre-conditions for effective creative or inventive thinking. Be that as it may, the outstanding thinker in any field is paid in the coinage of joy: a sudden overflow of excited feelings or a more lasting and quieter sense of profound fulfilment. After demonstrating the feasibility of protecting people against smallpox by vaccination, Edward Jenner wrote: 'The joy I felt at the prospect before me of being the instrument destined to take away from the world one of its greatest calamities ... was so excessive that I sometimes found myself in a kind of reverie.'

PART THREE
COMMUNICATION

Introduction

The major aim of this part of the book is to describe and explore the art of communication in such a way that you may feel inspired to set about a practical programme for improving your own communicating. Awareness and understanding of the principles of communication constitute the first steps towards becoming better at communication.

The art of communication is essentially a practical one. It includes skills such as speaking, listening, writing and reading which we all do, but which few do excellently. These basic skills can all be improved by the conscious effort of applying principles or rules to our daily practice of them. Like learning a new language, this conscious phase may seem awkward and full of mistakes at first. But it is not unnatural, for art lies in perfecting our natural gifts. Eventually these efforts will drift into the depth mind and continue to influence attitudes and actions without our being fully conscious that they are doing so.

Chapter 10 considers the nature of communication and the steps in our understanding of it which are most relevant for the practical leader. The skills of speaking, listening and writing are next defined in the context of leadership. Chapter 14 focuses upon the rôle of the leader as chairman of meetings, an especially important one for those in senior leadership positions. Then, the challenge of communicating the common task, maintaining team unity and relating each individual to the institution – the three-circles approach – is the subject of Chapter 15. Finally, you are invited in Chapter 16 to draw up your own action programme for improving your skills as a communicator in management.

10 The nature of communication

*The peoples of the world are islands shouting
at each other across a sea of misunderstanding*

GEORGE ELIOT

These words remind us that lack of communication is endemic
in our human condition. Loud shouting and even violence is a
symptom of the ailment, not a remedy. Without
communication we remain isolated, stranded on our islands,
divided rather than united. To diagnose the nature of
communication is as important for us now (as individuals,
groups and nations) as the discovery of the secrets of the atom
for our fathers. We have to discern the forces which create
human unity – not those which split matter with a crash –
invisible forces which can conquer the 'sea of
misunderstanding' and bind our hearts together. The technical
problems of long-range communication have been solved; the
more central and elusive nature of good communication in
human relations remains to be charted.

But what does this long, formidable word mean? Some verbal
archaeology may help. Using the *Shorter Oxford English
Dictionary* we can unravel the meanings that the word
'communication' has acquired down the centuries. First, it
comes from the same Latin root as 'common', namely the word
communis, whose own roots are shrouded in mystery. The first
part of it presents no difficulties, for 'com' is known to be an
English version of *cum* (with). The second part, *munis,*
descends either from *moinis* (bound), or from the early Latin
oinos (one). Dr Johnson defined the first and major family of
meanings of the word 'common' thus: 'belonging equally to
more than one'.

Our medieval forefathers used 'common' as a verb much as
we use 'communicate' nowadays. Until the beginning of the
first Queen Elizabeth's reign in the mid-sixteenth century an

Englishman might have spoken of 'commoning' with his friends about his work instead of communicating with them. He might equally have meant, however, by 'commoning' that he was eating with them at a common table in the great hall of some manor house or college, pasturing his pigs on the common land, or partaking in the Holy Communion or mass at the parish church. Behind all these uses is the central idea of *sharing:* something is available for all to share in it. Thus it is general and not private, a joint rather than an individual possession, one which is accessible freely to others.

'To communicate', which entered the language about the time that Henry VIII was having problems with his six wives, took over the senses of giving to another as a partaker, and making available something for a general sharing. 'Communication' came to mean the action of imparting, conveying or exchanging, or, concretely, that which is communicated, such as a letter or its contents. Although the Christian religion, always conservative when it comes to language, has retained 'communicate' and 'communion' for the sharing of the sacramental elements of the Eucharist, the words are now rarely used in regard to material things. Almost exclusively communication now refers to the giving, receiving or sharing of ideas, knowledge, feelings – the contents of the mind, heart and spirit of man – by such means as speech, writing or signs.

Quite early in its history, however, communication took on the extra job of denoting the access or means of access between two or more persons or places. By 1684, for example, it was used to describe an alley or passage; much earlier, in the English Civil War, the trenches and ramparts connecting the star-shaped forts around London were called the 'lines of communication'. When an army campaigned in the field, however, its lines of communication were the routes or means which linked it with base and with other allied armies: the roads, rivers or canals which made possible the essential communication or sharing of intentions, information and results. The term 'communications' now covers all the latter-day additions to the primitive trench or passage way: telegraph, telephone, radio, television. The distinguishing feature of these modern inventions is that they enable rapid communication between persons widely separated ('tele-' comes from a Greek word meaning 'far off').

Thus we may fruitfully distinguish three strands in the pedigree of communication, each of which still colours our use of the word. First, it means that which is shared, the 'commons', be they bread, land, ideas or life itself. More specifically, as the English language flowered, communication stood for the action of sharing in the mental or non-material realm, especially in and through the use of words. Lastly, anything which links two or more persons or places has come to be called a communication. In other words, communication has come to include the means used as well as the primary activity itself.

The roots of communication

We can perhaps learn more about the distinctive nature of communication in humans if we glance first at the world of animals, birds and fish. Wherever we look in the animal kingdom we find that communication through the senses is less liable to error than in man, but it is much more limited. Man, with his infinitely richer potential, is capable of attaining a communion with his fellows and his universe which is beyond the reach of even the most developed animal. Yet his communications are much more likely to go awry than those of his evolutionary cousins and his more distant relatives in the family of the living.

In her study of chimpanzees, entitled *In the Shadow of Man,* the zoologist Jane van Lawick-Goodall emphasised that speech sets humans far ahead of their nearest primate cousins, but that we retain many of the primitive methods of communication observable in the chimp.

In fact, if we survey the whole range of the postural and gestural communication signals of chimpanzees and humans, we find striking similarities in many instances. It would appear then, that either man and chimp have evolved gestures and postures along a most remarkable parallel, or that we share with the chimpanzees, an ancestor in the dim and very distant past; an ancestor, moreover, who communicated with his kind by means of kissing and embracing, touching and patting and holding hands.

One of the major differences between man and his closest living relative is, of course, that the chimpanzee has not developed the power of speech. Even the most intensive efforts to teach young chimps to talk have met with virtually no success. Verbal language does indeed represent a truly gigantic stride forward in man's evolution.

All the same, when humans come to an exchange of emotional feelings, most people fall back on the old chimpanzee-type of gestural communication – the cheering pat, the embrace of exuberance, the clasp of hands. And when, on these occasions, we use words too, we often use them in rather the same way as a chimpanzee utters his calls – on an emotional level.

It is only through a real understanding of the ways in which chimpanzees and men show similarities in behaviour that we can reflect, with meaning, on the ways in which men and chimpanzees differ. And only then can we really begin to appreciate, in a biological and spiritual manner, the full extent of man's uniqueness.[1]

A chimpanzee or an otter, however, are less likely to misinterpret one of their kind touching or clasping them in the presence of some anxiety-producing threat than, say, a pretty girl whose hand is suddenly held by her neighbour in a descending airliner. The repertoire of signs, gestures and postures is limited, and all the animals seem to know the code. The nature of man greatly confuses the issue. Not only is his speech an infinitely varied weaving and interweaving of forty different sounds, but the resulting words are capable of many different interpretations. Hence a man can convey or communicate much more widely and more deeply than a chimp can with his fellows, but at the risk of being more misunderstood and more isolated than any in the animal kingdom.

The limitations of animals can be further illustrated by considering the conditions which are necessary if they are to learn even the most elementary lessons. In 1959 Sir James Gray FRS summarised many experiments with animals by advancing five principles:

1 The response expected must not be unduly complex; the animal must be able to reach the food or escape the danger by making reasonably simple movements. In other words the problem must not be too difficult.

2 The lesson must be presented to the animal under conditions which ensure freedom from extraneous disturbance. An animal will not learn if its attention is constantly diverted by other changes in the environment.

3 The problem must be presented on an adequate number of occasions; the more frequent the lesson the fewer the mistakes.

4 There must be an 'incentive' to learn – a reward for success or a punishment for failure. Further, the reward must be related to the needs of the animal.

5 Finally, the experimenter must possess adequate skill and patience. Ability to learn depends to a very large extent on the personality and enthusiasm of the teacher.[2]

Humans far transcend animals, but we can trace some of the roots of human communication in such experiments: namely that factors in the content, situation, method, subject and teacher must all come into play. Certainly simplicity and repetition retain their value in all instruction or learning. But there is another legacy from our evolutionary past. Despite our development of language we retain *non-verbal communication* as an important auxiliary system.

Non-verbal communication

For some years Mr Michael Argyle, of the Institute of Experimental Psychology at Oxford University,[3] has been investigating the 'undercover language' of facial expressions, eye-contact and tone of voice. For example, films of conversations show that the talker tends to look away while actually speaking, but to glance up at the end of sentences for some reaction from the listener, which usually takes the form of a nod or murmur of assent. He gives the listener a longer gaze when he has finished what he has to say.

There are at least eight other factors involved in the non-verbal repertoire: physical touch, appearance (clothes, hair, etc.), posture, proximity, facial expression, hand and foot movements, head position and tone of voice. For the most part these are natural or unconscious expressions of our feelings, synchronised with what we are saying or doing consciously.

It follows that one can only change non-verbal behaviour by changing the inner nature which it is expressing. Courses or conferences which aim to teach you what Shakespeare called 'the craft of smiles' are to be regarded with suspicion, although Mr Argyle's work with mental patients suggests that one can help those whose synchronisation has gone sadly awry.

Courses for normal people in such matters as eye-contact or

gesture, could only induce self-consciousness, which works against natural communication. What is important, however, is the *awareness* that other people are receiving all our non-verbal behaviour, and perhaps finding it expressive of certain unseen inner states or attitudes which may or may no+ be there. One can legitimately strive to avoid sending out the wrong signs or signals through the variety of non-verbal channels. Fortunately we now have language, which can in part rectify our mistakes. But it is the original integrated combination of words and signs which make up the rich texture of human communication. We must now turn to our unique capacity for communicating through language – the prime means of human intercourse.

Communication as dialogue

Most people seem to regard spoken communication as getting a message across to another person: 'You tell him what you want him to know.' This concept implies a one-way traffic from one person to another, with all the emphasis being on transferring a message from one mind to another. Of course we all do this constantly, for example when we tell a taxi driver our destination. But there are some people who have a semi-conscious theory that this is what communication is all about. If this theory is combined with an ingrained self-centredness, it can produce the phenomenon of the bore: one who insists on monopolising the conversation to transmit *his* messages, regardless of the needs or interests of his hearers. Bores are an ancient social scourge. In 1611 the dictionarist Randle Cotgrave could define a 'monologue' as 'one that loves to heare himselfe talke.'

In its strict sense monologue means speaking alone. It became a theatrical term for a scene in which a person of the drama speaks alone, and hence to its modern use of a dramatic composition for a single performer. By the mid-nineteenth century it had extended its meaning to cover all talk or discourse which resembled a soliloquy. In theoretical terms monologue implies today an emphasis upon one-way communication, with a corresponding lack of awareness of the importance of dialogue: of listening as well as speaking, of sharing instead of giving.

'Dialogue', which means literally a conversation between two or more persons, comes from the same Greek verb as 'dialectic' – the art of critical examination into the truth of an opinion. In early English, dialectic was simply a synonym for 'logic' as applied to formal rhetorical reasoning; in later philosophy, however, it began to take on shades of meaning which still colour its use in our time. Hegel (1770–1831) applied the word dialectic to the process of thought by which the mutually contradictory principles of science, when employed on objects beyond the limits of sensory experience (e.g. the soul, the world, God), are seen to merge themselves in a higher truth which comprehends them. Thus we may speak of a dialectic method of critically inquiring into truth, one in which a dialogue between apparently conflicting views is more appropriate than a reflective soliloquy by a lone thinker.

It is important to distinguish between monologue and dialogue as *methods* of communication on the one hand, and as *theories* or *assumptions* about communication on the other. There is room for a diversity of methods, but we constantly need to rediscover the essential unity of the nature of communication as a shared or common activity. If you close your eyes now and stop reading you will effectively end the communication between us. You are involved in it as much as I am: we are partners in crime. Somehow I have to lead you to make up the deficiencies in my book with your thoughts. If one of us fails, then the communication falls to the ground. The real fallacy of the monologist philosophy is that it ignores your and my contribution to the communication process. Monologue sees us as a passive audience; dialogue knows that the other person holds some of the cards that will give to or withhold meaning from both of us. Thus one of the outward signs of a person who is truly convinced that communication is dialogue is that he will be as much interested in knowing about the person with whom he wishes to communicate as he is knowing about the subject in question.

Consequently an awareness of the other person or persons as active contributors to the 'commoning', and not as passive receivers, is an unseen *dimension* which can influence any form of communication. Sometimes it is difficult for the learned or wise to believe that their listeners or readers have anything to add except 'amen'. 'The monological argument against the dialogical process is that the ignorant and untutored have nothing to contribute, so that the addition of zero and zero equals zero', writes Dr Reuel L. Howe:

> This kind of comment, which is made by surprisingly intelligent and otherwise perceptive people, and too often

by educators, demonstrates how little they know about the processes of learning. Nor does it follow that the dialogical principle forbids the use of the monological method. There is a place for the lecture and for direct presentation of content, but to be most useful they should be in a dialogical context. Furthermore, it is quite possible for a person giving a lecture to give it in such a way that he draws his hearers into active response to his thought, and although they remain verbally silent, the effect is that of dialogue.

As a matter of fact, one should not confuse the different methods of teaching with the dialogical concept of communication. Both the lecturer and the discussion leader can be either monological or dialogical, even though they are using different methods. The person who believes that communication, and therefore education, is dialogical in nature, will use every tool in the accomplishment of his purpose. When the question needs to be raised, he may use the discussion method or perhaps some visual aid. When an answer is indicated, he may give a lecture or use some transmissive resource. But his orientation to his task is based on his belief that his accomplishments as a leader are dependent partly upon what his pupil brings to learning, and that for education to take place their relationship must be mutual.[4]

Dialogue is nothing more than good conversation: two persons face-to-face, talking and listening to each other, perhaps using gestures and signs as well. Seven characteristics of such conversations have been suggested:

It is face-to-face.
It is a two-way process.
It is informal.
It is sincere and open.
It is adapted to the situation in which it occurs.
It constitutes a means to an end.
It is desired and enjoyable.

Communication tends to be effective in situations which resemble the direct face-to-face conversation, and less effective the less similar they are. If one person cannot see the other, for example, something is already lost from the equation. Dialogue stands close to the heart of communication.

Feedback

A major contribution to our understanding of communication has come from the introduction of the concept of *feedback*. Norman Wierner coined this term in 1946 in an influential book entitled *Cybernetics: or Control and Communication in the Animal and the Machine*. In it he compared communication to a system which loops back on itself: the parts are linked together in a cycle of activity, like a child's electrical train set. Information does not just pass downwards or outwards: it curves backwards like a boomerang and affects the communicator. This phenomenon of bouncing back, the return of information through the system, Wierner called *feedback*.

This model, and instrumental metaphor from the electrical and electronics fields, emphasised the *two-way* or *dialogue* character of communication. According to this picture, communication was a process in which the sender received feedback from the hearer which might lead him to modify his approach. In diagrammatical terms the nearest representation to the model was a circle, and various forms of the circular model (ovals, rectangles with rounded corners) became popular in the 1950s. There are many versions of it, but the essential idea is the same. The example of the feedback process in Figure 10.1 comes from J. W. Humble's book *Improving Management Performance* (1969).[5] (p.158.)

It has been hoped that the circular model would portray communication as flexible, dynamic and democratic, as indeed to some extent it does. Moreover the electronics background to the Systems Model provided some good metaphors for some of the failings of communication in personal and organisational life. For example, William G. Scott could give this thought-provoking list of common faults or communication problems in organisations:

1 *Timing*, i.e. co-ordinating messages in such a way that they are received either simultaneously or sequentially by different receivers.
2 *Overload*, i.e. reception of messages in such quantity that the receiver is overwhelmed and unable to respond intelligently.
3 *Short-circuiting*, i.e. the omission of one or more persons in a vertical or horizontal communication chain.
4 *Distortion*, i.e. differences in meaning of messages as perceived by senders and by receivers, due primarily to

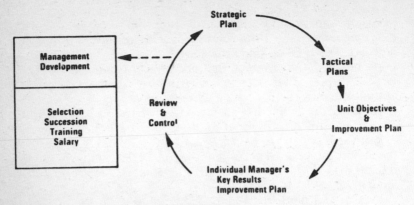

Figure 10.1 The feedback process

different job or positional orientations.

5 *Filtering,* i.e. conscious manipulation of 'facts' to colour events in a way favourable to the sender (especially upward communication).[6]

The circular or systemic model, however, does have certain drawbacks. Circles and systems can imply a concentration on social maintenance. The cyclic model also evokes some prevalent and largely unexamined assumptions about the nature of society and meaning of history. The circle image, of things returning to their starting points like the change of the seasons, has never entirely satisfied Western civilisation. For better or worse we want to push onwards along a line into the unknown. 'Better fifty years of Europe than a cycle of Cathay' as Tennyson declared in the last century.

More recently attempts have been made to develop the circular model while retaining the cybernetic dimension of communication as a dynamic process. A cork-screw? A mattress-spring? One ingenious suggestion, along these lines, comes from Frank E. X. Dance, the editor of a symposium entitled *Human Communication Theory* (1967). Having noted the limitations of the circular model ('a word once uttered cannot be recalled'), he suggested that the recently discovered structure of the DNA molecule might provide the clue, namely the double helix – or a spiral that looks like a coiled ladder. Professor Dance regarded the helix and spiral as essentially the same, however, and offered this model for communication:

'The helix combines the desirable features of the straight line and of the circle while avoiding the weakness of either', wrote Professor Dance:

> In addition, the helix presents a rather fascinating variety of possibilities for representing pathologies of communication. If you take a helically coiled spring, such as the child's toy that tumbles down staircases by coiling in upon itself and pull it full out in the vertical position, you can call to your imagination an entirely different kind of communication from that represented by compressing the spring as closely as possible upon itself. If you extend the spring halfway and then compress just one side of the helix, you can envision a communicative process open in one dimension but closed in another. At any and all times, the helix gives geometrical testimony to the concept that communication, while moving forward is at the same moment coming back upon itself and being affected by the curve from which it emerges. Yet, even though slowly, the helix can gradually free itself from its lower-level distortions. The communicative process, like the helix, is constantly moving forward, and yet is always to some degree dependent on the past, which informs the present and the future. The helical communication model offers a flexible and useful geometrical image for considering the communication process.[7]

If nothing else, Professor Dance's article illustrates how the contemporary student of communication often turns to the natural sciences for his metaphors or models.

Poor communication

Theirs not to reason why,
Theirs but to do and die:
Into the valley of Death
Rode the six hundred.

The proverbial schoolboy knows the story of the heroic but useless Charge of the Light Brigade at the Battle of Balaclava: 670 horsemen charged on that fateful afternoon of 25 October 1854; 247 men were killed or wounded and 475 horses slain. The immediate cause of the disaster was the misinterpretation of a written message. But behind that failure, so graphically described in the extract from Cecil Woodham-Smith's book *The Reason Why,* which follows, lay a history of strained relations between those who would have to communicate with each other in action.

Lord Lucan (commander of all the cavalry) and Lord Cardigan (the Light Brigade General) had had thirty years of quarrels behind them. More recently Lord Lucan and Captain Nolan (the messenger) had exchanged hot words before Balaclava. And these weak personal links must be set against the general lack of 'team maintenance' or cohesion between staff officers and line commanders, infantry and cavalry, the English and French allies. Thus this glaring instance of bad message writing and passing was but the tip of an iceberg of poor communication; it was upon this cold rock that the Light Brigade foundered.

To appreciate and learn from this disaster it is necessary for the reader to know the essentials of the situation. The Russians in the Crimean War were attempting to intervene in the siege operations before Sebastopol by cutting the British lines of communication to the seaport of Balaclava. The successful charge of the Heavy Brigade and the stubborn defensive resistance of some infantry regiments checked the Russians, but then Lord Raglan, the Allied Commander, spied the enemy attempting to remove some abandoned guns from some high ground to his right. The country is hilly and divided by valleys. Raglan's command post was on the high ground at the head of

the long winding North Valley. The Russians occupied the
heights on either side of it, and over two miles away, at its other
open end, their cavalry was regrouping behind twelve guns.
The Light Brigade stood quite near Raglan but, almost on the
floor of the valley, thus:

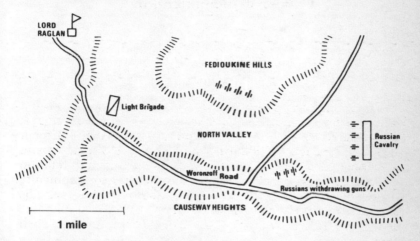

Throughout the story it may be helpful for the reader to bear in
mind all the time the simple fact that it was the guns on the
Causeway Heights that Raglan wished the Light Brigade to
secure – not those guarding the Russian cavalry at the end of
North Valley. How did Lucan set out towards the wrong
objective – and to tragedy? Cecil Woodham-Smith's account is
worth studying closely; it is an unforgettable parable of bad
communication.

The charge of the Light Brigade

The charge of the Heavy Brigade ended the second period of the
battle. The aspect of the action had been entirely changed by
Scarlett's feat. There was no longer any question of the Russians
penetrating to Balaclava, they had been pushed away from
Balaclava, even out of the South Valley altogether, and at the
moment their position presented difficulties. They held the
Causeway Heights and the redoubts, and they had infantry and
artillery on the Fedioukine Hills on the other side of the North Valley,
but between them the North Valley, 1,000 yards wide, was empty of
troops. The troops holding the captured redoubts on the ridge of the
Causeway Heights had therefore little support, and Lord Raglan saw
that this was the moment to recover the redoubts, the Causeway

Heights, and, with the Heights, the Woronzoff Road.

The two divisions of infantry ordered down two hours earlier should now have come into action, but, though the 1st Division under the Duke of Cambridge was present, the 4th Division under Sir George Cathcart lagged behind. He was still in a bad temper, and as he unwillingly left the heights, General Airey had brought him orders to assault and recapture the redoubts – So! he thought, his division, straight from the trenches and exhausted, was to attack, while the Guards were merely marched in support along the valley below. He refused to hurry.

Lord Raglan's anger was evident; indeed, William Howard Russell noticed that Lord Raglan had lost his usual marble calm and seemed fidgety and uneasy, continually turning his glasses this way and that and conferring with General Airey and General Estcourt. He now sent Lord Lucan a third order, of which two versions exist. The copy which Lord Raglan retained in his possession runs: 'Cavalry to advance and take advantage of any opportunity to recover the Heights. They will be supported by infantry, which have been ordered to advance on two fronts.' The order as it reached Lord Lucan and was retained by him is slightly different. The final sentence is divided into two. After the word 'ordered' there is a full stop and 'advance' is written with a capital 'A', so that the final words read 'They will be supported by the infantry which have been ordered. Advance on two fronts.' The change does not affect the issue. Lord Raglan expected Lucan to understand from the order that he was to advance and recapture the redoubts at once without waiting for infantry support, but that infantry had been ordered, and could be expected later.

Lord Lucan read the order in precisely the opposite sense. He was to advance when supported by infantry. Not only did the words of Lord Raglan's order seem to him to have this meaning, but Raglan's treatment of the cavalry throughout the campaign made it highly improbable that he would order an attack by cavalry alone. Again and again, at the Bulganek, at and after the Alma, on October 7th, the cavalry had been restrained, recalled, forbidden to take the offensive, prohibited from engaging the enemy. Only an hour or so ago Lord Raglan had withdrawn the cavalry from their position at the entrance to Balaclava, where they were preparing to engage the Russian cavalry, and placed them in an inactive position under the heights. It never crossed Lucan's mind that he was expected to launch an attack by cavalry with the prospect of being supported at some future time by the infantry. He mounted his division, moved the Light Brigade over to a position across the end of the North Valley, drew up the Heavy Brigade on the slopes of the Woronzoff Road, behind them and on the right, and waited for the infantry, which in his own words 'had not yet arrived'.

Ten minutes, a quarter of an hour, half an hour passed, and the infantry did not appear. Three-quarters of an hour passed, and still Lord Lucan waited. The attack which Lord Raglan wished the cavalry to make appeared to border on recklessness. Redoubt No. 1, on the crown of Canroberts Hill, was inaccessible to horsemen, Nos. 2 and 3 would have to be charged uphill in the face of infantry and artillery. The Heavy Brigade had earlier come within range of the guns in No. 2 and had been forced to retire. However, Lord Raglan, with his power to divine the temper of troops, perceived that the whole Russian Army had been shaken by the triumphant and audacious charge of the Heavy Brigade and that, threatened again by British cavalry, they would retire. Conversations with Russian officers after the war proved Lord Raglan to be right. A feeling of depression had spread through the Russian Army as they saw their great and, as they believed, unconquerable mass of horse-men break and fly before a handful of the Heavy Brigade. For the moment the British possessed a moral ascendancy, but the moment must be swiftly turned to account, and up on the Heights there were murmurs of impatience and indignation as no further action followed the triumph of the Heavy Brigade, and down below Lord Lucan and the cavalry continued to sit motionless in their saddles.

Suddenly along the lines of the Causeway Ridge there was activity. Through glasses teams of artillery horses with lasso tackle could be made out; they were coming up to the redoubts, and a buzz of excitement broke out among the staff. 'By jove! they're going to take away the guns' – the British naval guns with which the redoubts had been armed.

Captured guns were the proof of victory: Lord Raglan would find it difficult to explain away Russian claims to have inflicted a defeat on him if the Russians had not only taken an important position, but captured guns as well. The removal of the guns must be prevented, and, calling General Airey, Lord Raglan gave him rapid instructions. General Airey scribbled an order in pencil on a piece of paper resting on his sabretache and read it to Lord Raglan, who dictated some additional words.

This was the 'fourth order' issued to Lord Lucan on the day of Balaclava – the order which resulted in the Charge of the Light Brigade – and the original still exists. The paper is of poor quality, thin and creased, the lines are hurriedly written in pencil and the flimsy sheet has a curiously insignificant and shabby appearance. The wording of the order runs: 'Lord Raglan wishes the cavalry to advance rapidly to the front – follow the enemy and try to prevent the enemy carrying away the guns. Troop Horse Artillery may accompany. French cavalry is on your left. Immediate. (Sgd.) Airey.'

Captain Thomas Leslie, a member of the family of Leslie of Glaslough, was the next aide-de-camp for duty, and the order had been placed in his hand when Nolan intervened. The honour of carrying the order he claimed was his, by virtue of his superior rank and consummate horsemanship. The only road now available from the heights to the plain 600 or 700 feet below was little more than a track down the face of a precipice, and speed was of vital importance. Lord Raglan gave way and Nolan, snatching the paper out of Captain Leslie's hand, galloped off. Just as Nolan was about to descend, Lord Raglan called out to him, 'Tell Lord Lucan the cavalry is to attack immediately'. Nolan plunged over the verge of the heights at breakneck speed.

ANY other horseman would have picked his way with care down that rough, precipitous slope, but Nolan spurred his horse, and up on the heights the watchers held their breath as, slithering, scrambling, stumbling, he rushed down to the plain.

So far the day had been a terrible one for Edward Nolan; even its

sole glory, the charge of the Heavy Brigade, had been gall and
wormwood to his soul. He was a light-cavalryman, believing
passionately in the superior efficiency of light over heavy horsemen –
'so unwieldy, so encumbered', he had written – and in this, the first
cavalry action of the campaign, the light cavalry had done absolutely
nothing. Hour after hour, in an agony of impatience, he had watched
the Light Cavalry Brigade standing by, motionless, inglorious and, as
onlookers had not scrupled to say, shamefully inactive.

For this he furiously blamed Lord Lucan, as he had furiously
blamed Lord Lucan on every other occasion when the cavalry had
been kept out of action, 'raging', in William Howard Russell's phrase,
against him all over the camp. Irish–Italian, excitable, headstrong,
recklessly courageous, Nolan was beside himself with irritation and
anger as he swooped like an avenging angel from the heights,
bearing the order which would force the man he detested and
despised to attack at last.

With a sigh of relief the watchers saw him arrive safely, gallop
furiously across the plain and, with his horse trembling, sweating and
blown from the wild descent, hand the order to Lord Lucan sitting in
the saddle between his two brigades. Lucan opened and read it.

The order appeared to him to be utterly obscure. Lord Raglan and
General Airey had forgotten that they were looking down from 600
feet. Not only could they survey the whole action, but the inequalities
of the plain disappeared when viewed from above. Lucan from his
position could see nothing; inequalities of the ground concealed the
activity round the redoubts, no single enemy soldier was in sight; nor
had he any picture of the movements of the enemy in his mind's eye,
because he had unaccountably neglected to take any steps to
acquaint himself with the Russian dispositions. He should, after
receiving the third order, have made it his business to make some
form of reconnaissance; he should, when he found he could see
nothing from his position, have shifted his ground – but he did not.

He read the order 'carefully', with the fussy deliberateness which
maddened his staff, while Nolan quivered with impatience at his side.
It seemed to Lord Lucan that the order was not only obscure but
absurd: artillery was to be attacked by cavalry; infantry support was
not mentioned; it was elementary that cavalry charging artillery in
such circumstances must be annihilated. In his own account of these
fatal moments Lucan says that he 'hesitated and urged the
uselessness of such an attack and the dangers attending it'; but
Nolan, almost insane with impatience, cut him short and 'in a most
authoritative tone' repeated the final message he had been given on
the heights: 'Lord Raglan's orders are that the cavalry are to attack
immediately.'

For such a tone to be used by an aide-de-camp to a Lieutenant-
General was unheard of; moreover, Lord Lucan was perfectly aware
that Nolan detested him and habitually abused him. It would have
been asking a very great deal of any man to keep his temper in such
circumstances, and Lord Lucan's temper was violent. He could see
nothing, 'neither enemy nor guns being in sight', he wrote, nor did he
in the least understand what the order meant. It was said later that
Lord Raglan intended the third and fourth orders to be read together,
and that the instruction in the third order to advance and recover the
heights made it clear that the guns mentioned in the fourth order

must be on those heights. Lord Lucan, however, read the two orders separately. He turned angrily on Nolan, 'Attack, sir? Attack what? What guns, sir?'

The crucial moment had arrived. Nolan threw back his head, and, 'in a most disrespectful and significant manner', flung out his arm and, with a furious gesture, pointed, not to the Causeway Heights and the redoubts with the captured British guns, but to the end of the North Valley, where the Russian cavalry routed by the Heavy Brigade were now established with their guns in front of them. 'There, my lord, is your enemy, there are your guns,' he said, and with those words and that gesture the doom of the Light Brigade was sealed.

What did Nolan mean? It has been maintained that his gesture was merely a taunt, that he had no intention of indicating any direction, and that Lord Lucan, carried away by rage, read a meaning into his out-flung arm which was never there.

The truth will never be known, because a few minutes later Nolan was killed, but his behaviour in that short interval indicates that he did believe the attack was to be down the North Valley and on those guns with which the Russian cavalry routed by the Heavy Brigade had been allowed to retire.

It is not difficult to account for such a mistake. Nolan, the cavalry enthusiast and a cavalry commander of talent, was well aware that a magnificent opportunity had been lost when the Light Brigade failed to pursue after the charge of the Heavies. It was, indeed, the outstanding, the flagrant error of the day, and he must have watched with fury and despair as the routed Russians were suffered to withdraw in safety with the much-desired trophies, their guns. When he received the fourth order he was almost off his head with excitement and impatience, and he misread it. He leapt to the joyful conclusion that at last vengeance was to be taken on those Russians who had been suffered to escape. He had not carried the third order, and read by itself the wording of the fourth was ambiguous. Moreover, Lord Raglan's last words to him, 'Tell Lord Lucan that the cavalry is to attack immediately', were fatally lacking in precision.

And so he plunged down the heights and with a contemptuous gesture, scorning the man who in his opinion was responsible for the wretched mishandling of the cavalry, he pointed down the North Valley. 'There, my lord, is your enemy; there are your guns.'

Lord Lucan felt himself to be in a hideous dilemma. His resentment against Lord Raglan was indescribable; the orders he had received during the battle had been, in his opinion, not only idiotic and ambiguous, but insulting. He had been treated, he wrote later, like a subaltern. He had been peremptorily ordered out of his first position — the excellent position chosen in conjunction with Sir Colin Campbell — consequently after the charge of the Heavies there had been no pursuit. He had received without explanation a vague order to wait for infantry. What infantry? Now came this latest order to take his division and charge to certain death. Throughout the campaign he had had bitter experience of orders from Lord Raglan, and now he foresaw ruin; but he was helpless. The Queen's Regulations laid down that 'all orders sent by aides-de-camp ... are to be obeyed with the same readiness, as if delivered personally by the general officers to whom such aides are attached'. The Duke of Wellington himself had laid this down. Had Lord Lucan refused to execute an order brought by a member of the Headquarters staff and delivered with every assumption of authority he would, in his own words, have had no choice but 'to blow his brains out'.

Nolan's manner had been so obviously insolent that observers thought he would be placed under arrest. Lord Lucan, however, merely shrugged his shoulders and, turning his back on Nolan, trotted off alone, to where Lord Cardigan was sitting in front of the Light Brigade.

Nolan then rode over to his friend Captain Morris, who was sitting in his saddle in front of the 17th Lancers – the same Captain Morris who had urged Lord Cardigan to pursue earlier in the day – and received permission to ride beside him in the charge.

There was now a pause of several minutes, and it is almost impossible to believe that Nolan, sitting beside his close friend and sympathiser, did not disclose the objective of the charge. If Nolan had believed the attack was to be on the Causeway Heights and the redoubts, he must surely have told Captain Morris. Morris, however, who survived the charge though desperately wounded, believed the attack was to be on the guns at the end of the North Valley.

Meanwhile Lord Lucan, almost for the first time, was speaking directly and personally to Lord Cardigan. Had the two men not detested each other so bitterly, had they been able to examine the order together and discuss its meaning, the Light Brigade might have been saved. Alas, thirty years of hatred could not be bridged; each, however, observed perfect military courtesy. Holding the order in his hand, Lord Lucan informed Lord Cardigan of the contents and ordered him to advance down the North Valley with the Light Brigade, while he himself followed in support with the Heavy Brigade.

Lord Cardigan now took an astonishing step. Much as he hated the man before him, rigid as were his ideas of military etiquette, he remonstrated with his superior officer. Bringing down his sword in salute he said, 'Certainly, sir; but allow me to point out to you that the Russians have a battery in the valley on our front, and batteries and riflemen on both sides.'

Lord Lucan once more shrugged his shoulders. 'I know it,' he said; 'but Lord Raglan will have it. We have no choice but to obey.' Lord Cardigan made no further comment, but saluted again. Lord Lucan then instructed him to 'advance very steadily and keep his men well in hand'. Lord Cardigan saluted once more, wheeled his horse and rode over to his second-in-command, Lord George Paget, remarking aloud to himself as he did so, 'Well, here goes the last of the Brudenells'.

Conclusion

The word communication embraces a wide range of meanings centring on the concept of *sharing*. It includes the means as well as the ends of human intercourse. The major steps forward in our understanding of its nature in the past fifty years can be summarised by the sequence of the following sentences, which are the milestones, so to speak, marking the main road of research and inquiry:

Communication is one person giving a message to another.

Communication is essentially a dialogue: it takes two to communicate.

Feedback, or the response of the listener modifying the behaviour of the sender, is especially important.

Non-verbal communication, which can be studied in animals, continues as a dimension or aspect in human society.

11 Effective speaking

*Speak properly, and in as few words as you
can, but always plainly; for the end of speech
is not ostentation, but to be understood.*

WILLIAM PENN

Occasions for public speaking abound. In our working lives we
may have to give briefings or talks, take part in presentations or
even deliver formal lectures. Some occupations – notably law,
politics and education – make heavy demands on the speaking
abilities of their members. Others, including the managerial
and supervisory professions, are beginning to share this
characteristic as the art of communication becomes ever more
essential for getting results through working with people.

In industry, commerce and the public services, however, the
occasions for public speaking may be less formal – a few words
before a meeting, a question to a committee, a briefing to
initiate a special job – but these times call for effective speech
from the manager or leader.

Nor should the scope of this chapter be limited entirely to the
workaday world. Most of us live in communities; all of us
belong to families or have friends. We may never launch a ship
or open a bazaar, but few of us can avoid being asked 'to say a
few words' at some stage or another in our lives. Our words
may enhance the occasion, like a good speech at a wedding. Or
our contribution may sway a meeting of a society or
neighbourhood association. At work and in the local
community the ability to communicate or speak well is
inextricably bound up with good leadership and good
membership.

The search for rules

So important is public speaking that it would be surprising if a great deal of ink had not been spilt on the subject. The earliest writer on 'rhetoric', or the art of using language so as to instruct, move or delight others, is said to have been a Sicilian called Corax in the 460s B.C., but unfortunately his treatise has not survived. In the following centuries such practitioners as Demosthenes in Athens and Cicero in Rome brought 'rhetoric' to a high pitch of excellence according to the standards and expectations of their day. A study of their 'word skills' and writings, along with the efforts of the smaller fry of professional orators, formed the basis for later attempts at formulating the rules of 'the art of persuasion', as Aristotle called it in his own book – *Rhetoric.*

Perhaps the best way to get the flavour of this passionate search for rules is to take the most complete account of the art of oratory as our framework – Quintilian's *Institutio oratoria,* written about 95 A.D., when the Roman Empire was nearing its zenith. Like Caesar with Gaul he found his subject to be divided into three parts: the art of rhetoric, the speech itself and the situation that calls it forth.

Quintilian gave most attention to 'the art of rhetoric', which in turn he placed in five divisions. The first two he called 'invention' (collecting the material) and 'disposition' (arranging it in order). Then came the labour of putting it all into words, memorising it, and finally, delivering the finished speech. The speech itself should also have five phases: an introduction to gain the goodwill of the audience; a statement of the point at issue; arguments to prove your case; refutations of contrary arguments; and then a conclusion (peroration) which either recapitulated the main points or else appealed to the audience's emotions.

It was the third part of the art of rhetoric, the putting it into words, which received the most attention from Quintilian and other writers. They called this 'elocution', from the Latin verb 'to speak out'. For the Romans this meant roughly the same as our word 'style': only later did it arrive at its modern use, which virtually limits it to pronunciation. Style covered all the skills and tricks of constructing phrases and sentences so as to serve the content in hand and please the audience.

From the earliest times we can trace the tension between content and method, the Lion and the Unicorn of language, in the disputes of the rhetoricians. One school, the 'Asians', favoured a flowery and elaborate style, with plenty of verbal fireworks thrown in for fun. The other school, the 'Atticists', advocated a plain and unadorned 'elocution'. Allowing the content to speak for itself, they frowned on unnecessary frills. In architecture we may trace the same developments made visible: the ornate splendours of baroque on the one hand contrasting with the more austere line and proportion of classic Greek and Roman buildings on the other hand.

Demosthenes never added stylistic ornaments to embellish his own speeches but he kept the audience on the edge of their seats with a variety of devices: paradoxical arguments, dramatic outbursts, imaginary dialogues, the repetition of salient points and a wit which could be crude, scurrilous and bitter. But his language was simple, at times colloquial. Cicero, almost two centuries later, blended the Attic and Asian approaches. He was a master of the long, rolling, 'periodic' sentences, which he could break out upon the shores of his audiences' minds. When he was summoning up anger against his political opponents his sentences could sound clipped and staccato, like arrows rattling ferociously on a shield. While Cicero never lost sight of the immediate essential – the point he wanted to make – he could align words with such a fine ear that they sounded like poetry. Indeed we are told that on occasion, when he uttered a particular combination of syllables at the end of a sentence, the audience would leap to their feet in tumultuous applause.

By considering the third and last general category in Quintilian's treatise – the kind of speech – we can see the weakness in this whole attempt to construct a science of rhetoric or oratory. Quintilian recognised three main types of speech to which his rules would apply: show speeches (which he called 'demonstrative' ones), political or 'deliberative' ones, and legal pleadings. We only have to reflect that perhaps the greatest speech of all time, the Sermon on the Mount, delivered not a dozen years before Quintilian's birth, does not fit any of these categories, to realise how many kinds of speaking are left out of the traditional classification. As the centuries passed these limitations became more apparent. Rhetoric became backward-looking; it ossified by failing to adapt to the changing situation and the consequent needs of practical men. From politics and public life the concept of rhetoric retreated into the law courts and academies. It became increasingly identified with form (or methods) rather than content, with the mannerisms of speech and gesture which owe more to the Asians than the Atticists. Not only the kinds of speeches but also the audiences changed, and these alterations rendered the more static corpus of books on rhetoric out-of-date. The same is true for modern manuals on public speaking in our own dynamic world. Even Winston Churchill's oratory now sounds a little dated.

Yet the thoughts of the Greek and Roman masters on the six elements of human communication are well worth attending to. For example, they never saw public speaking as a mere string of techniques, gimmicks or tricks of persuasion. They focused attention upon the moral as well as the intellectual and educational gifts of the communicator. As Cato said, a true orator is 'a good man skilled in speaking'. The integrity and kindliness of Quintilian still shines through his pages.

Secondly, the Greek and Roman masters were aware of the importance of the content: they knew that truth or justice communicates better than lies or evil. Of course they knew also that a skilful speaker could cause an untruth or injustice to be accepted, and some believed that the good of the state sometimes justified such advocacy. But they recognised this as being in some way an inversion of the natural order. Values such as goodness, happiness, justice, and moderation were the 'places' where arguments could be found. One word – 'topics' – comes from the Greek word for 'places' used by Aristotle in this way.

Thirdly, the traditional theorists of ancient times stressed the advantages of knowing your audience, and that remains equally valid today. They were especially interested in the psychology of emotions, such as anger or pity. In our own times, when we have witnessed the effects of the emotion-arousing oratory of Hitler and Mussolini, and at a cultural phase when if anything we rather distrust emotional displays, this aspect of knowing people may not greatly appeal to us. But it is the abiding message of the past great masters that a thorough knowledge of people in general and the audience in particular is essential if the aims of public speaking are to be achieved. In the terse words of Cicero these aims are *docere, movere, delectare:* to instruct, to move and to delight.

Five principles of good speaking

Should we abandon the search for principles or rules and rely upon the mind's general thinking abilities of analysing, synthesising and valuing? For two reasons I do not think so. First, the gap between our mind's general faculties and the highly specific actual situations of speaking aloud to one or more people is too wide: we need some bridges across it, some ready-made shapes into which these abilities can flow. Merely to tell someone to analyse (content, audience, and situation) and synthesise (content with methods) is not enough. Such advice would be too general. Secondly, although each communication is unique – unlike any before or after – to some extent they can be grouped into families. The wedding speech situation, for example, has a habit of cropping up repeatedly. Thus it should be possible to make some generalisations.

But what sort of generalisations? Rules come in assorted sizes and shapes. 'Love your neighbour' is qualitatively different from 'Brush your teeth after meals'. The danger of being too specific is that you ignore the situational variables. The rule then has the advantage of being concrete and practical, but it accumulates a 'tail' of 'ifs' and 'buts'. As the months pass it can die the proverbial death of a thousand qualifications. If, on the other hand, the rules are too general they become too abstract, and the mind cannot get a purchase on them. We may agree but we do not buy them in the auction of practical ideas. 'Think!' may be a good rule, but it does not help very much.

The answer may lie in the identification of the appropriate values. Values come in different galaxies and clusters. Where communication is concerned we need to be able to call into play a certain family of values, so that they intermingle with the intellectual and practical work of analysing and synthesising content, methods, communicants and situation. Values are not victims to changes in fashion or to the whims of particular situations: they last. From the point of view of training it is essential that we build these values into our semiconscious or depth minds. We can best do this by a conscious phase when we treat the values in question as principles or rules. Verbally we can express this harnessing of will-o'-the-wisp values by prefixing each with the imperative 'Be'. An additional advantage of changing values into principles, or seeing them as the primary rules, is that we can use them for evaluating communication as well as for shaping it.

Be prepared

In a sense this principle covers all our working life: it is an expression of practical wisdom. As such the praises of its virtues or value have been sung throughout history. Most of us, for example, can recall the Parable of the Wise and Foolish

Virgins. The possibility of preparation springs from our endowment with foresight and imagination: because we can see ahead we can also prepare for what is to come.

Our immediate preparations in speaking will focus on collecting, surveying and arranging our material, finding out about the communicants or receivers and considering the situation. They will usually include making a *plan* of the communication, be it long or short. This may be on paper: an outline of the main phases or stages of a speech or lecture, annotated with the illustrations or examples used to buttress the salient points. Or the plan may be constructed in one's head if time does not allow for even an outline on the back of an envelope.

The bare essentials of the plan are the identification of the central *aim* or *objective* of the communication – what you really want to say – the arrangement of the material to this end, and the 'methods of instruction' to be employed. It is vital to have some sort of plan. By itself a good plan – one that satisfactorily promises to achieve its end – does not guarantee success, but not having any plan can virtually guarantee failure.

There are no particular rules for such plans, except the suggestion that formal speeches should include a *beginning, middle* and *end*. Cicero ignored the complicated rules of structure current in his day, but his speeches always contained an introduction, some sort of main body and a concluding peroration. A good meal, as opposed to a snack, should consist of a 'starter', an entrée and a sweet. Apart from the general principle that the material should be so presented as to fulfil the objective, the three-point programme of beginning, middle and end is worth keeping in mind.

Thorough preparation should also include a visit to the scene of the crime, and a meeting with those whom one is to talk to. Situations are so varied, however, that this is not always necessary: one may know the room and the people extremely well. If not, however, it is essential to reconnoitre the place, checking the seating arrangements, lighting and acoustics, potential external or internal distractions, and any equipment which is being supplied for your use. You should not be satisfied until you (or someone you trust) have seen the equipment in question working. In my experience the things that can go wrong with film projectors, tape recorders, closed-circuit television, and overhead projectors are legion. 'I'm sorry, I am not used to this particular model', hisses the operator apologetically as the machine breaks down. But it is the communicator who carries the responsibility: he has already communicated to his audience that he has failed to observe the first principle: Be Prepared. Of course, you will gain marks if you show unflappability, or even fish out the odd spare part from your pocket – but who wants to live dangerously?

John Casson makes this point well in his description of 'setting the stage'. Of course most speakers have to be their own stage-managers, but the advice holds good when applied to oneself:

> In a theatre, stage-management is the organising of mechanics of effective presentation. It includes setting the stage, lighting it, providing the right properties at the right time and in the right place. The stage-manager's job is so to manage all these mechanics that the actor doesn't have to think about them or be distracted by the lack of them. If anything goes seriously wrong every member of the audience is going to see it and there is no possible way in which the stage-manager could explain why it has gone wrong or to justify its going wrong. It had just gone wrong and from that moment it is irretrievable in the minds of the audience. If something happens for which he feels he needs to apologise, or should apologise, then he has failed. A good stage-manager's attitude of mind is therefore at all times one of using his imagination to anticipate every conceivable disaster that could or might occur. He does it by mentally going through every operation that every actor and every member of the stage staff might have to perform, and checks to see that everything has been done to see that the operation can be performed as easily and as safely as possible. It's his job to see that nothing happens that will distract actors and audience from their close interaction with each other.[1]

Planning and the material advance preparations necessary to implement the plan are the immediate or tactical applications of the Be Prepared principle. They transform raw meat into a tender, succulent and garnished dish, set on a clean warm plate on an attractively laid out table. By good preparations we also make it easier for our guests to enjoy the common meal. But there are also the more strategic or longer-term applications of the principle. All education and training should be preparing us to communicate more effectively. Training refers to skills and techniques; education signifies the stocking of our depth minds with potentially relevant ideas, facts, experiences, pictures and information.

The depth mind, however, like the sea does not always disgorge its treasures at our command. For those who must speak often, either in formal settings or else in committees and discussions, it is a good idea to keep a filing system or perhaps a *common place book,* an ordinary notebook in which one records ideas, thoughts, illustrations, jests or newspaper cuttings – anything which might prove to be useful. To extend its usefulness, make it also a record of *lessons* in communication: your own observations on what works and what does not, along with the tips and rules of thumb which come your way. As well as the value of the contents in what will be your own book on communication, this method keeps the mind constantly preparing for the sudden short moments of speaking. This preparation should be a continuous process.

Time is often in short supply for preparations, but it is rare to find yourself without even a minute to make a plan. Such crisis occasions do have the advantage of revealing the person who is more-or-less always ready to speak in certain areas if called upon to do so. But the good communicator seeks to avoid these surprises.

In summary: the principle of Be Prepared should be applied specifically by making some sort of workable plan for the speech or talk, one which at least fully covers the main points you want to make. The traditional framework of beginning, middle and end is a good start, although the time available may compel us even to chop down this skeleton. Second, no one is prepared until the materials, setting and administrative details have been made ready, checked or settled. Third, Be Prepared should govern our long-term work: the slow and unhurried mastery of our aims and subject, all the relevant background knowledge, the skills and methods of instruction or dialogue, and understanding of people's needs and wants. Lastly, preparation should encompass our own selves – the personality which must refract the light of even the most faint truth, the less obvious aspects of our life which will communicate whatever cosmetics we paint on to disguise them. Can they be changed? Yes, of course they can, but only over a longish period of time.

Be clear

Clarity is the quality of being unclouded or transparent. A clear sky is one free of clouds, mists and haze. With reference to speech it means free from any confusion and hence easy to understand.

Being clear is not primarily a matter of sentences and words. The value of clarity is an inner one: it should act as a principle, purifying thought at its source, in the mind. Clear thinking issues in a clear utterance: if one's ideas or theories are basically muddy or muddled, then it will be a miracle if the external communication of them is easily understood. Thus the application of this principle begins a long way back from the board room or executive office, in the struggle to achieve a piece of clarity in the uncertain weather of the mind. This entails mastering the intellectual skills of analysing, synthesising and valuing.[2]

It should not be supposed that what is clear is automatically true. Someone once said that George Bernard Shaw's head contained a confusion of clear ideas. Be that as it may, truth does not always come purified and translucent, and 'all that glitters is not gold'. Clarity is a mercenary value: it serves well whoever is prepared to pay the price for it. That price includes the willingness to suffer muddled confusion before the clouds part, the dust settles and the issue, problem or course of action becomes crystal clear. If it becomes a matter of communicating to others, the combination of truth and clarity is well-nigh irresistible, certainly so in the long run.

One of the masters of our time in applying the principle of Be Clear was Field-Marshal Montgomery. His wartime 'briefings' became a legend for those who heard him. As a boy at St Paul's School in 1947 I heard Lord Montgomery when he returned to his old school to describe his D-Day plans. It was the building he had used during the war as Allied Headquarters, indeed in the same lecture room he and the other generals had used for their final presentations to King George VI and Churchill, and so it was not difficult for a boy of fourteen years to capture the 'atmosphere', as Montgomery liked to call it. Above all his refreshing clarity lingers. Brigadier Essame emphasised it in his account of Montgomery at work:

> He could describe a complex situation with amazing lucidity and sum up a long exercise without the use of a single note. He looked straight into the eyes of the

audience when he spoke. He had a remarkable flair for picking out the essence of a problem, and for indicating its solution with startling clarity. It was almost impossible to misunderstand his meaning, however unpalatable it might be.[3]

The principle of Be Clear needs to attack like sulphuric acid the corrosions which discolour the work of arrangement, reasoning and expression in our minds. The arrangement or structure of what you are saying should be clear, so that people know roughly where they are and where they are going. The reasoning should be sharp and clean cut, without the blurred edges of those who gloss over the issues. Above all the value dimension of the matter in hand should be clarified, for it is this realm which releases most mud into the pools of thought. Lastly, the principle of lucidity invites us to shun the obscure reference, the clouded remark, the allusion which few will understand, or the word which is fashionable but all too muddy in its meaning.

Be simple

The third principle — simplicity — is a first cousin to clarity. It means uncomplicated. Its cardinal importance for communication stems from the fact that our minds find it easier to take in what is simple. The simple is that which is composed of one substance, ingredient or element: it is not compounded or blended with 'foreign bodies' or unnecessary additions.

Again this principle should be applied to the fountain of our words, our minds and their thoughts. The search for simplicity in thinking is the same as the search for the essence of a subject, that which is specific to it and not composite or mixed up with other matters. Such a quest demands skills of analysing. We have to dissect, discard, blow and burn before we isolate the essential simplicity of a subject.

At this point we may fruitfully distinguish between being simple and being *simpliste* or simplistic. The French version we can use for those who present a complicated matter in the false clothes of a bogus simplicity. Oversimplification is not the same as being simple; simplicity should not be mistaken for simple-mindedness. To be simple requires a lot of hard work, especially if we have to present a subject which has many complications when studied in detail. But even if the subject is inherently complex we still have the choice to make between presenting its complexities in the simplest possible way, or reflecting the complications in both the arrangement of our talk and the language we employ. The ability to speak simply about difficult subjects – without oversimplification – is one of the marks of an effective speaker. We should certainly not fall into the trap of equating simplicity with superficiality. It is quite possible for the simple to have depth and the sophisticated to be empty.

In practical matters, where the desired result of communication is action, the more simple the instructions or plans the more likely people are to remember them and therefore carry them through. Writing to Lady Hamilton in October 1805 from HMS *Victory*, Nelson described the reaction of his captains to the strategy he outlined for the impending battle of Trafalgar:

> I joined the Fleet late on the evening of 28th of September, but could not communicate with them until the next morning. I believe that my arrival was most welcome, not only to the Commander of the Fleet, but also to every individual in it; and when I came to explain to them the *'Nelson touch'*, it was like an electric shock. Some shed tears, all approved – 'It was new – it was singular – it was simple!' and, from Admirals downwards, it was repeated – 'It must succeed, if ever they will allow us to get at them.'[4]

It is important, however, that the communicator should have been aware of all the difficulties and worked his way through the complexities to the heart of the matter, to the essential simplicity of the phenomena. This is as true for the scientist as for the military leader. Max Perutz, himself a Nobel Prize winner in chemistry, commentated on the capacity of Professor Sir Lawrence Bragg in this respect:

> His mind leaps like a prima ballerina, with perfect ease. What is so unique about it – and this is what made his lectures so marvellous – is the combination of penetrating logic and visual imagery. Many of his successes in crystal structure analysis are due to this power of visualizing the aesthetically and physically most satisfying way of arranging a complicated set of atoms in space and then having found it, with a triumphant smile, he would prove the beauty and essential simplicity of the final solution.[5]

Wherever we look we find the same story: good speakers

naturally apply the principle of Be Simple, and it is the less good ones who lose themselves and their audience in a maze of complications, real and imagined. Chancellor Willy Brandt of West Germany said of Jean Monnet, the father of the Common Market: 'He had the ability to put complicated matters into simple formulae.' Doubtless in politics simplicity is a sign of statesmanship just as it accompanies outstanding ability in the arts and sciences.

Apart from content and arrangement the principle of Be Simple should also be applied to language. Here we have to fight an endless battle against the thoughtless use of jargon in public conversation or speeches. But again the price of freedom from this particular piece of professional tyranny is the knowledge of the complications and ramifications which the trade vocabulary, signs and symbols have come to stand for. Otherwise the talk will be *simpliste*. Perhaps we have to earn the right to speak simply.

'I am allowed to use plain English because everybody knows that I could use mathematical logic if I chose', wrote Bertrand Russell in *Portraits from Memory*. 'I suggest to young professors that their first work be in a jargon only to be understood by the erudite few. With that behind them, they can ever after say what they have to say in a language 'understanded' of the people.'[6] His advice applies equally well to all who have to speak to their fellow men about technical matters.

Be vivid

The principle of vividness covers all that goes to make what we say interesting, arresting and attractive. From the Latin verb *vivere,* to live, the word vivid means literally 'full of life'. The characteristics it points to spring from the presence of young kicking life in both the speaker (whatever his age) and the subject: vigorous, active, enthusiastic, energetic, strong, warm, fresh, bright, brilliant and lively. When the subject or content is clear and simple it is already well on the road to becoming vivid, but we may still have to let it come to life.

Thus vividness is not something that can be lightly superimposed when all the other preparatory work is completed. Nor is it the result of giving one's personality full play to express itself, like a fountain playing in the sunlight. All public speaking, however slight the occasion should be 'truth *through* personality'. It is the truth which we have to vivify or bring to life for the other person, never ourselves. Only then can the speaker produce what the poet Thomas Gray called 'thoughts that breathe, and words that burn'.

The first application of the principle Be Vivid is to be interested in what one is talking about and the persons to whom one is talking – in that order. Interest, one of the forms of life itself, is a magnetic quality which is in people and not in subjects. It is true, of course, that genetic inheritance, family upbringing and education predispose us to being interested in certain subjects or topics rather than others. But these fields are as broad as the plains: people, things, ideas, the past, present or future. Within such expanses there are many camping grounds. Moreover, we share some common or universal traits, and if one human person is genuinely interested in some subject it will be surprising if he can find no one to share his interest.

Interest, however, can be a quiet and unassuming movement of the mind. We may acknowledge it in others, but not be necessarily moved to share it. Not all those who have an interest in what they wish to communicate also possess the gift of kindling interest in an audience. But we all find it hard to resist enthusiasm, which is interest blazing and crackling with happy flames. It is extremely difficult for an enthusiastic speaker to be dull: quite naturally he is applying the principle of Being Vivid.

Enthusiasm originally meant in the old Greek the quality of 'being invaded by the divine spirit'. As St Paul records, some of his spirit-possessed congregations babbled away incoherently, like drunkards filled with new wine. They were enthusiastic, but the spirit did not connect and flow into the ordinary language of the day: 'I would rather speak five intelligible words, for the benefit of others as well as myself, than thousands of words in the language of ecstasy', Paul assured his Corinthian readers. The problem for the enthusiast is often how to channel his surging 'ecstasy' into the five intelligible words. At least his face and voice should 'give him away'; they proclaim that – take it or leave it – he finds the subject interesting, even absorbing and fascinating. John Casson writes:

> Enthusiasm consists of a permanent, intense delight in what is happening in the life around us at all times, combined with a passionate determination to create something from it, some order, some pattern, some artefacts, with gusto and delight. It means attacking problems, puzzles and obstacles with gumption and with relish.

We can develop this drive in ourselves by consciously looking for the enthralling, the exciting, the enchanting, the emotionally moving in even the most routine or most trivial matters, and applying ourselves to it and with all the vigour of which we are capable. We don't have to display a frenzy of histrionics and so become a menace to our friends. But we do need to enjoy unashamedly and uninhibitedly whatever we are doing.[7]

Beyond these essentials quite how you apply the principle of vividness depends upon your creative imagination. Where mass communications are involved, a theatrical sense for the 'drama' may be the way forward. Montgomery and Nelson both 'stage-managed' their communications. 'Monty', alone on the stage, tiers of coloured medal ribbons on his battledress, could communicate the inherent drama of battle. Nor was it perhaps just chance that Nelson loved a former actress, or that he insisted on donning his dress uniform of blue laced with gold on the fateful day of Trafalgar. Above all, he had the ability to capture a great moment and let it speak for itself, with all the flair of a great actor on the stage.

In smaller gatherings or groups and in less intrinsically dramatic situations the attempt to be dramatic can soon land us on the rocks of amateur theatricals. Thus the first step is always to look for *relevant* vividness in the subject. For example, I recall one afternoon's instruction in the Army on digging trenches. After a talk on the theory of it, we recruits were marched to the middle of a large field, given spades and told that in thirty minutes a machine gun would sweep the field with fire. None of us had ever dug so fast in our lives ... It was a lesson on a fairly humdrum subject, but the instructor had discovered and released the vividness within it.

Thus vividness springs from the interest and enthusiasm in the mind and heart of the communicator. But it has to become visible in the methods and language which the communicator recruits for his purpose. Audio or visual aids can help a lot, yet they ought to remain *aids* for vividness, not substitutes for it. As we have seen, the structure of the communication, or the order in which the content is presented, can induce vividness. The art here is so to arrange material that the form itself, not the ornaments or aids, convey the life-breath of interest and enthusiasm. Form includes not only the life-less structure of the talk or briefing as it lies inert on the planning-board, but the sense of proportion and timing which allows you to give the

right emphasis to each part of the whole. Vividness is served if
there is an effortless speed; it is destroyed by the two ugly
sisters – Hurry and Worry. Thus, to quote from the
advertisement for a famous make of motor-car, a
communication should have 'Grace, Pace and Space'.

When the structure and timing is clear and the visual aids
sorted out, there remains what could be called the tactics of
vividness – the style or language of the speaker. Many
textbooks at this point give long lists of figures of speech and
idioms to avoid. My own difficulty with such lists is
remembering them in heat and excitement when I am actually
speaking. Fortunately the principles of Be Clear and Be Simple
attack these porridge-like expressions, and they may be
conveniently left until later for consideration in Chapter 13.
Here it remains for us to look at the heart of the matter when it
comes to vivid speech, and that rests upon the fact that perhaps
the majority of people have visual minds: they see things in
pictures and not by hearing abstractions. Thus for the
communicator, as Confucius said, *A picture is worth a
thousand words.*

Best of all is the actual picture, plan or visual symbols
supported by words; second best is the word picture. These
come in various sizes, from the story or description to the
metaphor or simile – the phrase or word which flashes a vivid
picture on the inner screen of the mind. Stories or parables can
be extremely telling, but they require considerable powers of
imagination to invent or adapt, and qualities of voice and
timing which are uncommon. Try to invent a new parable like
'The Good Samaritan' or 'The Prodigal Son' and you will see
what I mean. Count the number of friends you have who can
really tell a joke well, and compare them to those who think
they can! Vivid stories and parables are invaluable, but they
should be relevant, clear and simple.

Metaphors and similes are essentially comparisons. With
metaphors the comparison is introduced neat and sudden; with
similes it is signalled in advance by the words 'like ...' or 'as
...'. They can help in two ways. First, they can aid clarity,
because our progress in any field often depends upon our
ability to relate the unknown to the known. If we can place the
unfamiliar beside the familiar, so that we can explore the 'likes'
and 'unlikes' of the comparison, it helps us to understand what
the communicator is getting at. For example the prize-winning
journalist Robert Heller could work into an *Observer* piece on
management technology: 'A great deal of this essential

technology is financial: those who feel that finance is seldom sensible should consider Discounted Cash Flow. That supposedly sophisticated technique is based, roughly, on the simple old adage that a pound in the hand is worth two in the bush.'[8]

Thus we must distinguish between intrinsic and ornamental metaphors and similes. Intrinsic metaphors, like sheep-dogs, work for their living; ornamental ones may add a touch of grace or colour, but they are more like poodles. Of course metaphors can be both useful and attractive: when this happens they bring a refreshing life to whatever is said. In the bread-and-butter communications of our daily professional lives I believe that the priority must go to the intrinsic or working metaphors.

It is difficult for us to bring colour and vitality into our daily speech through striking and apt metaphors because we are so conditioned to think of all such words as poetic extravagances or artificial devices. The cure is to remember that all language has its roots in the concrete: scratch almost any word, lift the Latin varnish from it, and you will find a ready-made picture. For example, 'company' (from *cum panis*) meant originally people who 'shared bread' together, while 'salary' signifies the money a Roman soldier received in place of his *salus* or salt ration. Whether we like it or not our language is photographic already, and in applying the principle of Be Vivid we only have to release the picture power which is already gloriously there.

Power is probably the right word, because our metaphors and similes often come kicking and struggling into the world with a life of their own. Language should serve meaning as method should serve content. But both meaning and content are constantly in danger of 'take-over' bids from language and methods, such as visual aids. The test is always the practical one: do people remember the message or do they only chuckle over the illustrative story or the memorable phrase?

Mixed metaphors are to be avoided unless they are announced. For they betray a muddled mind; they break the principles of clarity and simplicity. Secondly, they are witnesses to the metaphor struggling to dominate the message. We can see this by comparing two examples of personification, the first cousin to metaphor. John Bright M.P., speaking on the eve of the Crimean War, made his hearers in the House of Commons sit up with this vivid image: 'The Angel of Death has been abroad throughout the land; you may almost hear the beating of his wings.' Compare that with the mixed metaphor of an excited Irish politician of a later decade who could solemnly warn his fellow members:

> Mr Speaker, I smell a rat. I see it floating in the air;
> and if it is not nipped in the bud, it will burst forth into
> a terrible conflagration that will deluge the world.

Humour can also add vividness to speaking. No one has yet
succeeded in defining humour, nor do we understand all the
causes of laughter. Yet we all recognise humour when we see or
hear it, and our response is all the more pleasing because it is
involuntary. We are being temporarily robbed of our
composure, and we surrender it instantly and willingly.
Besides bringing light relief and vitality to speaking humour
also can serve the secondary purpose of attracting and earthing
the tension – sometimes electric – which is present in the
situation. Laughter enables us to explode the tension within us,
and we are grateful to the jester.

Thus a natural humour may help to make a point vividly and
defuse a situation at the same time. Countless illustrations of
this twofold rôle of humour in communication could be given.
We enjoy them so much that we pay professional comedians to
demonstrate this single attribute of the good speaker for our
entertainment, but it is better to observe how practical men use
their humour. Arthur Ellis, a World Cup football referee now
retired, recently recalled one such incident. Having
commented on the problems of maintaining discipline he
continued:

> I used to love the humour of the Shackletons and the Laws
> ... real showmen who put extra sparkle into the game.
>
> There are a score of anecdotes I could tell you about
> Shack but the one that sticks out in my memory came
> when he was partnering Trevor Ford against Derby
> County.
>
> Shack drew the defence and pushed a precise pass to
> the feet of Ford. I reckoned he was fractionally offside and
> blew up.
>
> As Shack ran past me he shouted for my hearing: 'That
> was a bloody awful decision, wasn't it, Trevor?'
>
> I smiled to myself and got on with the game. Some time
> later Shack beat three men in a magnificent run but
> mis-hit his shot and almost put the ball against a corner
> flag. 'And that was a bloody awful shot,' I shouted, and we
> all laughed out loud.[9]

Thus the principle of Be Vivid starts in the heart, in the

interest, enthusiasm and commitment which the subject has
kindled in the potential communicator. But it has to find
expression in arrangement and delivery. Pictures bring
vividness, be they actual or verbal. The visual metaphor or
simile is a short and vivid picture, which also aids clarity and
simplicity. Humour can also enliven working communications,
for laughter and boredom cannot live long together.
Communication is a serious business, but it need rarely be a
solemn one. But the vividness of image or humour should be
such as not to draw attention to itself. Far from taking off on an
independent life of its own, and becoming 'art for art's sake', it
should always serve the *aim* of the communication.

Be natural

To a large extent the first four principles can be applied before a
talk or speech begins, even though there are only a few minutes
to consider what you are going to say and how you will put it.
The principle of Be Natural, however, belongs primarily to the
stage of delivery: it governs our manner of speaking. Of course
it can also influence all our preliminary thinking, for both the
subject and the methods chosen should be natural to use, or
have become so.

When it comes to speaking, art (like all grace) should not
destroy nature but perfect it. Here the influence of the situation
on occasion can be especially troublesome. We all know how
difficult it can be to act naturally in certain circumstances. We
should think nothing of jumping a four-foot-wide stream, but a
similar gap several thousand feet up on a mountain cliff can
make us freeze with nerves. The principle of Be Natural invites
us to shut off the danger signals from the situation, and speak as
naturally as if we were standing before our own hearths. Easier
said than done. Yet the art of relaxing can help to fight off the
strained voice. The natural and relaxed manners of the
experienced television entertainers give us plenty of models for
observation.

The principle of naturalness is not, however, a licence to be
our own worst selves before a captive audience. Relaxation can
so easily slip into sloppiness, just as 'doing what comes
naturally' may be sometimes rightly interpreted by the
audience as an inconsiderate lack of adequate preparation. Nor
should friendly mumbling or inconsequential chatter, laced
with 'you knows', be mistaken for naturalness. The principles
must be taken together. Speaking distinctly is the principle of

Be Clear applied to the actual activity of speaking: it is our ordinary natural speech magnified to meet the larger situation.

Many of the textbooks on communication devote much space to the techniques of breathing, intonation, pronunciation and gesturing. Doubtless there is much to be learnt here, but it is possible to overstress the importance of these elocutionary actions. Beyond the essentials of clear and distinct speech there is little that must be said. Variety in tone and pitch stem from one's natural interest and enthusiasm. If they are 'put on' or practised in front of the mirror, the result can seem self-conscious and even theatrical – in a word, unnatural.

Being natural should not be equated entirely with vocal relaxation. It includes giving expression in our speech to the natural emotions that human flesh is heir to. Our education and culture teach us to suppress any public display of emotion, and this can make communication sound stilted and artificial. It is unfashionable for orators to weep in public nowadays, although Churchill brushed the odd tear from his eye on more than one occasion. But naturalness follows if we allow the emotions of the moment – interest, curiosity, anger or passion – to colour our voices and movements. Yet they should serve the voice and not master it. 'I act best when my heart is warm and my head cool', declared the actor Joseph Jefferson, and all who speak might echo his sentiment.

Summary

It would be possible to put forward fifty or more rules for public speaking, with sub-rules to cover the 'set piece' situations and the more 'off the cuff' ones which characterise the working life of managers, supervisors and shop stewards in all kinds of organisations, besides the wider community. But nobody could remember such a list, let alone apply them. It is much better to have before us the five memorable principles. These principles take the values most relevant to communication and put them to work:

BE PREPARED

BE CLEAR

BE SIMPLE

BE VIVID

BE NATURAL

Mere techniques cannot reproduce these principles. The starting point is to recognise their value and importance: not merely for writers or journalists, but for the practical ends of everyday life. Peter Drucker puts it like this:

> Managers have to learn to know language, to understand what words are and what they mean. Perhaps most important, they have to acquire a respect for language as man's most precious gift and heritage. The manager must understand the meaning of the old definition of rhetoric as 'the art which draws men's hearts to the love of true knowledge.' Without ability to motivate by means of the written and spoken word or the telling number, a manager cannot be successful.[10]

12 Better listening

Many of us, like Falstaff, suffer from 'the disease of not listening'. All too often listening is regarded negatively as what you do while you are awaiting your turn to talk. Yet listening is such a positive contribution to the total business of 'commoning', or attaining the common aim, that it deserves our attention in its own right. Thus we must start with a clear distinction between hearing and listening. The first is mundane; the second is rare. To be good listeners means essentially the same as to be good communicants or receivers.

Most books on communication seem to ignore listening altogether. The few which deal with it launch straightaway into 'Do's' and 'Don'ts'. But it is worth pausing to recollect that listening is a vital ingredient in the creative pattern-making of all human communication. Indeed William Pitt went as far as to declare that 'eloquence is in the assembly, not in the speaker.'

Nine symptoms of poor listening

Of course it is possible to find people who do not suffer at all from Falstaff's 'disease of not listening,' but they are uncommon. Most of us, having fought an uncertain war against our self-centredness, succumb to minor bouts of 'not-listening' at any time; some are as permanently incapacitated by it as are the physically deaf to sounds. What can we do about it? The first step is to diagnose one's own case; or, better still, ask an honest husband or wife to help us to do so. You may like to use the following nine symptoms of poor listening as a guide to some self-analysis. Should you score 100 per cent under each heading, being totally void of all the nine failings in the judgement of even your most perceptive and honest critic, then you can safely ignore the rest of this chapter!

1 Condemning the subject as uninteresting without a hearing

'There is no such thing as an uninteresting subject,' wrote G. K. Chesterton, 'there are only uninteresting people.' Sufferers with this symptom disagree with Chesterton: they have defined their own 'interests' and built them like town walls around their lives. You have to storm the gates to get in. The remedy is to realise that condemning any subject as uninteresting is a public acknowledgement of being an uninteresting person. Of course there are shades and grades: we develop our own pattern of interests. But the failure comes when we do not add to the judgement 'uninteresting' the qualifying phrase — 'for me'. If we admit that the universe is so designed that interest impregnates it, then a subject is always potentially interesting — however dull the speaker may be, or however impoverished our own bank balance of interest at the time.

A variation on this symptom is to pre-judge a speaker as uninteresting for some reason or another. 'Can any good come out of Nazareth?' asked the Pharisees. So we condemn large numbers of people to silence, because we do not believe they have an interesting contribution to make. Or because their last efforts have been unconstructive or long-winded. Yet in organisations of all kinds much of the conversation revolves around work, and people's jobs are sources of endless interest. We all have only one piece of the jig-saw of meaning. Other people have always learnt some skills, some insights or some facts which we know not, and thus — strictly speaking — we never meet anyone who has nothing to teach us. Persuading him to give us a free lesson is the art of listening. The more he cares for his work the more he will respond. Plato, one of the world's top ten intellects, loved to listen to seamen, farmers and craftsmen talking about their skills. There is no record that he ever condemned anyone or anything as incapable of arousing his interest.

2 Criticising the speaker's delivery or aids

One way of expressing one's non-listening ability is to fasten on the speaker's delivery or the quality of his audio-visual aids.

Some trick of pronunciation, an accent or impediment, involuntary movements or mannerisms: all these can be seized upon as excuses for not listening to the meaning. Or the audio-visual aids, which like Hannibal's elephants can be a terror to their own side, can go on rampage and distract a weak listener. It is hard to listen when the delivery is bad and the audio-visual aids out of control, but such occasions do sort out the hearers from the listeners.

3 Selective listening

Selective listening should not be confused with listening in waves of attention, which is in fact a characteristic of the good listener. Selective listening means that you are programmed to turn a deaf ear to certain topics or themes. Adolf Hitler achieved a unique mastery in this field: he only wanted to hear good news. Those who brought him bad news, or told him the truth, encountered a glassy look and personal insult, if not worse. The danger in selective listening is that it can become habitual and unconscious: we become totally unaware that we only want to listen to certain people or a limited range of ego-boosting news, or that we are filtering and straining information. But our friends and colleagues know full well. And they start pre-digesting the material for us, omitting vital pieces and garnishing the rest with half-truths. And in the corridors they may mutter, 'You can't tell him the truth – he doesn't want to know.'

4 Interrupting

Persistent interrupting is the most obvious badge of the bad listener. Of course interrupting is an inevitable part of everyday conversation, springing from the fact that we can think faster than the other person can talk. So the listener can often accurately guess the end of a sentence or remark. The nuisance interrupter, however, either gets it wrong or else – even worse – he elbows in with a remark which shouts out the fact that he has not been listening to the half-completed capsule of meaning. He may often be working on his own next piece of talk, and therefore be literally too busy to listen. Once the remark is ready, or even half-fitted, he lets it fly and starts winding up for the next one.

5 Day dreaming

Day dreaming may be a natural escape from an intolerable situation, but it can also be a symptom of poor listening. It is difficult to think two things at the same time. The day dreamer has 'switched off,' and his attention is given to an inner television screen. Some inner agenda has gained precedence over what is being said to him. The poor listener has a monkey always on his mental shoulder. There is a disconnected chatter going into his left inner ear – that holiday, what Mr Jones said, did I switch my car lights off, if only I was managing director I would ... Emotions can project colour pictures on the inner-screen and turn up the sound. Then – farewell to listening.

6 Succumbing to external distractions

Uncomfortable chairs, noise, heat or cold, sunlight or gloom: the situation can master the listener and drown the speaker and the content. The good listener will try to deal with the distraction in some helpful way; the poor one allows it to dominate his mind and rob him of attention. The higher the quality of listening the less power externals have over the relationship of communicant and communicator. Listening affirms or builds the relationship in the teeth of forces at work to disintegrate it. The weak listener has no extra reserves to call upon to counter such trying circumstances as falling bombs or cocktail parties.

7 Evading the difficult or technical

Such is our addiction to the clear, simple and vivid that none of us cares for the difficult, long and dull presentation, and we throw the sponge in too soon. We have a low tolerance for anything which even threatens to be difficult, coupled with an impatience at the inability of the speaker to save our time and energy by applying the principles of good speaking. But what is at issue is not merely his ability as a speaker but our skill as listeners. If the path has to be tortuous and uphill, the stout-hearted listener will follow. The lazy listener gives up at the first obstacle.

8 Submitting to emotional words

A symptom of the poor listener is his vulnerability to trigger words. Words enter the atmosphere carrying certain associations, pleasant or unpleasant. An unskilled speaker can trigger off a minefield in the minds of an audience, and yet be as innocent as a child out at play. Our minds are like a convoy in this respect, and the poor listener gives in at the first mine explosions! At once thought stops, and his ready-made responses come into play. The man or the topic is instantly categorised; emotions rise and throw us out of tune with the speaker. Once lost, that harmony of relationship, the essential partnership, is not easily restored.

9 Going to sleep

Or the Mad Hatter Syndrome. When indulged in frequently, nodding off to sleep can be a symptom of a poor listener. For the art of listening requires a background of sufficient sleep, a fact which the poor practitioner habitually ignores. His late nights and impressive tiredness may be signs that he has not understood the importance of listening. Tiredness does affect our listening. The tactical remedy lies in that neglected commodity, will-power; the strategic answer is to insist upon enough sleep. The poor listener is chronically short of both.

Towards better listening

Awareness that in varying degrees we are all victims of poor listening habits is a necessary if painful start to a programme of self-help in this area of communication. But once the 'disease of not listening' has been diagnosed we may have to do more than treat the symptoms, for the root of the malady sometimes lies deep inside us, in basic attitudes to life, other people and ourselves. No form of management training and perhaps no kind of medicine, can reach down into those depths and change us entirely. We can split the atom, but we do not know a technique for transforming the nucleus of self-centredness into other-centredness. Yet most of us are not such hopeless cases, and beneath our superficial pre-occupation with self there lies a ready and willing spirit waiting to share in the experience and life of others. It is more a question of projecting ourselves into orbit.

In order to escape the forces of gravity which pull us back to our own centre we can be helped by some common-sense guides. Ten of these are listed and discussed briefly later in this chapter. But first we must consider again the importance of planning and preparation for creating the essential background to good listening.

Being prepared to listen

'A busy man', the saying goes, 'finds time for everything.' Somehow the 'still life' picture of a person intent on listening does not seem to fit in with the contemporary image of the business man as Busy Man. Like the White Rabbit in *Alice in Wonderland* the latter always seems to be 'late for a very important date'. Frenetic activity, telephones ringing, secretaries hovering, typewriters clattering: these are so-called realities. All these externals can provide most respectable excuses for becoming poor listeners. 'So sorry – I should *like* to have listened to you, but I just do not have time' ...

The answer, of course, is to make the time. To have the necessary leisure to listen attentively and not merely hear what is said requires a well-kept life. The application of the principle of making time might begin with ruthless examination of where one's time goes, and a total or partial reorganisation of the working day. It is difficult to listen unless you have with you the right person, at the right time and in the right place. Consequently this first principle is not a mere exhortation: it is an invitation to consider priorities against purpose, aims and objectives.

In her book *Managers and Their Jobs* (1967) Dr Rosemary Stewart has presented the evidence from 160 managers which confirms the need to plan one's time if the necessary conditions for listening are to be created:

> A manager may be able to save more time by organizing his discussions with other people efficiently than in any other way. The research findings underlined the truth of the statement that managers work with other people. The average amount of time that the 160 managers spent with other people was 66 per cent. Is this a high proportion of the working day well spent? To answer this ... the manager must know who are the people he should be seeing and how much time he should normally spend with them. He should know to whom he should be available, and when. He and his secretary should know who ought to have immediate access to him.

When a manager has a visitor his secretary should know in what circumstances he is to be interrupted, but should otherwise ensure that the conversation is undisturbed. His visitor should never need to resort to the strategy reportedly adopted by Keynes in a visit to Roosevelt. The story, which may be apocryphal, is that Keynes paid a visit to Roosevelt, which was interrupted by frequent telephone calls. After some time Keynes left the room and telephoned Roosevelt, who expressed surprise. Keynes replied, 'I realize that the telephone is the only way to get your attention.'[1]

Through good planning and diary control it is possible to lessen the frittering away of one's own time, and – what may be worse – to keep the interruption of other people's time down to the essential minimum. We have no more precious gift to offer another person than our time, and the art lies in spending it both carefully and generously.

Sometimes, however, the programme goes wrong or events crowd in upon one. The 'set-piece' interviews and meetings, with their times thoughtfully budgeted, do make better listening possible, but what about the less structured and less predictable parts of a busy person's life? Here the answer is to create opportunities in the midst of the hustle and bustle, to make time and space just as a great footballer can find that fraction of a second to turn on the ball and score where many lesser players just cannot react fast enough. In other words, the principle of making time can apply to minutes and seconds as well as hours or mornings. Sometimes it is possible to clear a minute or five minutes to listen, which will be worth half-an-hour or more of fitful interrupted hearing to the person concerned.

In these moments, which we create out of nothing, the rank or importance of the person should count not at all. What is vital is that the person wants to say something which matters to him and concerns us, however indirectly. If one cannot guarantee to listen immediately it is always possible to fix an appointment when one can. It takes a well-kept life to be free to listen in the cracks and crevasses of a full timetable, but it can be done. For without making some time totally available there can be no listening.

Preparations may be compared to ploughing up the ground in order to make it more receptive. Background knowledge about the subject and the speaker can aid listening. More often than not one's preparations must be general rather than particular, but sometimes it is possible to do some preliminary reading or discussing which helps one to select what will be the areas meriting special attention in the forthcoming meeting.

Adequate sleep and general fitness may also contribute to the production of attention. Listening, if properly done, can be physically demanding. 'Efficient listening is characterized by a quick action of the heart, a fast circulation of blood, and a small rise in body temperature. It is energy-burning and energy-consuming. It is dynamic and constructive. Therefore, if you would listen well, you have to expend some energy in the process.'[2] Planning and control of the written or unwritten timetable, preliminary preparations and physical freshness: under such treatments the 'disease of not listening' must begin to respond.

Thus, like any game or battle, the outcome of a meeting as far as the communication goes is largely determined before play or action begins. As we have seen, this is as true for the listening part of the equation as it is for the speaking rôle. And, of course, we usually play both parts in alternation. Thus a good listener is made in solitude, in times of reflection and thought far removed from the dust and heat of conversation.

The clearest evidence of his existence is the shape of his diary, by the careful but generous use of his time and the flexible control he maintains over interviews or meetings. Also his mind is well-kept: skeletons are not rattling in the cupboards of his mind. Internal and external distractions can be often foreseen and dealt with, but there are times when we just have to brace ourselves and deliberately compartmentalise our minds. The seas may be flooding the fo'c'sle but we have to slam and screw a hatch, and turn with our back to it in order to listen. As actors say, 'the show must go on.'

Ten guides to good listening

Based on a study of the 100 best and the 100 worst listeners in a freshman class at the University of Minnesota, Ralph G. Nicholas has produced ten useful guides to listening.[3] Although I have retained his headings and most of his comments (given in quotes) I have added some of my own. They can be described briefly, as most of them are positive versions of the negative symptoms of poor listening.

1 Find area of interest

From the discussion above it can be seen that this is almost the golden rule of good listening. It is a rare subject which does not have any possible interest or use for us, our friends or families. We naturally screen what is being said for its interest or value.

2 Judge content, not delivery

'Many listeners alibi inattention to a speaker by thinking to themselves: "Who would listen to such a character? What an awful voice! Will he ever stop reading from his notes?" The good listener moves on to a different conclusion, thinking, "But wait a minute … I'm not interested in his personality or delivery. I want to find out what he knows. Does this man know some things that I need to know?"'

3 Hold your fire

'Overstimulation is almost as bad as understimulation and the two together constitute the twin evils of inefficient listening. The overstimulated listener gets too excited, or excited too soon, by the speaker. The aroused person usually becomes preoccupied by trying to do three things simultaneously: calculate what hurt is being done to his own pet ideas; plot an embarrassing question to ask the speaker; enjoy all the discomfiture visualized for the speaker once the devastating reply to him is launched. With these things going on subsequent passages go unheard.'

4 Listen for ideas

The good listener focuses on the main ideas. He does not fasten on to the peripheral themes or seize on some fact or other, which may block his mind from considering the central ideas.

5 Be flexible

There is no one system for making notes. The good listener may employ four or five methods, depending on the factors, such as the content and situation.

6 Work at listening

Good listening takes energy. Attention is a form of directed energy. 'We ought to establish eye contact and maintain it; to indicate by posture and facial expression that the occasion and the speaker's effort are a matter of real concern to us. When we do these things we help the speaker to express himself more clearly, and we in turn profit by better understanding the improved communication we have helped him to achieve.'

In his rôle, silence can be as expressive of the listener's personality as words are for the speaker. If a sculpture is a work of art compounded of materials and space, so communication is made up from words *and* silence. Silence is not a negative vacuum; it can convey warm and positive feelings which can help or hinder the communicator. The best silence, corrected and deepened by asking the right questions, is an influence felt by the other person, willing him to give of his best.

7 Resist distractions

'A good listener instinctively fights distraction. Sometimes the fight is easily won – by closing a door, shutting off a radio, moving closer to the person talking, or asking him to speak louder. If the distractions cannot be met that easily, then it becomes a matter of concentration.'

8 Exercise your mind

Good listeners regard apparently difficult or demanding presentations or speakers as challenges to their mental abilities.

9 Keep your mind open

Effective listeners try to identify their own prejudices, blind spots and semiconscious assumptions. Instead of turning a deaf ear, they seek to improve upon their perception and understanding precisely in those areas.

10 Capitalise on thought speed

'Most persons talk at a speed of 125 words per minute. There is good evidence that if thought were measured in words per minute, most of us could think easily at about four times that rate.

The good listener uses his thought speed to advantage; he constantly applies his spare thinking time to what is being said. It is not difficult once one has a definite pattern of thought to follow. To develop such a pattern we should:

- Try to anticipate what a person is going to say.
- Mentally summarize what the person has been saying. What point has he made already, if any?
- Weigh the speaker's evidence by mentally questioning it. Ask yourself, "Am I getting the full picture, or is he telling me only what will prove his point?"
- Listen between the lines. The speaker doesn't always put everything that's important into words. The changing tones and volume of his voice may have a meaning. So may his facial expressions, the gestures he makes with his hands, the movement of his body.

Not capitalizing on thought speed is our greatest single handicap. Yet, through listening training, this same differential can readily be converted into our greatest asset.'

The ethics of listening

Cato's definition of an orator – 'a good man skilled in speaking' – can also be adapted and applied to listeners. There are indeed skills in listening, but it would be a mistake to reduce good listening to a matter of techniques. Professional listeners – priests, doctors and journalists – are bound by their own codes of ethics. But the natural activity of listening itself may possess its own intrinsic morality. The good listener, for example, is one who can be trusted to keep a confidence, or to use what he hears only to the advantage of the speaker. Certainly we feel betrayed if someone has misrepresented us, broken a confidence or in any way diminished the poles of trust which must support the slender line of communication. Integrity is as essential for the good listener as it is for the communicator.

Conclusion

A person's listening will express his attitude to other people as surely as the way in which he speaks to them. Indeed, writes Robert T. Oliver, 'for the real master of communication ... listening and talking are interwoven ... like the warp and weft of a piece of cloth. When he is listening, he is standing at the threshold of his companion's mind; and when he is talking, he invites his auditor to stand at the doorway of his own thought.'[4] To be able to move easily and flexibly from one position to the other in pursuit of a common subject or theme, such is good communication.

Above all listening should be a positive influence which enables or supports the speaker in the difficult business of transferring thought, with all its shades of meaning, into the coinage of sentences and words. Silence can be made to express positive and warm encouragement, or it can lamely convey negative feelings or indifference. Silence and attention form the basis of listening, but the mind is not a blank page or empty barrel. Listening is only valuable because it creates the necessary conditions in which the mind can get to work to sort out, restructure and digest what is being said. Lastly, it could be added that attentive silence should bear in it the seed of willingness to make an appropriate response, be it action, understanding or unity. 'The effective listener', concludes Dominick Barbara, 'is one who *uses* silence as he uses talk – with an eager, alive and generous desire to share.'[5]

13 Clear writing

*For a man to write well, there are required
three necessaries – to read the best authors,
observe the best speakers, and much exercise
in his own style.*

BEN JONSON

Ben Jonson's words remind us that there are no sharp divisions between the different modes of communication: our competence with the written word depends to some degree upon our abilities as speakers, listeners or readers. Certainly managers or leaders in all fields have plenty of occasions for 'much exercise' in writing: letters, memoranda, reports, minutes and notes abound. Research confirms the common-sense observation, as Dr Rosemary Stewart's survey of 160 managers has witnessed:

> Managers varied enormously in the amount of time they spent on writing, dictating, reading, and figurework. The average was 36 per cent of total working time, with a range from 7 to 84 per cent. The average is made up of 26 per cent spent on writing, dictating, and reading company material, 8 per cent on figurework – though in some jobs it may have been difficult to separate figurework from writing – and 2 per cent on reading external material for work purposes.[1]

Such devices as books, reports, letters etc. are *methods* for conveying a content from communicators to communicants. The situation or context in which the paper will be read cannot always be known or predicted. Nor can the writer watch the face of the reader, and adjust his message and delivery in the light of his reactions. Thus it is possible to become extremely suspicious about the usefulness of the written word. 'Paper does not communicate', as one manager bluntly declared to me once.

On the other hand writing it down does have some obvious advantages. The written word is at least potentially permanent. The reader can refer back to it and ponder the meaning. Moreover, especially through the medium of print in all its forms – from typewriter to printing press – the written word can convey meaning to those widely separated in distance from the writer, and in a more readily accessible way than – for instance – the recorded spoken word. Lastly, whether we like it or not, writing is here to stay for the foreseeable future as an essential ingredient in working and personal life.

The importance of style

Writing is obviously made up of words, phrases and sentences. There are certain rules and conventions over such matters as punctuation, spelling and arrangement. Many or all of these we learn in elementary and secondary education, or teach ourselves later on. But the combinations of parts are so varied that we each develop a method of writing which can be as distinctive as our finger-prints. Our writing computer gets programmed with certain favourite words, phrases or constructions, which trigger off certain other lines of language when they appear on the blank sheet before us. For this manner of expression, characteristic of a particular writer, we can best use the word *style,* borrowed from *stylus,* the name of the Latin tool for incising letters on wax tablets.

Style bears two main meanings. It can stand first for an individual's unique mode of expression, and secondly for the general mode which distinguishes some class of writers or writings. A discussion of the first belongs properly to the art of literary writing, but we should be wary here as elsewhere of making a false dichotomy. Although the aim of business writing (in any sphere) is to get a message over (and not 'to express oneself'), it is important to be aware that – again like it or not – our style will communicate to the reader something about ourselves as persons. An ill-chosen word can jar like a wrong note; a sloppy sentence can suggest muddled or woolly thinking. 'Reading between the lines' is an unavoidably human activity. 'Use what language you will,' wrote Emerson, 'you can never say anything but what you are.'

Thus the first priority of the working writer is to concentrate on the general characteristics – or style – needed for business writing. Only secondly should he study some of the literary 'tricks of the trade' and then only to avoid accidentally conveying the wrong message about himself to the reader. Yet that does not mean that his writing should be totally devoid of grace. Pleasure boats or gilded yachts were no rivals in beauty to sail clippers. Yet those tall ships carried cases of tea or bales of cotton stacked within their holds. Working books, reports or letters must also carry cargo, but they too can do it with elegance.

In one important respect the stylistic demand is more severe for the manager than the literary writer. The manager is dealing more explicitly in the commodities of money and time. Long letters or memos cost money in terms of secretarial wages and postal charges. Thus conciseness is an essential for the business writer. Not for him the luxury of spreading himself over many pages. Of course the professional writer should also wage war on unnecessary length, although his definition of 'necessary' may include a larger place for self-expression through the tricks and skills of his trade. For he is being paid to delight as well as to instruct and move his readers. But both manager and author are drawing upon the precious limited time of the reader, those minutes and hours which measure out our lives. Wasting time is wasting life. Thus, above all, the manager has to aim at an accurate brevity, or (as Herbert Spencer said) at the 'economy of the reader's or hearer's attention'.

The prose revolution

The Prose Revolution, like the Industrial Revolution, owes much to the impact of science on life. As early as the seventeenth century the first historian of the Royal Society, Thomas Spratt, mentioned their rejection of the 'amplications, digressions and swellings of style' in contemporary writers in favour of a 'close, natural and naked way of speaking'. But the preference for such a style has its roots deep in history. The Prose Revolution, as we may call its triumph into an orthodoxy, in this century, was fed by many underground streams.

As in the case of science the Revolution was founded upon a search for immutable laws which could yield a list of 'Do's and Don'ts' guaranteeing an effective and pleasing style for the busy writer. In 1906 H. W. and F. G. Fowler opened the first chapter of *The King's English* with this salvo:

Any one who wishes to become a good writer should endeavour, before he allows himself to be tempted by the more showy qualities, to be direct, simple, brief, vigorous, and lucid. This general principle may be translated into practical rules in the domain of vocabulary as follows:-

Prefer the familiar word to the far-fetched.
Prefer the concrete word to the abstract.
Prefer the single word to the circumlocution.
Prefer the short word to the long.
Prefer the Saxon word to the Romance (i.e. Latin)

These rules are given roughly in order of merit; the last is also the least.

Another influential writer, Sir Arthur Quiller-Couch, in his Cambridge lecture 'On the Art of Writing' published in 1916, added one more rule:

Generally use transitive verbs, that strike their object; and use them in the active voice, eschewing the stationary passive, with its little auxiliary is's and was's, and its participles getting into the light of your adjectives, which should be few. For, as a rough law, by his use of the straight verb and by his economy of adjectives you can tell a man's style, if it be masculine or neuter, writing or 'composition'.

At the invitation of the Treasury in 1948 Sir Ernest Gowers produced his paperback *Plain Words,* a guide to the use of English by civil servants. Gowers, in common with Quiller-Couch, suspected pedantry in the last two rules proposed by the Fowler brothers, but he was equally critical of Quiller-Couch's substitutes. Instead he suggested that the essence of both the sets of advice could be summed up in three rules:

Use no more words than are necessary to express your meaning, for if you use more you are likely to obscure it and to tire your reader. In particular do not use superfluous adjectives and adverbs and do not use roundabout phrases where single words would serve.

Use familiar words rather than the far-fetched, for the familiar are more likely to be readily understood.

Use words with a precise meaning rather than those that are vague, for they will obviously serve better to make your meaning clear; and in particular prefer concrete words to abstract, for they are more likely to have a precise meaning:

Meanwhile Rudolf Flesch had translated and popularised Fowler and Quiller-Couch for American readers in a series of books, beginning with *The Art of Plain Talk* in 1946. His message had a marked effect, for American 'businessese' was ripe for the sickle as Whitehall 'officialese' had been. Flesch condensed his advice into no less than twenty-five rules:

Write about people, things, and facts.
Write as you talk.
Use contractions.
Use the first person.
Quote what was said.
Quote what was written.
Put yourself in the reader's place.
Don't hurt the reader's feelings.
Forestall misunderstandings.
Don't be too brief.
Plan a beginning, middle, and end.
Go from the rule to the exception, from the familiar to the new.
Use short names and abbreviations.
Use pronouns rather than repeating nouns.
Use verbs rather than nouns.
Use the active voice and a personal subject.
Use small, round figures.
Specify. Use illustrations, cases, examples.
Start a new sentence for each new idea.
Keep your sentences short.
Keep your paragraphs short.
Use direct questions.
Underline for emphasis.
Use parentheses for casual mention.
Make your writing interesting to look at.

To measure progress in the Anglo-American war on verbiage Flesch and others developed some quantifiable methods of estimating readability by counting up certain kinds of words in limited samples and calculating a score which was then checked against a scale. But readability is not the same as comprehensibility. Whether or not people understand does not depend primarily on the choice of root words, but on the quality of thought behind the language. The quantifying techniques 'will certainly not stop a bad writer from producing an illogically constructed text.'[2]

The less happy results in the 'prose-engineering movement' come from the human tendency to treat as literal rules what should really be regarded as principles. We need to be able to break down abstract principles into more concrete rules, but the impulse in many people is then to forget the principles and fasten exclusively on the rules, holding them to be 100% applicable in all cases. But this policy soon lands a writer on the rocks. A rule such as 'Prefer the short word to the long', for example, if taken too far ignores the fact that sometimes the long word is the right word. Thus the superficial application of the Flesch formulas could result in a deliberate 'talking down' (or 'writing down') to a supposed level of intelligence and vocabulary in the reader. The outcome in America, according to *Fortune* magazine, has been a kind of managerial pidgin English or an inverted form of gobbledygook. In other words a new orthodoxy, full of autocratic rights and wrongs, has begun to emerge.

Rules do have their place, but they ought to be concrete expressions of principles and not substitutes for them. One cannot make lasting improvements in style by manipulating language in a superficial way. The principles have to govern how the mind works, or what it seeks. Take simplicity as an example. Most of Flesch's rules seem to guarantee the golden egg of simplicity. But slavishly followed do they not end up by producing only broiler chickens capable of *simpliste* writing or talking? As the *Fortune* article on 'The Language of Business' perceptively comments:

> Simplicity is an elusive, almost complex thing. It comes from discipline and organization of thought, intellectual courage – and many other attributes more hard won than by short words and short sentences. For plain talk – honest plain talk – is the reward of simplicity, not the means to it. The distinction may seem slight, but it is tremendously important.[3]

Thus we are led back to the principles which should govern both speaking and writing. Be Prepared, Be Clear, Be Simple, Be Vivid and Be Natural. These should not be seen as separate or detachable guides or rules: they ought to qualify each other like checks and balances in any situation, and it is the complex of all five that matters. Be Prepared, for example, ought to include a knowledge of the way other men have written effectively, distilled into such rules as 'prefer the active to the passive verb', as well as the accepted customs over spelling and punctuation. But this should be balanced by the principle Be Natural. The best writers, like the naturally good soldiers of ancient days, are those who have undergone the formal drills and manoeuvres of their discipline, and then been allowed to revert to their former ferocious selves.

As another example, the need for simplicity in language must be balanced against the first principle, which is clarity. All communication, like sketching or painting, involves leaving some things out. The substance and aids to accuracy – stating all the relevant facts, defining terms, following logical steps – demand that certain things should be kept in, even at the expense of brevity. Over-brief or mutilated writing inevitably creates the need for further correcting communications, and so nothing is gained.

In the case of writing we should have swallowed the drill book of grammar (or usage), punctuation, spelling, idiom and composition during our schooldays. The problem, of course, is that we do not have anything much to write about then, and so it can all seem a rather pointless exercise. Only later, when we try to say what is important, or vital, and when the octopus of gobbledygook wraps its long arms around us, do we wish that we had paid more attention to those Ancient Mariners, our teachers. Many textbooks on business communication seek to remedy this deficiency with chapters on such topics as punctuation, spelling and syntax. But these should have been mastered at school. Fortunately there are plenty of good cheap books which can either remedy early deficiencies in our education or provide 'refresher courses' in the more detailed customs of idiom and punctuation. But the spirit matters more than the letter. 'The formal rules of grammar can be taught,' wrote G. H. Vallins, 'but not the indefinable spirit that underlies usage.'[4]

When actually writing it is difficult to remember all these rules and regulations anyway. With plenty of practice and friendly critics the rules governing the selection of words should have become as habitual as the proverbial 'dotting of *i*s and crossing of *t*s'. Certainly in practice we do need such rules as those proposed by Fowler, Flesch, Quiller-Couch and others, for they form the bridge in writing between the more abstract principles and the tangible bricks-and-mortar of nouns and verbs. They provide techniques for injecting mental clarity, simplicity and vitality into the medium of the written word.

Word power

The principle of preparation implies an expanding vocabulary. Many of the rules advocated choices of words from many possibilities, e.g. 'prefer the concrete word to the abstract.' Obviously such rules imply a certain vocabulary. But there is a dilemma over selecting the 'right' word. The 500 most common words, according to *Webster's Dictionary,* have some 14,000 meanings between them. Thus if you use any one of them it may be necessary to hedge it with definitions or qualifications. On the other hand the rarer but more accurate word may be unintelligible to the other person without translation. Most people in the United Kingdom use around 8,000 words. But they can understand many more than they use. Thus the writer is not limited to the colloquial language, even though he must eschew the obscure word that will leave his reader in ignorance or waste his time looking it up in the dictionary.

The writer must master the words that are within reach of the reader although they are never on his lips. Cultures and societies, trades and professions, tend to stretch the language, with their own labour-saving words. The Bedouins, for example, have over 300 words for camel; the Eskimo have 23 names for snow but only one word for flower. Our English ancestors produced a wide vocabulary for horses – yet how many city-dwellers today could accurately define a hackney, roan, gelding or piebald? Still, we have evolved 220 variants for 'said', and no less than 11,000 words to describe human personality traits.

Television, radio, newspapers, books stamped in the public libraries: all these conspire to maintain the latent vocabulary of the reader. Both the nation's and the individual's vocabularies are rather like stopping commuter trains, with new words getting in and old words alighting at each station. This process is a natural one, but the business writer has to be aware of it. These fashionable newcomers are rarely useful for him, because they are so often already on the way to becoming clichés, smart-sounding words which mean little. The valuable words, those which will keep you company to the end of the journey, are those which you recruit yourself because you like them: they prove useful, intelligible and full of life. The writer has to collect words like other men collect stamps. He also needs to compile his own Rogue's Gallery of words and phrases he does not want to meet, even on a dark night. Yet the final verdict lies with the language as a whole. The words, *mob, sham, banter, bully* and *bamboozle* did not please Dean Swift, nor did Dr Johnson care for *clever,* which he called a 'low word'. But the victory of all these words has been almost complete. We need to fight our own rear-guard actions, but we have to avoid the danger of pedantry, of losing touch with genuine mutations in the language. As the first Queen Elizabeth's tutor Roger Ascham put it:

> He that will write well in any tongue, must follow this counsel of Aristotle, to speak as the common people do, to think as wise men do; and so should every man understand him, and the judgement of wise men allow him.[5]

New phrases for old

Few of us have the time or originality to coin new phrases. Thus the advice to avoid the ready-made phrase is pointless. Rather we should shop for them like discriminating housewives. Clichés are phrases that were once striking metaphors or figures of speech which have become so worn with constant use that their face value has diminished. Sometimes, however, such as in our griefs or joys, when we least feel like searching for words, truth can flood back into these dry seaweeds of language. The words we speak to the bereaved may *sound* like clichés, but if sincere they are charged with truth and meaning. Sometimes language must go into mourning. At other more joyful times we have better things to do than to mint new phrases.

For these reasons one should never shut one's mind to someone who writes in clichés. But their reduced capacity as bearers of meaning makes them suspect in most situations. Repetition is subject to the law of diminishing returns. Thus, the principle of Be Vivid is not an invitation to showing off; it should be the prompter of a refreshing variety in phrases. The really dangerous clichés are those which you harbour and use repeatedly without thinking about them.

The language also contains a whole range of ready-made adverbial phrases which do take up space without conveying very much, such as 'by and large', 'on the whole', or 'all things being equal'. These have come under much fire during the Prose Revolution, perhaps rather unjustly. For writing should echo our conversation, and most of us do use such everyday phrases. It seems rather purist to insist on their deletion in favour of a single word, like chopping down some endearing and harmless hedges. One can be too neat, as the poet and critic Geoffrey Grigson has observed:

> In a sense I find it easier to write as I grow older. I'm less mystified by what I'm doing. I have more verbal resources and I manage to avoid my own clichés as well as everyone else's. Finding the proper form isn't just a matter of mathematical proportions. I used to write poems which were rather slick – neatly finished off and full of internal rhymes. But now I seem able to avoid that ultra-neatness, as well as the sloppiness that lies in the other direction. There's no longer any feeling of strain, and I suspect it's because I know more surely what it is I want to say.[6]

Tone in business letters

The physical conventions for setting out a business letter need not detain us, nor the common-sense importance for deploying a style that is lucid and clear, so that the reader is left in no doubt as to your meaning. But the demand for economy, which I have stressed, can lead to a charge of terseness. It is vital that the *tone* of the letter should reflect your true feelings. The *Oxford English Dictionary* defines *tone* as 'a particular quality, pitch, modulation, or inflexion of the voice expressing ... affirmation, interrogation, hesitation, decision, or some feeling or emotion.' Business letters are more likely to be effective if they are written in a tone of courtesy.

Thus courtesy is not an 'optional extra' of good style; it belongs to its very heart. For good style shows that you are at least taking the reader's interest seriously. Quiller-Couch made this point himself in *The Art of Writing*:

> Essentially style resembles good manners. It comes of endeavouring to understand others, of thinking for them rather than yourself – of thinking, that is, with the heart as well as the head ... So (says Fénelon) ... 'your words will be fewer and more effectual, and while you make less ado, what you do will be more profitable'.[7]

But what is good manners, as opposed to formal politeness? 'Courtesy results from a balance between *cordiality* and *tact; cordiality* being the warmth and friendliness you show toward your reader, *tact* the sensitivity and discretion you show', wrote W. W. Wells in *Communication in Business*.[8] He offered an ominous list of 'Courtesy blunders':

CURTNESS	The flaw which results from inordinate brevity and implies unconcern for your reader.
SARCASM	Most people dislike being on the receiving end of this special form of wit, which is ridiculing by saying the opposite to what you mean.
PEEVISHNESS	Includes such whining remarks as 'You ought to know better.'
ANGER	The roar of anger usually provokes an answering roar, even if it is under your breath.
SUSPICION	Often takes the form of being suspicious about motives.
INSULT	Intentional insults are rare, but unintentional ones are not uncommon — especially in replies to applications for jobs.
ACCUSATION	It is obviously difficult to point an accusing finger and maintain courtesy.
TALKING DOWN	'In an establishment as large as ours, Miss Smith ...' The didactic or instructional tone grates in letters, and any teaching has to be done with a light touch.
OVER FAMILIARITY	Cultural differences abound here, e.g. over the use of first names.
PRESUMP-TUOUSNESS	Anyone might be offended by a letter which assumes that he will do something before he has made up his mind to do it. The line between confidence and presumption is a fine one.

Writing business letters implies the desire to do business. One of the tests of a successful business transaction is whether or not the parties are willing to do business with each other again. Lack of courtesy, as exhibited in any or all of the ten symptoms listed above, will diminish this mutual desire to do business or fail to create it in the first place. Thus courtesy has a solid practical and business rationale. But it can also be used to express the 'house style' or ethos of the company and the individual manager. The writer should be able to echo Shakespeare's words in *Timon of Athens:* 'No levell'd malice infects one comma in the course I hold.'[9]

In personal letters especially the note of sincerity is vital. The word means literally a clean or pure sound, and it is an obvious cousin to clarity. Deception, pretence and dishonesty are the opposites to sincerity. Symptoms such as over-humility, obvious flattery, exaggeration and effusiveness betray the presence of insincerity. There are no verbal signs of sincerity: it exists in the writer's mind or not at all. The flavour of the genuine is there or not, according to your palate.

Therefore courtesy, sincerity and a positive firmness make up the tone of the best working correspondence. Examples quoted in this book of such a distinctive tone are the letters of Abraham Lincoln later in this chapter.

In his book *Communication in Business* (1968) W. W. Wells has graphically summed up the ingredients which go into the making of an effective letter (see Figure 13.1).

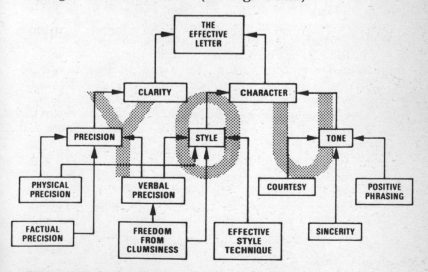

Figure 13.1 The effective letter

Writing reports

Few executives in any kind of organisation evade writing reports. We cannot do without them. In essence a report is a formal statement of the results of an investigation, or any matter on which definite information is required, made by some person or body who is instructed or asked to do so. The outcome of a report will depend upon a variety of factors: the intellectual skills of the communicator, the responsiveness of the communicants, the intrinsic merits of the contents, the situation at the time, and the use made of the report method. It is with the last factor we are concerned here.

The first step is to establish whether the report must stand alone or serve in a supporting rôle to oral communication of some kind – a talk, lecture or a briefing. The latter might take the form of the presentation of a draft report to a small committee, followed by another meeting some time later, when the outline and modifications are explained. The report then acts more as an aide-mémoire. If the situation allows it, some such combination of oral communication and report is much to be preferred, especially if some action is envisaged as a key result.

The principles of clarity and simplicity should be applied in a common-sense way to the structure of the report. It should begin with an introduction, which sets out the essential background and crystallises the aim and objectives of the report. The latter will have been already foreshadowed by the title. The format, like a book in miniature, should include the name of the author and the date of compilation. The middle body of evidence, information, issues and discussions should be clearly and succinctly arranged in a simple order, sign-posted by chapters, major and minor side headings and numbered paragraphs. The concluding section must leave the reader in no doubt as to the writer's conclusions and recommendations.

The writer's key assumptions should be made manifest at the appropriate places; difficult or technical terms should always be defined. Illustrations, sharing the characteristics of a speaker's good visual aids, can save time and space in the main text, but complicated supporting data should appear as appendices at the end. The minimum requirements for style are not different from those needed for letters or any other forms of business writing. Above all, the report should achieve its stated objective with economy of words, especially where the written word is to be used in alliance with speech.

It is essential that the quality of thinking is reflected in the report, together with the writing ability to arrange and convey it lucidly and concisely to the reader in the right proportion to the spoken word. A victim of many a Whitehall report bulging with undigested evidence, Winston Churchill took the offensive on 9 August 1940 with a famous circular to all Government departments, entitled 'Brevity':

> To do our work we all have to read a mass of papers. Nearly all of them are far too long. This wastes time, while energy has to be spent in looking for essential points.
>
> I ask my colleagues and their staff to see that their reports are shorter.
>
> 1. The aim should be reports which set out the main points in a series of short, crisp paragraphs.
>
> 2. If a report relies on detailed analysis of some complicated factors or on statistics, these should be set out in an appendix.
>
> 3. Often the occasion is best met by submitting not a full report, but a reminder consisting of headings only, which can be expounded orally if needed.
>
> 4. Let us have an end to such phrases as these: 'it is also important to bear in mind the following considerations ... or consideration should be given to the possibility of carrying into effect ...' Most of these woolly phrases are mere padding, which can be left out altogether, or replaced by a single word. Let us not shrink from using the short expressive phrase, even if it is conversational.
>
> Reports drawn up on the lines I propose may at first seem rough as compared with the flat surface of officialese jargon, but the saving in time will be great, while the discipline of setting out the real points concisely will prove an aid to clearer thinking.

Winston Churchill may have enjoyed an unfair advantage over his civil servants in that he had worked for many years as an author and journalist. Both as writer and orator he had indeed immersed himself exuberantly in the English language as in a tin bath. But the clarity and felicity of his letters and memoranda published later in *The Second World War* issued from a long struggle with the resistances of language to thought, just as the famous Churchillian voice bore the marks of a victory over a childhood speech slur.

For the manager who has grasped the need to be aware of the nature of communication and the five principles of speaking, the writing of a report should present few difficulties. Of course Churchill's demand for brevity makes for harder work and greater skill. The long-winded and complicated report takes far less effort. Easy reading makes hard writing. Moreover false marketing doctrine may persuade us that a thick sheaf of paper, pompous prose and unintelligible diagrams may somehow advertise the importance of the subject and the weight of the conclusions. In fact Albert Sloan's report on General Motors – perhaps the most influential management report ever written – was not a lengthy or superficially impressive document. The effectiveness of his report lay in the accurate location of the issues raised by organisational size and the practical solutions he proposed. With economy of words the report conveyed the clear thought of the writer, and he had ample opportunity to expand it in discussion. Such are the hallmarks of a good report.

Lincoln's letters to Hooker and Grant

One of the harder tasks of communication is to express confidence to a person while at the same time rejecting some of his words, actions or policies. Lincoln, a master of direct simple communication, demonstrated his ability to face and overcome this problem in his letter to 'Fighting Joe' Hooker. Lincoln had considerable difficulty in finding a General up to the standard necessary to beat such Confederate leaders as Robert E. Lee and 'Stonewall' Jackson. By 1863 General Wingfield Scott, the first over-all commander, and Generals McClellan and Burnside in the eastern theatre of operations, had all retired or been discarded by the President. Despite his careless conversation and insubordinate mien Hooker had commended himself to Lincoln on account of his offensive spirit. As 1863 unfolded, it became apparent that Hooker was not the man that Lincoln was looking for, but his letter is an eloquent testimony to the President's firm attempt to make the most of Hooker's strengths and to minimise his weaknesses by revealing his knowledge of them and a willingness to discount them for the sake of the common cause.

Executive Mansion,
Washington,
January 26, 1863

Major General Hooker.

General

I have placed you at the head of the Army of the Potomac. Of course, I have done this upon what appear to me to be sufficient reasons. And yet I think it best for you to know that there are some things in regard to which, I am not quite satisfied with you. I believe you to be a brave and skillful soldier, which, of course, I like. I also believe you do not mix politics with your profession, in which you are right. You have confidence in yourself, which is a valuable, if not an indispensable quality. You are ambitious, which, within reasonable bounds, does good rather than harm. But I think that during General Burnside's command of the Army, you have taken counsel of your ambition, and thwarted him as much as you could, in which you did a great wrong to the country, and to a most meritorious and honorable brother officer. I have heard, in such a way as to believe it, of your recently saying that both the Army and the Government needed a Dictator. Of course, it was not *for* this, but in spite of it, that I have given you the command. Only those generals who gain successes, can set up dictators. What I now ask of you is military success, and I will risk the dictatorship. The government will support you to the utmost of its ability, which is neither more or less than it has done and will do for all commanders. I much fear that the spirit which you have aided to infuse into the Army, of criticizing their Commander, and witholding confidence from him, will now turn upon you. I shall assist you as far as I can, to put it down. Neither you, nor Napoleon, if he were alive again, could get any good out of an army, while such a spirit prevails in it.

And now, beware of rashness. Beware of rashness, but with energy, and sleepless vigilance, go forward, and give us victories.

Yours very truly,

A. Lincoln

By 1864 Lincoln had found his man in General Ulysses Grant. Again the President showed his consummate skill as a communicator, expressing the right balance of direction, encouragement and caution without in any way detracting from the full delegation of executive action. Like its predecessor this letter illustrates the principles of simplicity and clarity.

Executive Mansion,
Washington,
April 30, 1864

Lieutenant General Grant.

Not expecting to see you again before the Spring campaign opens, I wish to express, in this way, my entire satisfaction with what you have done up to this time, so far as I understand it. The particulars of your plans I neither know or seek to know. You are vigilant and self-reliant; and, pleased with this, I wish not to obtrude any constraints or restraints upon you. While I am very anxious that any great disaster, or capture of our men in great numbers, shall be avoided, I know these points are less likely to escape your attention than they would be mine. If there is anything wanting which is within my power to give, do not fail to let me know it.

And now with a brave army, and a just cause, may God sustain you.

Yours very truly,

A. Lincoln

Conclusion

Letters and reports do not exhaust the opportunities for writing well in professional life. Articles, pamphlets, books: a versatile manager may tackle them all in the course of his career. In so doing he will evolve his own methods of work. But any of these forms will be filled by his style, which may become as distinctive as his signature. While aware that he is no Michelangelo, a stonemason can still have a craftsman's pride in his handiwork; so can a business writer. He may first have to overcome an ingrained belief that he cannot communicate well on paper, and that there is some art mystique inherent in forging a good style. A training course may give such a person more confidence than reading this book. But it may help him or her to recall Matthew Arnold's encouraging remark: 'People think that I can teach them style. What stuff it all is. Have something to say and say it as clearly as you can. That is the only secret of style.'[10]

14 Meetings: the leader as chairman

He that complies against his will
Is of his own opinion still.
Hudibras, SAMUEL BUTLER

From the preceding chapters it is evident that a manager or leader in any kind of organisation is going to find himself in the 'hot seat' as chairman or initiator at a whole range of meetings: briefing groups, consultations, committees and conferences. Managing the exchange of information and ideas has become a vital aspect of leadership in contemporary society. More than that, the leader must seek and direct a true union of minds, wills and actions.

The work of leaders in any setting is the provision of the necessary functions to achieve the common task, to build the team and to meet the needs of its individual members. These needs, present in the whole organisation and in its more permanent groups, are also alive briefly in the *ad hoc* working parties, meetings or committees with which we are concerned at this point. But there are no invisible boundaries around the meeting room: the wider needs and values of the organisation will invade the small group discussion, and what the leader has, or has not done in the larger setting will influence the *ad hoc* meeting for good or ill.

Whether the leader is appointed, elected or emergent (or some combination of these possibilities), he still has to prepare for the meeting and exercise positive leadership within it. The principle of Be Prepared includes thinking about the organisational context of the forthcoming meeting: why it is being held, who is coming and what is to be discussed or decided. A key question is how far the meeting is concerned with actually taking a decision, rather than with airing views, making suggestions, stimulating creative ideas, or exchanging information.

If the group is to be concerned with decision making it is important to be clear from the off-set about the relative 'shares' which the leader and the group members will have in the decision.[1] For example, a policy decision may have been made by the main board and the heads of departments called together to co-ordinate their implementing of that decision. In other words, although the group may not share in the actual decision, there is plenty of room for participating in the lesser but still major decisions on how to realise the policy in the most effective, efficient and satisfying way.

The main functions necessary to meet the three areas of leadership responsibility are the same for any purposeful activity, but the meeting situation does call for particular applications of them, such as the skills of clarifying, summarising and testing for consensus. Consequently it is worthwhile to consider briefly the main functions of leadership in relation to the management of information, ideas and decisions.

The leader is responsible for the provision of such functions, but that does not mean he supplies them all himself. Indeed he cannot do so. If the group members have had opportunities in training to develop their own natural awareness, understanding and skill as leaders, they should be better able to supplement and buttress the work of the appointed or elected leader in all three over-lapping areas of responsibility. Paradoxically if people aim at becoming better leaders they cannot help becoming better followers, because they can use their knowledge and experience to complement and support the man or woman who carries the main burden of accountability. On the other hand, the provision of at least the essential parts of the general leadership functions by one person does save time leaving the other members free to devote all their 10,000 million or more brain cells to the matter in hand.

Initiating

Be it a single decision or a series of them, the exchange of opinions or the stirring of the creative depth mind, a meeting is usually about something. In the early stages it is fitting for the leader to state (or perhaps re-state) *what* the meeting is for and *why* it is necessary, valuable or desirable.

It should not be supposed, however, that this function can be

performed satisfactorily by a ritual incantation at the start of
the proceedings. Despite a lack of comments, questions or
interruptions from them in those initial opening minutes
members may voice their uncertainties about the aim or
objective of the discussions at any point in the meeting. The
leader should not be surprised or annoyed by such
interventions. All of us, at some time or another, have lacked
the courage to say that we do not know what it is all about,
especially when everyone else seems quite happy. If time
allows, the leader should counter these doubts with a succinct
re-formulation of the task and the relevant constraints. Or, if
the failure lies in the vocabulary of the leader, it may be that
somebody else can interpret the objective into language which
the hesitant person can grasp.

Wise leaders anticipate these delayed reactions by checking
for comprehension. In other words, they seek early feedback on
the success or failure of their efforts at conveying the objective
of the meeting and the values implicit in it. 'Any questions?' is
one direct method. But it is always profitable to supplement
this question with a swift glance at the faces around. Often the
feelings which accompany uncertainty or doubt find
expression in the looks of people, and a leader should open
himself to these non-verbal communications which fill the air
as invisibly as radio music. One way of helping a leader is by
not assuming a poker face, or – even worse – a mask of smiling
and positive assent, when inwardly there is nothing but mental
fog. At this early stage some *dialogue* – spoken or glanced – is
essential.

The only test of how well the objective or intention of the
meeting has been explained is the result or outcome of the
discussion and subsequent action. If the group charges – like
the Light Brigade at Balaclava – in the wrong direction, and
finishes up in total disintegration as an assortment of angry or
frustrated individuals, we may be reasonably certain that the
leader fell at the first functional hurdle.

Incidentally, during the Crimean War battle at Inkerman, the
'thin red line' of British soldiers frequently drove back hordes
of Russians. Many of the latter fell down, pretending to be
dead, and the British soldiers – returning to their own heights
in the mist – encountered these 'resurrection boys', as they
called them, scampering back to the Russian positions. There
are 'resurrection boys' in committee meetings: members who
assent vocally to the objective and then 'jump up' later,
showing that they were only pretending to agree. The leader

may be forgiven if he succumbs to more irritation in re-stating the objective for these 'resurrection boys', who must of course be distinguished from those who genuinely thought that they had understood, but only subsequently discovered that they had not checked their listening sufficiently well.

Planning

Once the task is seen and accepted a plan is needed. A plan means the allocation of resources in the constraints of time and space to achieve an aim or objective. Thus a plan is a way of structuring the meeting, so that it tackles the work in hand with order. To use a musical analogy, the function of planning may be compared to hammering out a musical score which orchestrates a theme; so that all the talents and contributions of the group's players are integrated to the maximum effect within the available time.

Making a plan involves decisions about the framework or skeleton of the meeting. Again it is important for the leader to think out in advance how much participation in these decisions of method would be appropriate. Sometimes he may announce all the plan; sometimes he may be willing to go along with almost any plan providing that it promises to command the assent and whole-hearted involvement of the group's members. But he cannot evade his responsibility for ensuring that there is some workable plan adopted or accepted for the meeting.

Planning can never be a mechanical function. It depends as much upon the valuing faculty of the mind as the analysing and synthesising abilities. For a plan should reflect the priorities of the task: what *must* be done, what *should* be done and what *might* be done. According to Aneurin Bevan '75 per cent of political wisdom is a sense of priorities', and that is true about planning. Without this sense of priorities a plan can easily become rigid and inflexible, for priorities can change in a shifting situation and the leader has to watch them all the time. Establishing these priorities and retaining an awareness of them, however, prevents such over-planning, which can be as damaging as under-planning.

Another activity naturally associated with planning is the allocation of sub-tasks or functions by the leader to group members. Sometimes the custom or practice of the organisation or society will have already ensured that certain minimal tasks will be performed, e.g. taking notes or minutes. But the leader should always check these arrangements. In addition he may delegate jobs to others where this is appropriate.

Planning may well include – explicitly or implicitly – the establishing of work standards or norms. These are the stated or informal rules which can eliminate a lot of unnecessary discussion or work. For example, one such method of working would be the parliamentary practice of addressing all remarks to the chair. A less formal example would be the rule that if possible speakers are not interrupted, or the injunction to keep contributions brief and to the point.

The leader's responsibility for planning starts before the meeting in question begins. By using his common sense, laced with some visual imagination, he should be able to foresee what will be required in or near the place of meeting. In particular he ought to look at the seating arrangements, because sometimes these can impose their own (often unwelcome) pattern on the exchange of information and ideas, as one of King James I's chief ministers – Francis Bacon – observed over three hundred years ago:

> A long table and a square table, or seats about the walls, seem things of form, but are things of substance; for at a long table a few at the upper end, in effect, sway all the business; but in the other form there is more use of the counsellor's opinions that sit lower. A king, when he presides in council, let him beware how he opens his own inclination too much in that which he propoundeth; for else counsellors will but take the wind of him, and, instead of giving free counsel, will sing him a song of 'I shall please'.[2]

Controlling

The function of controlling describes the pattern of words and actions which keep the discussion on course. Any group of people talking is liable to follow red herrings, or to linger on the easier slopes rather than pushing on to the heights. An effective group, however, will not need much spurring or whipping: a slight pressure, a subtle hint or even a look will suffice to re-unite it with the objective of the meeting.

Sometimes unruly members, inflamed by strong feelings, may ignore even these gentle signals. Or a veteran bore may seize the group by the throat. In such situations a firm but friendly exercise of the controlling function is expected or required from the chairman. A touch of humour can sweeten the sharp medicine. This point is well illustrated by the practice of a former Speaker of the House of Commons, Mr Selwyn Lloyd:

> One of the most useful weapons in a Speaker's armoury is a sense of humour and a wit which, if used in the correct way and at the right moment, can bring the Commons to heel like a hunting horn with a pack of hounds. Those who did not know Mr Lloyd well a year ago suspected that he would be found wanting in this respect. How mistaken they were. Time and again during the past year the Speaker's dry wit has thrust home to take the sting out of many a nasty situation or to deflate pomposity.
>
> Once, when Mr Wilson and Labour MPs were in hot pursuit of Mr Heath over his yachting activities and the exchanges across the table were getting more and more bitter and less and less relevant, with talk about half-time Prime Ministers, Mr Lloyd intervened to tell the House: 'I think it is time we got back on to the fairway.' The reference to Mr Wilson's golfing pursuits was not lost on MPs and when the laughter from both sides had died down, the Commons returned at once to more serious matters.

The leader at industrial meetings, even at shop-floor bargaining encounters, will rarely face the difficulties faced by the Speaker, for political passions run high and can erupt into physical violence or threats thereof during the long debates. Yet any chairman, manager or trade union official has to be able to exercise control without appearing to be autocratic or insensitive. Again a good reputation will aid him. Certainly Mr Selwyn Lloyd's experience in Parliament had given him the right sort of credit.

> His spell as Leader of the House earned him a high reputation for reasonableness and fairness and he was recognized as having the interests of the Commons always at heart. It was the regard of his fellow MPs gained when he was leader which had much to do with setting the seal on his election last year.
>
> Remembering at all times that his powers stem from the Commons themselves, he must control the House in a way that is never dictatorial. Mr Lloyd does this superbly, with

just the right touch of natural modesty to crush the most arrogant intervention.[3]

Sarcasm, facetiousness or slighting remarks are inappropriate methods of controlling the path of a discussion. Nor does any form of hectoring or bullying contribute much to task achievement, team maintenance or the individual needs of members. These blunt weapons inflict grievous wounds and produce no good results. Far better is a quiet reminder of the time constraints, a firm tone of voice or a re-statement of the problem or decision which lies on the table.

One important way of guiding the discussion is to *summarise* progress so far, so that the remaining issues or agenda stand out clearly. Thus a summary given during a meeting (rather than in conclusion) can act as a trumpet sounding the recall. But the summary has to be accurate, simple, clear and vivid. With all his other responsibilities it requires a high level of natural ability and practice for a leader to be able to summarise succinctly at the right time, in such a way that the summary is instantly accepted as a true account of the proceedings to date.

Although summarising is an especially important skill for a chairman, all listeners can find it useful on occasions. A summary is a sign of listening because it establishes whether or not a communicant can select the salient points to the satisfaction of the speaker and the rest of the audience, if there is one. A summary not only chops away much of the dead-wood and foliage, but it also provides a listening check, for other listeners will either accept your abbreviation or reject it. Thus a summary helps the process of thought and digestion.

The singer, however, takes a piano note and transforms it into a vocal sound. Another chairmanship asset is the distinctively human ability to *interpret* from one language into another, without loss of fidelity to the original. The interpreter must be able to divine meaning and translate it into a different language. For example, an economic spokesman may have to translate a difficult complex financial matter into language simple enough to be understood by laymen with reasonable effort. His ability to do so will test his powers as a listener. But a timely interpretation can contribute to the over-all direction of the discussion.

Supporting

Supporting is a general or portmanteau word for a host of minor functions which give a group a sense of being a team while at the same time enhancing the value of individuals and maximising their personal contribution. Quite literally supporting means to strengthen the position of a person or community by one's assistance, countenance or adherence. Supporting covers all those words and actions of encouragement which sustain organisations, groups or individuals in testing times or circumstances.

Groups as wholes are always stronger than the sum of their individual parts. The social force of feeling and opinion is so powerful that grown men can fall sick and die if they are ostracised by their fellows. Indeed in primitive societies to turn your face away from someone is a severe punishment. For we need people who will 'countenance' us, or turn a friendly face towards us. In groups we remain aware of these primeval forces in our depth minds: hence the shades of our reactive feelings, which range from shyness through to a proper respect for the power of the community.

For this reason individuals may find it difficult to speak their minds in groups. The leader, who has a certain counter-balancing power vis-à-vis the group, can support the individual in a variety of ways. For example, he can act as a door-keeper, noticing a silent individual and checking with him, verbally or by a quizzing look, whether or not he wants to contribute in speech. This would be the reverse of the parliamentary practice of 'catching the Speaker's eye'. During and after his contribution a speaker may well need a sustaining atmosphere of interest and encouragement. Of course not everyone has to speak at a meeting; there are plenty of ways of sharing and contributing without opening one's mouth. But people should feel free to talk if they wish, and to know that the leader will support them against, if necessary, the combined power of the group.

The leader may also respond to the group's need for maintenance and support in the teeth of difficulties. Common enterprises are fraught with natural hazards, and even a one-hour committee meeting can have its quota of despondent moments. Some meetings seem to take place in Doubting Castle under the gloomy presidency of Giant Despair. The calmness of the leader and his confidence in the fundamental goodness of the group can sustain it in its trials, just as the greater resources of faith and hope released in any meeting of true minds will both refresh and encourage the leader.

Of all necessary functions in our corporate life, supporting is the one most open to full participation. The response of a group to individual speakers is a sure sign of how far it is holding a positive and creative philosophy or set of values. With a smile or a glance one member can support another, and each can do his bit to maintain a cohesive but easy unity of relationship as well as purpose. By setting a high standard by his own listening, for example, a leader can encourage others to listen in a business-like yet positive way.

Informing

The function of informing concerns the import of relevant information into a group, and the passing of information from a group. It touches upon the rôle of a leader as a representative of the group or organisation, either informally or as an appointed delegate, which rôle has as a corollary the bringing back of information from those other councils.

In briefing groups and joint consultations this function of leadership has pride of place. In the former the leader is passing down information (directives, policies, facts, rules etc.) to a meeting; in the latter he is gathering facts, ideas and opinions for upwards or sideways transmission. Part of his skill in performing the function lies in the ability to interpret information into a form suitable for the new audience without any loss of central meaning or intended overtones, or the addition of any unintended glosses or flavours.

Except in management and union negotiations, where the meetings may need a sequence of a constant flow of information in the shape of reactions from their parent groups to new proposals, the leader can perform this function mainly before or after the planned discussion. In other words he can ensure that the necessary information is available or easily attainable. And, secondly, he can work out how the information gathered at a meeting will find its appropriate destinations.

Thus the leader passes freely over the boundary or frontier of a group in that he may have to speak for or from it as an ambassador or impart information into it. Of course this function may be delegated to a group member, or shared in rotation. But the leader of the organisation retains responsibility for this function and usually participates fairly fully in it. During the course of a meeting he is the natural communication channel for messages flowing either into a group or out of it. More than a channel, he may have to filter what should be reported to the meeting, or be allowed to pass from it before the conclusion of the discussion.

Evaluating

Evaluating means testing the worth or value of something. We may usefully distinguish between 'quantifiable evaluation', where there is some measure or yard-stick which can be applied, and 'quality evaluation' involving a judgement based on a set of (individually) imperfect criteria. In most organisations or groups someone has to evaluate the proceedings, otherwise there is no way of knowing whether or not the task is being achieved.

Within the context of small group meetings the leader shares responsibility with the other members for testing their conclusions against certain standards or values. It may be necessary for the leader to spell out these standards, or they may be implicit. In most cases there is a mixture of explicit and semi-implicit criteria which measures the quality of the content of the communication.

Where decisions are to be taken the general function of evaluating includes checking the feasibility of proposals against the accepted values. Thus this function may involve the rational and practical activity of testing the consequences of a proposed course or solution. In groups which are seeking to stimulate creative ideas and suggestions such valuing should be tentative or even temporarily suspended altogether, for constant appraisal inhibits the shy denizens of our creative depth minds.

An important skill, which changes this general function into the small coinage of detailed action, is *testing for commitment.* Not all decisions should be made by consensus, or even by majority vote, but in a democratic society many should be. Moreover the closer a group comes to consensus the more its members will tend to feel involved, committed or responsible for the outcome. Consensus, incidentally, does not mean total 100 per cent agreement on the part of each individual. Rather consensus stands for the decision which everyone will accept and go along with as the best in the circumstances. In physiology it means the general accord of different organs of the body in effecting a given purpose.

Some leaders possess a natural awareness of the consentive

feeling in a group; others develop it over a life-time. Of course, knowing where the consensus lies does not necessarily mean that the leader accepts the group direction. He may seek to change, or influence it, or – in the last resort – tender his resignation. But whatever his ultimate response it is a good start for him if he can sense the invisible consensus. Groups, like moving shoals of fish, have an unseen centre point; a constantly shifting pole which draws the fish together as if by magnetic influence. Consensus in human groups is a similar centre of feelings. No leader can afford to be so oblivious of this point or so far ahead of it that all contact is lost.

Thus, like Moses, the leader has to know when and where to strike the water of consensus from the rock of outward appearance. It is not always evident where the water lies, and the leader of any meeting should be able to test for consensus. Like water divining, this is an inexact science. It is made up of simultaneously asking for people's views while watching their faces and expressions. Views may be elicited either by direct questions, or else putting forward a trial consensus and judging the reactions. In this case testing for consensus is akin to summarising.

What has to be avoided like the plague is a mistaken assumption about group consensus, made from a misinterpretation of one or two nods or smiles, a few murmurs of approval or the out-pourings of a voluble self-appointed spokesman. When the leader seizes upon such straws he either reveals his incompetence or (even worse) his own wishful thinking about the result. Worst of all, it may look as if he is seeking to impose his own will by underhand methods.

The process of finding consensus is fraught with hazards, especially if some sort of consentive action is desperately needed. In particular the leader may have to guard against unfair pressures being brought to bear on individuals. 'We do *all* agree, don't we Mr Jones ...' As the clock warns that the end of the meeting is nigh it is common for waves of hostile or angry feelings, separated by troughs of honeyed smiles, to wash against the opposition in a last attempt to wear it away. Like the false prophets, such groups show themselves anxious 'to cry Peace, Peace, where there is no peace'.

In the absence of consensus some groups or organisations may have alternative systems for making up their minds. The most common of these is voting. Depending on the rules, a vote may be carried either by a simple majority, even if it is only one, or else a pre-determined proportion, e.g. two-thirds, or even 75 per cent. This method is said to have the disadvantage that it leaves an unconvinced minority. But this is mitigated where the minority, having had their say, are willing to go along with the majority decision and do their best to make it work. Where they will not the leader has to balance the disruption of the group against the gains stemming from the majority decision. Such conflicts between the values of unity and harmony on the one hand, and the onwards call to advance on the other hand, can cause leaders of all ranks and shades in an organisation many thoughtful hours, and there are no easy answers.

Whether or not the leader should initiate or co-operate in an evaluation of the way the group has worked together – its relationships and performance – depends upon the kind of group and the situation. In the training setting it would be natural to do so. If the committee, working party or consultative group is a standing one, then some time could profitably be spent on the analysis of 'process' as opposed to 'content', because it may lead to more effective performance 'the next time'. But such evaluation requires a delicate touch; it has to strike a balance between protecting individuals against too much or too unskilled feedback and an unwelcome form of paternalism which consists of over-protection of the group or the individual in the face of unpleasant facts.

So much for the six basic functions of leadership in small group meetings. Each is essential. None may be performed exclusively by the leader. All are his responsibility.

Conference leadership

A conference is simply the bringing together of a number of people for a serious (but not necessarily solemn) conversation. For my purposes I should define it as a group which must sub-divide in order to enable communication to take place. It is easy to have a discussion in which everyone is able to participate if there are less than a score of people. If there are many more, however, it is best to sub-divide into small groups for at least part of the time. The art of planning a good conference lies largely in blending the small-group and plenary sessions to perfection.

The old-style conference which consisted of a series of lectures or speeches from the platform, followed by questions from the floor, has died a peaceful death. Its *alter ego*, the 'informal' or 'structureless' conference, which floated like an amoeba in a sea of chaos, has also largely fallen out of fashion. We are left with the conviction that if one looks after the essential ingredients of structure, then the outcome of the conference will almost look after itself. These ingredients include thorough preparation and planning, followed by a flexible leadership which allows for changes in the programme if they become necessary.

Preparation includes choosing the right subject, delegates and speakers. Naturally it overlaps with planning, which centres first on the programme and ends with the last administrative details. It is at this stage that the balance between small-group work and plenary sessions has to be achieved. The pattern of 'lecture – questions – small groups – plenary report-backs' should never be regarded as fixed and inevitable. The sequence of 'small group – plenary discussion – lecture – questions' may be much more appropriate, especially in subjects where the delegates or members already have considerable knowledge or experience.

All conferences should have some sort of 'wash-up' at the end. A plenary session gathering the threads together is usually needed. Not infrequently such a session will soundly test the leader's powers of summarising and establishing consensus. Moreover he will have to support the conference in the face of its impending physical disintegration, always difficult when the meetings have been conspicuously enjoyable and successful. This may entail an evocation of the purpose which sustains the enterprise, consciously or unconsciously, and which threads all meetings together, like pearls on a string, so that they form a progression and a unity.

Leadership manner

Manner, derived distantly from the Latin word *manus*, a hand, means primarily 'mode of handling', or the way in which something is done or takes place. It used to embrace the meanings of our present words for moral conduct and character, but this flavour has faded into the background. In leadership, as in any other aspect of living, it is not only *what* is done or said but *how* it is said or done which is important. How the six leadership functions are done can vividly communicate non-verbally what the leader really thinks about the relative values of task, the group, individuals and himself.

It is a pity that the phrase 'leadership styles' has become so inter-twined with the attempt to prove that one degree of participation in decision making is 'better' than any other. As many recent writers have suggested, the appropriate 'shares' in a decision depend (or should depend) upon the situation, the subordinates and the kind of organisation which forms the matrix for the group. It is regrettable also that the expression 'leadership styles' conjures up the unconvincing efforts of psychologists and sociologists to place leaders into such imaginary or over-simplified categories as Authoritarian, Autocratic, Bureaucratic, Democratic or Charismatic. In fact style is an individual matter, and it is always unique if one looks close enough. We should firmly resist the idea that leaders (or anyone else) should be 'styled' like motor cars.

On the other hand, just as certain general architectural styles seem to belong with or reflect an age, it may be that there is a wide style or manner which strikes a chord in a generation. This may be a national phenomenon, or it may be shared between certain nations or cultures. If so, it is little more than a reflection of the general principle that a leader tends to (or should) personify the qualities which are necessary or admired in a group, organisation or society. Even if he does not possess them they may be ascribed to him by a grateful public.

From the leader's point of view it is important to remember that his manner will exert influence as well as the necessary functions he performs. Like the mannerisms of a public speaker, the manner of a leader is expressive of personality: it gives away at least some of the contents of his depth mind. The only remedy is to endeavour to make one's manner reflect those inner convictions beliefs and values.

Conclusion

Effective communication in any organisation or society implies a number of meetings. These may vary in purpose and sail under many different flags: briefing groups, committees, joint consultations, creative 'brainstorming' sessions, and conferences – to name but a few. Yet they all require some form of leadership. For any inter-personal communication has to be managed in the right way if it is to achieve the desired results.

In the meeting situation some or all of the general leadership functions will be required, namely initiating, planning, controlling, supporting, informing and evaluating. The principles which govern how far these should be shared are well-known, and it is possible to conclude that good leadership will ensure that members participate as fully as possible in the response to task, team and individual needs.

Lastly, the leader's manner may do as much if not more than his words to encourage (or discourage) genuine communication. Humour, modesty and firmness have their own part to play. As the leader's own task encompasses the creation of a warm, friendly but business-like atmosphere it is vital that he too should check whether or not his manner aids and abets him in promoting good communication.

Perhaps the sixth century B.C. poet Lao-tzu sums up well the necessary direction and manner of leadership for today in these lines:

> A leader is best
> When people barely know that he exists,
> Not so good when people obey and acclaim him,
> Worst when they despise him.
> 'Fail to honour people,
> They fail to honour you';
> But of a good leader, who talks little,
> When his work is done, his aim fulfilled,
> They will all say, 'We did this ourselves.'

15 Communicating in large organisations

The first function of the executive is to develop and maintain a system of communication.

CHESTER BARNARD

For a variety of reasons, predominantly economic, the prevailing tendency towards the growth in size of human organisations in almost every sector of life looks like continuing. Indeed some prophets have forecast that by the turn of the century we shall all be working for about 300 universal giants. Be that as it may, the speed towards corporate bigness has certainly accelerated in the last decade.

But what is a 'large' organisation? Would you call a firm of 3,000 employees large, small or medium? As in the case of hills and mountains, where there is no agreed 'height' which divides them, it is a matter for individual judgement. Experience suggests that people have very different internal scales for measuring 'small' and 'large' in human groupings. To put my own cards on the table, I regard any organisation of more than about 500 people as large, for that number is already getting beyond the maximum that any one leader can hope to know by name.

Although it solves many problems by the well-known 'economies of size', the increased bulk of organisational life creates other ones no less thorny. Foremost among these is the problem of communication. In the group or small organisation this can be done simply by word of mouth. In the modern corporation even communication has to be organised and managed.

The larger an organisation grows the more time and energy it must devote to communication among its parts. Matters concerned with creating or maintaining the spirit and practices of unity must occupy a bigger share of the communication content. The rules, procedures or meetings which ensure co-ordinated effort will inevitably take up more time in the communications within larger organisations than in very small ones. The result is that issues like human relations, work on problems of communication and of people understanding one another, which we used to think of as the frills of a business organisation, now become absolutely central.

Communication and consultation are particularly important in times of change. The achievement of change is a joint concern of management and employees and should be carried out in a way which pays regard both to the efficiency of the undertaking and to the interests of employees. Major changes in working arrangements should not be made by management without prior discussion with employees or their representatives. When changes in management take place, for example, following a merger or take-over, the new managers should make prompt contact with employee representatives and take steps to explain changes in policy affecting employees.

Change means the intrusion of the new, the unfamiliar or the unknown into the ordered working world; as such it can produce the symptoms of fear, anxiety or insecurity. But the pace and scope of change has accelerated: we all have to live with it and cope with the consequences. Whether or not it is perceived and accepted as progress or rejected as a loss of a way of life will depend as much on the integrity and trust which has been built up in the relationships within the organisation, and the presence of good communications, as on the intrinsic merits of the change.

Good communicators

Chairmen and Managing Directors of large organisations who claim that they have no time to leave their offices or that they are too busy to communicate with ordinary work people should study the example set by General Eisenhower at the end of the Second World War:

At times I received advice from friends, urging me to give up or curtail visits to troops. They correctly stated that, so far as the mass of men was concerned, I could never speak, personally, to more than a tiny percentage. They argued, therefore, that I was merely wearing myself out, without accomplishing anything significant, so far as the whole Army was concerned. With this I did not agree. In the first place I felt that through constant talking to enlisted men I gained accurate impressions of their state of mind. I talked to them about anything and everything: a favourite question of mine was to inquire whether the particular squad or platoon had figured out any new trick or gadget for use in infantry fighting. I would talk about anything so long as I could get the soldier to talk to me in return.

I knew, of course, that news of a visit with even a few men in a division would soon spread throughout the unit. This, I felt, would encourage men to talk to their superiors, and this habit, I believe, promotes efficiency. There is, among the mass of individuals who carry the rifles in war, a great amount of ingenuity and initiative. If men can naturally and without restraint talk to their officers, the products of their resourcefulness become available to all. Moreover, out of the habit grows mutual confidence, a feeling of partnership that is the essence of esprit de corps. An army fearful of its officers is never as good as one that trusts and confides in its leaders.

One day I had an appointment to meet five United States senators. As they walked into my office I received a telegram from a staff officers stating that a newspaper article alleged the existence at the Lucky Strike camp of intolerable conditions. The story said that men were crowded together, were improperly fed, lived under unsanitary conditions, and were treated with an entire lack of sympathy and understanding. The policy was exactly the opposite. Automatic furloughs to the States had been approved for all liberated Americans and we had assigned specially selected officers to care for them.

Even if the report should prove partially true it represented a very definite failure to carry out strict orders somewhere along the line. I determined to go see for myself and told my pilot to get my plane ready for instant departure. I turned to the five senators, apologized for my inability to keep my appointment, and explained why it was necessary for me to depart instantly for Lucky Strike. I told them, however, that if they desired to talk with me they could accompany me on the trip. I pointed out that at Lucky Strike they would have a chance to visit with thousands of recovered prisoners of war and that at no other place could they find such a concentration of American citizens. They all accepted with alacrity.

In less than two hours we arrived at Lucky Strike and started our inspection. We roamed around the camp and found no basis for the startling statements made in the disturbing telegram. There were only two points concerning which our men exhibited any impatience. The first of these was the food. It was of good quality and well cooked but the doctors would not permit salt, pepper, or any kind of seasoning to be used because they were considered damaging to men who had undergone virtual starvation over periods ranging from weeks to years. The senators and I had dinner with the men and we agreed that a completely unseasoned diet was lacking in taste appeal. However, it was a technical point on which I did not feel capable of challenging the doctors.

The other understandable complaint was the length of time that men were compelled to stay in the camp before securing transportation to America. This was owing to lack of ships. Freighters, which constituted the vast proportion of our overseas transport service at that stage of the war, were not suited for transportation of passengers. These ships lacked facilities for providing drinking water, while toilet and other sanitary provisions were normally adequate only for the crew. The men did not know these things and it angered them to see ships leaving the harbor virtually empty when they were so anxious to go home.

So pleased did the soldiers seem to be by our visit that they followed us around the camp by the hundreds. When we finally returned to the airplane we found that an enterprising group had installed a loudspeaker system, with the microphone at the door of my plane. A committee of sergeants came up and rather diffidently said that the men would like to see and hear the commanding general. There were some fifteen to twenty thousand in the crowd around the plane.

In hundreds of places under almost every kind of war condition I had talked to

American soldiers, both individually and in groups up to the size of a division on that occasion I was momentarily at a loss for something to say. Every o... ...r those present had undergone privation beyond the imagination of the normal human. It seemed futile to attempt, out of my own experience, to say anything that could possibly appeal to such an enormous accumulation of knowledge of suffering.

Then I had a happy thought. It was an idea for speeding up the return of these men to the homeland. So I took the microphone and told the assembled multitude there were two methods by which they could go home. The first of these was to load on every returning troop-ship the maximum number for which the ship was designed. This was current practice.

Then I suggested that, since submarines were no longer a menace, we could place on each of these returning ships double the normal capacity, but that this would require one man to sleep in the daytime so that another soldier could have his bunk during the night. It would also compel congestion and inconvenience everywhere on the ship. I asked the crowd which one of the two schemes they would prefer me to follow. The roar of approval for the double-loading plan left no doubt as to their desires.

When the noise had subsided I said to them: 'Very well, that's the way we shall do it. But I must warn you men that there are five United States senators accompanying me today. Consequently when you get home it is going to do you no good to write letters to the papers or to your senator complaining about overcrowding on returning ships. You have made your own choice and so now you will have to like it.'

The shout of laughter that went up left no doubt that the men were completely happy with their choice. I never afterward heard of a single complaint voiced by one of them because of discomfort on the homeward journey.

In the Second World War more than one commander noted that intelligent soldiers fought much better when they were told what was going to happen. The conditions of modern warfare made close control impossible, and the soldier who knew the plan could use his initiative in carrying it out, even though he was separated from his officers. Moreover it was noted that the simple act of telling men what was the task, and the problems involved in it, had a profound motivational effect. The allied soldier of the Second World War could be driven only with difficulty, but he was easy to lead.

A major difference now is that an ever-growing majority of men and women at work expect not only to be told what they are doing but also why it has to be done that way. In addition they expect to be consulted much more often, if not about the aims at least about the objectives and methods of their daily work. Managers, supervisors, foremen, shop stewards and work people expect their leaders to communicate with them on a regular and thorough basis, just as they recognise the increasing demands made on them to communicate with others both within and without the organisation. But *any* communication will not suffice. There are certain areas or topics that people want to hear about and discuss.

The purpose of communication in organisations is usefully defined by the three circles on p. 12: to achieve the common task, maintain the unity of the whole body and to meet individual needs. Thus the *content* of communication falls into the three (over-lapping) areas:

- Purpose, aims, objectives, plans and policies.
- Procedures, rules and normal standards.
- Conditions of service, performance, progress and prospects.

This conclusion is supported by some research which suggests that these are the subjects people at work want to hear about. A study of two big American firms made by Princeton University in 1949 showed the employees could put to best use these three types of information:

1 Anything which gave them a better insight into their work, and its relation to the work of others in the firm.
2 Anything which gave them a sense of belonging to the firm.
3 Any information which improved their sense of status and importance as individuals in the firm.

Priorities for communication

All managers have to think in terms of priorities, not least when it comes to communications. The three general topics outlined – matters concerned with the common task, team (or organisational) relations and individual needs – have to be constantly scanned in order to select the priorities, which must then be matched by the best-grade methods of communication available. The less important matters can be married off to the less effective communication methods. The manager or management may find it useful to bear in mind three concentric circles of priority to balance the three over-lapping ones (see Figure 15.1):

There will be a mass of material which deserves to be communicated in any organisation so it is important at a given time to break it down into:

MUST KNOWS: vital points necessary to achieve the common aim.

SHOULD KNOWS: desirable but not essential.

COULD KNOWS: relatively unimportant.

Figure 15.1 Circles of priority

In industrial organisations there is room for debate on what should fall into the MUST, SHOULD and COULD circles in a specific situation, but generally speaking there is wide agreement on the areas which have to be constantly considered for such priority decisions. Peter Masefield, a former chief executive of British European Airways, has listed – and commented on – these important main categories of key information to the effect that an effective two-way process within a company should deal with this type of information under seven main headings:

> *First* – the policy and objectives of the company, both in broad terms and in their detailed components right down to floor level.
> *Second* – the results and achievements – both financial and general – gained already from the application of the company's policy — together with such modifications of policy as are suggested by experience.
> *Third* – plans and prospects for the future and the basic assumptions on which forward estimates are based.
> *Fourth* – aspects of conditions of service and improvements which are desirable and can be attained.
> *Fifth* – ways and means by which efficiency and productivity can be improved.
> *Sixth* – problems of industrial safety, health and welfare among staff.

Seventh – education – general and specialised.

Under each of these headings we can ask ourselves 'What do the men – and the women – on the shop floor want to know about this aspect of the business'? And we can also ask ourselves, in addition – 'What do we want to know about their reactions on this subject?' If we are wise, we shall want to know a lot.

In the case of policy in my experience the important thing is 'Why'. The 'why' of the business can range from commercial policy dictating why prices are set at the figures they are, down to such items as why re-equipment is being pressed forward or postponed, why a competitor may have established a particular lead, why advertising is concentrated on certain lines and why profits are ploughed back.

On policy matters above all else, one thing inevitably leads to another. In my experience a full and free discussion can work wonders in improving morale. Such an exchange alone can bring to light facts that lead to a proper understanding of the reasons for given action. Without this background, our decisions may very easily be misunderstood. 'To know all is to support all' – provided management is sound and knows how to express itself.[1]

The key importance of integrity and trust

The ability to communicate implies the equal ability *not* to communicate. There are good reasons as well as bad ones why certain information cannot be briefed or spread throughout an organisation. The words 'good' and 'bad' bring us back to the realm of moral judgements. It is important to consider these value dimensions, because they are bound up with the creation and maintenance of trust. If anyone wishes to create good communication in organisations the first essential for consideration is the line of relationship which joins the potential senders and receivers. If that line is strong in trust it will have the necessary reserves to overcome the occasional necessary non-disclosure of information to avoid industrial espionage, for instance. It also will cope with the odd distortion or failure in communication, such as we as fallible humans are prone to commit.

But 'bad' reasons, for example withholding financial information to prevent wage claims, breeds mistrust and impugns the integrity of management. And integrity is the foundation of good communication; techniques are only its servants. Peter Drucker has rightly stressed its importance for the manager or leader of tomorrow in any organisation or field:

> 'The more successfully tomorrow's manager does his work, the greater will be the integrity required of him ... Indeed the new tasks demand that the manager of tomorrow root every action and decision in the bedrock of principles, that he lead not only through knowledge, competence and skill but through vision, courage, responsibility and integrity.'[2]

Without such leadership our organisations will tend to become impersonal pieces of technology, never achieving full operational effectiveness, let alone mutual understanding and a sense of satisfaction and true involvement for each individual member.

Methods of communication in organisations

Methods are ways of doing things, especially according to regular plans or procedures. A system is a group, set or aggregate of things, natural or artificial, forming a connected or complex whole. Thus any organisation has a system of communications, although few managers may be aware of all its ramifications. In order to understand the system in a given organisation it is necessary to study it in an objective way. This kind of research is still the exception rather than the rule. Once the profile of the system has been established its strengths can be confirmed and its deficiencies made good. To achieve these improvements, however, it is important to grasp the characteristics and functions of the main methods which form strands in many contemporary organisational systems.

We must first distinguish at this point between the method and the people who are involved in it. A railway network may be judged a good one, even though the diesel engines are slow, the train drivers incompetent and the buffet-car food bad. But the remedies for these ills would not include tearing up the tracks.

The six sections below deal with some of the main methods or systems which many larger organisations have evolved or adopted for handling the increased load of communication that contemporary business and the rising expectations of employees require. Doubtless the reader will be able to add other systems to the list, such as the regular meetings of trade union representatives and management, or annual general meetings.

Line management

An obvious line of communication in any organisation follows the structure of rôles or the hierarchy. The pyramid or tree structure persists, despite the under-mining activities of recent years, simply because large organisations need it for their work. It is true that the degree of participation in policy decisions has increased, and will do so much more in the coming years. But, if nothing more, the implementation of decisions does require a structure of rôles with a definition of accountability. Nor should we imagine that a measure of clarity in such matters is antagonistic to human values. Professor D. S. Pugh and his University of Aston colleagues drew this conclusion from their extensive research into organisations:

> Most important of all is the finding that work groups having many standard procedures and rules do not necessarily become dissatisfied and disunited ... This supports the view that a reasonable amount of job definition and control by procedures does not lessen readiness to innovate ... It is our hope that the publication of our work may help to modify what may be a current over-emphasis on the informal aspects of group behaviour.[3]

Thus, despite its military overtones, the 'chain of command' allows for essential information to flow downwards or upwards in any kind of organisation. Moreover this exchange can happen in a series of personal interviews or conversations, which may or may not be formalised. In an age which rather favours group meetings and group discussions it is important to retain the centrality of the one-to-one transmission of instructions, information or ideas. In vital matters there is often a tendency in organisations to revert to fundamentals: to communicate directly to the individual, supporting the spoken word with a letter, memo or report as necessary.

One source of confusion in communication is a lack of understanding of the distinction between *line* and *staff* management. Line authority is exercised by any manager, over his immediate subordinates, and carries the right to direct their work. Staff authority is exercised by a staff manager only over other managers who report to a line manager in common with him, and carries with it the right to advise on how previously agreed policies, plans or procedures should be carried out. Thus the line of authority can be shown in Figure 15.2, though of course the Staff Manager in it will have a direct line of communication with Line Manager (B) as well.

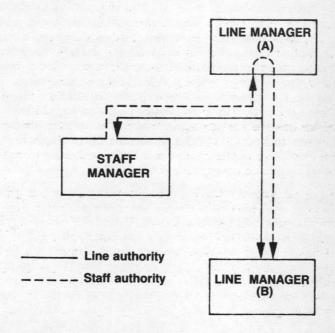

Figure 15.2 The line of authority

Team briefing groups

The personal one-to-one link works well, but in large organisations it needs to be supplemented by team briefing groups, just as the modern university has had to introduce seminars to augment the traditional one-to-one tutorial system. Briefing groups are the method whereby one communicator passes on orally some instructions or information to a small number of communicants (i.e. not less than two, not more than about 30). It is usually assumed that the communicator will be of a senior status to the group – their leader, manager, supervisor, foreman or chargehand. On the military analogy, such meetings may be *ad hoc* briefings (i.e. before some particular exercise), or they may be formalised so that everyone belongs to a briefing group which meets regularly, not unlike the Army's 'O-Groups' (Order Groups).

Despite its current military use the word 'briefing' comes from the legal world. A brief (from the Latin *breve*) was originally a writing issued by an official or legal authority, such as king or pope. The term survived in the legal profession to mean a summary of facts and points of law, drawn up by a solicitor for a counsel in charge of a case. Thus paradoxically 'to brief' originally meant to put something down on paper. It has always included the notion of brevity, for the ancient documents or letters were comparatively short and terse.

Such is the triumph of oral communication that briefing now stands for a spoken passing on or interpretation of instructions, whether explicit or not. The Industrial Society has played a leading part in advocating the introduction of such purposeful meetings. In his booklet *The Manager's Responsibility for Communication* the Society's Director John Garnett proposed the following 'drill':

> Each department will organise its systems of face to face communication differently depending on the number of levels and the work arrangements, numbers involved and whether on shifts or days. The system for each department should be written down and made known to all concerned. A typical arrangement would be for a works manager to see his deputies and section heads together; they in their turn would see their plant managers and foremen together, and the foremen would then see the men and act as management's spokesmen. In this way five levels of management would be covered in three steps. It might be possible to get the whole management team together at one time but the groups should not be larger than 18. *Understanding* of policies and decisions is only achieved if the group is small enough to allow questions and discussion. Eighteen is normally the maximum.

On many occasions the manager or supervisor will need a written brief to guide him, which may be an abstract of a much larger and complicated administrative document. How often should briefing groups meet? John Garnett suggested these guidelines:

> Briefing sessions should ideally only be held when there
> is something important to communicate. If it is merely left
> to this, however, there is a danger that in practice sessions
> will be held only when there is something to tell which is
> to the employees' disadvantage such as the coming of
> redundancy or the tightening of an incentive scheme. It is
> therefore essential to stipulate that a minimum number of
> meetings are held – at least four a year which, because of
> holidays, are not necessarily spread equally through the
> year. Down to the level of supervisor the minimum
> frequency is eleven times a year.

Lastly, the Industrial Society has emphasised the importance
of brevity, proposing thirty minutes as an ideal. Two-thirds of
this time should be spent on covering the decisions and
policies which affect the work – the nature of his job and the
conditions of employment – leaving one-third for questions
and points which the working group may want to raise.

Joint consultation

Decisions in any group or organisation must be taken by the
leader and the members in varying proportions amongst
themselves, depending upon the situation, the knowledge of
the subordinates, the nature of the decision and the philosophy
of the organisation. The more people share in decisions which
affect their working lives the more they are inwardly moved to
carry them out. Enthusiasm, involvement, commitment, a
sense of responsibility: all these are strengthened by
participating in the process of decision making. Although the
final decision may rest elsewhere, and may turn out to be other
than an individual member would have desired, the fact that
his voice has been heard-and-listened-to is a positive incentive
in itself.

Consequently there is a solid case for meetings where the
main emphasis is upon upwards communication. Three
possible aims for such consultative or representative meetings
have been succinctly defined by John Garnett:

- to give employees a chance to improve decisions by
  contributing comments before decisions are made;
- to make the fullest possible use of their experience and
  ideas in the efficient running of the enterprise;

– to give management and employees the opportunity to understand each other's views and objectives.

Characteristically these are meetings where discussion takes place on any matter influencing the effectiveness or efficiency of the enterprise prior to decisions being made. Sometimes the group's views will be passed upwards; sometimes the decision will be made by the manager or supervisor on the spot and in the presence of those who have contributed to his judgement.

Consultative meetings may be distinguished from formal management/union discussions on such topics as wage systems, job evaluation, hours of work, holidays and holiday pay. In the latter instance elected representatives of work people in trade unions are seeking to reach formal agreement on matters relating to the 'individual needs' circle in the trefoil or three-circles model. In consultations the active working members of an organisation are being asked to contribute towards decisions mainly in the field of the common purpose, aims and objectives, and the shape of the structural organisation necessary to achieve those short- and long-term ends. As the circles over-lap it is not always possible in practice to separate matters of concern for trade unions from those which belong to the individual as a member of a particular organisation. But there is a distinction, and it is worth bearing it in mind.

It is usually assumed that a consultative group, formalised into a consultative committee, should exist on a factory or plant basis, although in very large organisations there may be a case for regional, national or international councils. Normally one might find one joint consultation committee, consisting of representatives from management and shop floor, in a factory employing perhaps 1,000 men and women or more. Thus it would act as a forum of debate, rather than as a cabinet for decision. Except in schemes for industrial democracy, where the committee becomes the governing council, the final decisions and the ultimate accountability will still rest with the board of directors.

Personally I think that the formally elected 'constitutional' consultative system needs to be supplemented by the flexible use of briefing groups in a secondary rôle as consultative groups, engaging in such activities as discussion, problem solving and creative thinking. So that at some briefing meetings as much as two-thirds of the time might be reserved for *upwards* consultation in all the various degrees or shades of that word. The formal consultative meeting or committee has a 'safety net' rôle to play, especially where for some reason there is a majority or significant minority of non-union members. But we should expect to see its importance declining as the quality of leadership in working groups improves, the membership of white-collar unions grows, and the actual concerns of trade unions reach out beyond their present pre-occupations with pay, hours, safety and job security.

Committees

Committees have come under such heavy fire in recent years that it is worth recalling that in their heyday between 1900 and 1939 they were hailed by industry with as much enthusiasm as briefing groups are today. From the turn of the century they have inspired much faith as a method for running large organisations with the maximum involvement of individuals and departments.

The reasons for their present disfavour include the identification of committees with a particular method of making decisions by majority vote or consensus. They are associated with the institutions of democracy, in that Parliament does much of its work through committees, such as the Committee of Ways and Means, and has done so for centuries. Bodies which set out to copy Parliament, such as church synods and county councils, also adopted the committee method as one means of bridging the gap between the legislative and executive functions.

The emphasis upon individual accountability and the growing appreciation of the necessarily undemocratic (but not anti-democratic) nature of most working organisations, have drastically affected the image of committees. They are seen often as time-consuming chores. Yet the board of directors is a committee, and it often needs to appoint sub-committees. Contrary to the prevailing orthodoxy it is necessary to assert with Albert Sloan that large organisations cannot run without committees, in the general defined sense of 'a body of persons appointed or elected for some special business or function.'

The part played by committees in the total decision-making activity of an organisation depends upon the purpose, structure and ethos of that organisation, and discussion of it lies outside the present scope of this book. But committees do have an important function in communication which is neither primarily downwards (briefing) or upwards (consultative) but *sideways* or lateral.

This aspect of communication becomes especially important in large organisations, where individuals, departments or divisions are separated by large distances. Upwards and downwards communication may be taking place perfectly well, but it is also necessary for lateral discussions to happen as well. The mixed history of 'combined operations' between army, navy and air force amply illustrates how essential is the work of communicating for *co-ordination.* For besides being subordinates we are also co-ordinates one with another.

House journals and bulletins

Letters, memoranda, reports and the like, follow the main trade routes of communication – upwards, downwards and sideways. Sometimes they travel the channels alone; at other times they act in concert with the spoken word. Their contents do not concern us here. For, to revert to the railway analogy, it is the network of tracks that we are considering, not the type of train which is travelling on them. Company magazines, bulletins or news letters, however, providing they appear at regular intervals do merit attention, because they form another distinct line of communication.

Usually companies pay for most of the costs of their magazines and it is therefore not surprising that in the past they should be seen mainly as promoting downwards and sideways communication. In terms of the priority circles, the MUST and the better part of the SHOULD areas ought to be covered by personal encounters or small group meetings along the 'chain of command'. But that leaves the SHOULD–MIGHT shades to be conveyed by such means as bulletins, notice boards, news letters or house journals. This paperwork will be enhanced by illustrations, photographs and diagrams. In the future they may be increasingly supplemented by films or closed-circuit television programmes. We cannot help being interested by the people we work with or for, and such methods help us to understand the personal and social nature of our organisation, however vast. Fortunately there are plenty of examples of good company journals and much sound advice on producing them.[4]

Although expensive in terms of time and money, surveys do have a part to play in the life of large organisations. But, like all public opinion polls, their interpretation requires specialist knowledge – and some pinches of salt.

The grape-vine

Informality is one of the keynotes of our age. It conjures up a picture of relaxed ease, and a brave dispensing with all pompous and rigid formalities. But its history cannot support this edifice of value judgement. Indeed when Shakespeare wrote of 'these poor informal women' he probably meant that they were disordered in mind. Rather unflatteringly, the dictionary defines *informal* as, 'not done or made according to a regular or prescribed form; not observing forms; not according to order; irregular; unofficial, disorderly.'

It is common knowledge that alongside the network of official or regular lines and junctions of communication there exists an unofficial or informal exchange of ideas or information. The unreliability of this method is notorious. Indeed, during the American Civil War a 'despatch by grape-vine telegraph' – later shortened to 'grape-vine' – meant an extravagant or absurd story circulated as a hoax, or a false report.[4]

Passing any message from person to person is liable to lead to distortion, even if only two people are involved, as the following examples of secretarial errors illustrate:

WHAT THE MANAGER SAID:	WHAT THE SECRETARY TYPED:
I can *heartily* reciprocate your good wishes.	I can *hardly* reciprocate your good wishes.
It is not wise to *mix* type *faces.*	It is not wise to *skip* type *spaces.*
He *acceded* to these restrictions.	He *exceeded* these restrictions.
Archimedes said ...	*Our committees* said ...
This will *enable* us to close the contract.	This will *unable* us to close the contract.

The more people in the lines of communication the more the content tends to lose its shape. In a legendary trench on the Western Front during the First World War a colonel asked his men to pass down the line an oral message to the neighbouring regiment a mile away, which said: 'Send reinforcements – we are going to advance.' At the time the message had been exchanged by three hundred cold and wet soldiers manning the trench it had become: 'Send three-and-four-pence – we are going to dance.'

Thus informal communication allows rumours to snowball especially if they contain threats to individual needs and hopes. Bad news travels fast. For these reasons managers have traditionally looked upon the factory grape-vine with a suspicion amounting to hostility, over-looking the fact that they have their own grape-vines and 'old-boy nets'. But these informal contacts should be positively welcomed as a valuable 'alternative system' to the formal system of communications. In other words, the grape-vine ought to give upwards feedback on how well the main channels of communication are working, and whether or not they are carrying the information which is necessary in the situation.

Secondly, the grape-vine can bear good news as well as bad. Truth can leap along its branches, especially when the 'official channels' are clogged thick with green slime and mud. Sometimes leaders can choose to send messages along the grape-vine, or relay them through those who use that medium most. Only good coins will drive out a debased money. Rumour originally meant a widespread report of a *favourable* or *complimentary* nature, and it only came later to have its more neutral tone, as general talk or hearsay not based upon definite knowledge or clear evidence circulating in a community. Obviously the better rumours are those which act as advance-guards preparing the way for good news. The only way to scotch or control bad rumours is to produce the knowledge or evidence, or the reasons why it is not available, and explain the general policies of the organisation in that field. But this work should be done through the normal and formal system, not through a series of 'crisis' meetings.

Any organisation needs much informal exchange of ideas and opinions upwards and downwards, and no system of communication has yet been invented which can bear all the growing volume of that legitimate traffic. We shall always need the coffee breaks, lunch meetings and conversations on the train. What we hear between the words, and what we project non-verbally in confidence or anxiety is as much part of the total communications in an organisation as the briefing group or the company telephone system.

These informal contacts are especially important for lateral communication. It is perhaps salutary for those of us engaged in management training to reflect on the fact that a major value for the participants in staff-college courses, and in-company and in-service programmes lies precisely in the opportunity such get-togethers provide for the exchange of ideas and attitudes, names and jobs on the sideways or lateral-communication dual carriageway. Relationships forged at such times facilitate the intercourse of information by hook or by crook. Of course bad leaders always fear their subordinates getting together to compare notes, because they fear the exposure of their own incompetence and because they entertain a low view of human nature anyway. Fortunately the number of organisations with such helmsmen at the tiller is dwindling rapidly.

Besides the hierarchical structure of rules, which acts as the primary communication framework, the large organisation needs other methods. The shape or form which these take will vary according to the kind of organisation, but we can identify them as Briefing Groups, Joint Consultation, Committees, House Journals and Bulletins, and the Grape-vine. In the anatomy of communication each of these deserve careful study, for they have a vital part to play in the over-all health of the organisation. Owing to their poor communication systems the dinosaurs became extinct. No one system is necessarily right for all organisations. What is important, however, is that the methods making up the present system as appropriate to the needs of a given enterprise should be understood, maintained, modified where necessary. Management, employee representatives and trade unions should co-operate in ensuring that effective communication and consultation take place, but it is the responsibility of the top leader to see that it happens.

16 Action programme: how to improve your communication

Personally I am always ready to learn,
although I do not always like to be taught.
SIR WINSTON CHURCHILL

The preceding chapters may well have achieved their objectives and developed in you the reader both a greater awareness of the elements in communication, and an increased understanding of the art which blends them into ever-new patterns and harmonies. But it is by practice or *doing* that we learn most, and, as the end of this book is near, you may now wish to begin to formulate your own plan for improving communication.

As a preliminary it is helpful to diagnose as accurately as possible the areas in which you would like those improvements to take place. Communication is such an all-embracing subject that it is easy to be too general about it. Some limitation or narrowing of focus is necessary. Therefore it is suggested that you should set your sights on some few limited objectives, attainable in the next three months or so, and not frame altruistic New Year's resolutions, or seek to reform the entire organisation in which you work (unless you happen to be a chairman or managing director).

Once you have identified your own training needs (with or without some friendly help), mark the chapters or pages in this book which deserve to be re-read in the light of them. Then read them extracritically, adding your own notes or observations if necessary, so that the conclusions become your own. At this point scan ahead in your timetable to see if there is an occasion, time or opportunity which naturally suggests itself for practical experiment. For example, your diary may tell you that on such-and-such a date you must give a talk to a group, or chair a meeting: golden opportunities for applying some lessons.

Having written down your own programme of not more than, say, five points – each with time limits – the next step is to mark down a day for a progress review. Again this appointment with yourself (and this book) can best be made firm by writing it in your diary in red ink. So that in about three months time you have fixed to review your own Five-Point Programme against your conclusions or decisions stemming from your reading of the above chapters.

During this exercise in 'self-management by objectives' (as we could call it) it is important to inoculate yourself in advance against discouragement. We suffer from forgetful minds, and our reach always exceeds our grasp. At the end of three months you may only have discovered just how unaware you are of the dimension of communication, and how noticeably you lack some or all of the skills which others exercise so gracefully. As teachers know so well, that will be your crucial moment. Either you give up the struggle or you resolve to go on come what may. Blame this book, curse your lack of time, wait for an easier method: these are useful alibis for those who choose the former course. But, if you embrace the second one, you will have gained from the 'self-management by objectives' exercise a far more valuable weapon than any technique: a much greater willingness to go on practising and learning even although you now realise – with humility – that it will take a lifetime to make much progress.

You may already have decided long ago upon such a lifelong strategy, in which case this book may only suggest some more tactical moves. Or you may be embarking on the enterprise of seeking to master the art of communication, not without a sense of excitement or freshly rekindled interest. In the latter cases it may be helpful to set down alongside your own 'action programme' a more general strategy which can be the source of new ideas for later programmes. Such a strategy can also act as a framework, reminding you of the unfinished business on the agenda, even when you have honestly won gains in one or two of the areas of your choice. The following ten suggestions may serve as such a guide. They should not be regarded as infallible, but simply as ways of translating the message of good communication into a form so that you can use them yourself. In writing them I have followed the excellent headings of the 'Ten Commandments for Good Communication', published by the American Management Association, but I have re-worded the comments underneath them and added some observations and suggestions of my own.

1 Seek to clarify your ideas before communicating

The more thoroughly we analyse the problem or idea, the clearer it should become. This search for preliminary clarity is the first step toward any effective communication. Only as a result of a considerable amount of thinking (and sometimes hard wrestling with problems) does the content yield up its treasures of clarity, simplicity and vividness.

In this respect communication is often faulty because it is like a house built on weak foundations. The remedy is to check mentally each communication to see whether or not it is as clear and as simple as possible. If it can be colourful as well, that is an extra bonus. If it still seems unduly complicated or vague, then the matter may not yet be ready for communication. Thought should dispel these opaque and diffuse facets, so that the matter becomes crystal clear and reveals its natural order.

2 Examine the true purpose of each communication

Ask yourself always what you really want to accomplish with your message. It may be to initiate action, to win commitment, to enlarge understanding or to change attitudes. Once you have identified the most important target – the MUST bull on the target opposed to the SHOULD and COULD inner and outer rings – then your plan, language and tone should reflect that goal. The art of communication lies not least in the ability to fashion means to fit ends neatly and appropriately. But this message implies the prior activity of defining the objective as precisely as possible. It is a common mistake to attempt too much in any one communication. The sharper the focus of the intention the greater its chances of being realised.

3 Consider the total physical and human setting whenever you communicate

This guide-line embraces the two key elements in the communication process of the recipients and the situation. The receivers or communicants bring their own past history, education, frames of reference, meanings and expectations to the communication. It is a sign of a good communicator (to repeat the point) if he spends as much time on understanding people as he does grasping his subject.

Also the communicator can fruitfully develop a greater sensitivity to the total physical and human situation which forms the context of the actual or proposed communication. The situation is simply the particular combination of circumstances. Most situations share some general features in common, otherwise it would be pointless to frame any rules at all. It is very rare for us to find ourselves in a situation without any kind of parallel in human experience or history. But conversely all situations have certain particular features, their unique aspect.

From the standpoint of a communicator it is important to check your sense of *timing* against the situation. The circumstances in which you make an announcement or ask a question will affect its outcome. As the old saying puts it, there is a time and place for everything. If waiting is often included in the strategy of a good communicator then timing is part of his tactics. To a large extent timing is a natural talent, like an ear for music. But it can be developed by a constant attention to the actual situation – its present weather or mood, hopes and fears, as well as the more permanent attitudes and values which sustain it.

The principle that the situation influences the relationships of people (and therefore communication), and is conversely controlled and modified by them, reaches down to the *physical* environment too. Should you communicate in private, for example, or otherwise? Improving the physical conditions for a communication can contribute considerably to its outcome.

Within an organisation this principle includes understanding thoroughly the total communication system, the sum of all the methods outlined in Chapter 15 and how they interact with each other in a living way. So that we know instinctively in a given situation what are the appropriate channels for sending messages upwards, downwards or sideways. Thus we avoid the twin errors of communicating to too few on the one hand and too many on the other.

4 Consult with others, where appropriate, in planning communication

One of the best and simplest ways of improving the methods you employ in communication is to discuss them and even try them out with others first. These discussions, trial runs or rehearsals may additionally throw up questions about the aim and the content, but they are especially valuable for exposing the drawbacks or weaknesses of the method employed.

As a principle, the sooner that others are involved in planning a communication the better. If it is left until the eleventh hour the form of the communication (including the audio-visual aids) may have so 'hardened' in the communicator's mind that he will be reluctant to make substantial changes. Or it may be literally too late. Far better, present your tentative draft and sketches first, and then have one or two more rehearsals later. Even if it is only a matter of asking a question or making a complaint it is a good self-training practice, if time allows, to check the wording with someone else. Wives, colleagues and secretaries will often agree to act as consultants in this way before a communication takes its final shape.

5 Be mindful, while you communicate, of the overtones as well as the basic content of your message

All that we can do over our non-verbal communication is to be aware that it is going out from us all the time, like radio waves which the communicant can pick up. Then we can endeavour to tune these transmissions into the intentions of minds and hearts. In practice this means eliminating or controlling the distractors, such as mannerisms. Also it entails allowing the natural tone of voice, facial expression and gesture to integrate freely into the message.

This awareness or sensitivity should extend to language as well. The emotional overtones of some words are well known: they have the power (because we give it them) to conjure up the feelings they signify. A 'trigger' word or phrase can explode like a detonator in another person's mind. All words have their attendant aura tails, like stars or tadpoles. A sense of these shades of meaning can be developed easily by turning often to a fat and well-fed dictionary. Such a habit also aids clarity.

There is also the possibility that whatever is strongly in your personality, but not necessarily expressed in word or outward sign, will be picked up by the other person. People who are not themselves very articulate can be experts at sensing what is in your mind, just as babies seem to pick up their mothers' emotions. Fear is especially contagious, as are all the negative attitudes or emotions, such as hostility or embarrassment. Most of us recognise the presence of these feelings by physical sensations of tenseness, heart beating or going hot-and-cold. Conversely, we may feel warm, stimulated or better – we know not why. It is important for the communicator to sense when the atmosphere is charged in this way, and to be aware that his own total communication is flowing into it, like a river into a sea. To some extent, we can practise changing the atmosphere by selecting our own attitudes more carefully.

6 Take the opportunity, when it arises, to convey something of help or value to the receiver

It is easy (but fatal in the long-term) to reduce this guide to a formalised and insincere ritual of 'praise first, them criticise'. A few sugary phrases of flattery before the 'But' … which starts the real point of the meeting: all too often appraisals take this unimaginative form. Yet communication depends on the strength of the line of relationship between two or more people. And the way to build up that relationship is by using it frequently to convey helpful or valuable ideas or information, so that the positive attitude behind all good communication becomes manifested.

This practice stems best from the habitual attitude of 'doing unto others as we would have them do unto us'. We like to receive helpful suggestions, or communications which enhance our own sense of the worth-whileness of our contributions. If we have made some kind of special effort we appreciate the finishing touch of a genuine 'thank-you' from those who have benefited. Yet we are often slow to take up our daily opportunities for giving help, bringing something valuable to or showing a lively concern for another person or persons.

It is true that communicants will be more willing to receive criticism or ill-tidings from a person whom they have grown to trust through the tenor of his general communication with them. But if they detect that this positive communication is developed only with ulterior motives in mind, the results will be disastrous. Eventually want of sincerity breeds want of trust. In a faithless atmosphere even offers of help, gifts and compliments will be greeted with suspicion and perhaps fear. If we entertain positive attitudes towards people it is natural for us to want to bring them good news or constructive help whenever we can, simply because we like them.

7 Follow up your communication

We shall not be able to improve our communication unless we find out how effective it has been. You can actively follow up some communications by encouraging feedback from the receiver through asking questions and by a positive attitude to any opinions he may offer. But should you rely upon the immediate verbal feedback? Try asking the same questions some days or weeks after the communication.

Another useful yardstick is to review behaviour or performance. If the original communication aimed at some change in the way someone does something, look over the heads of their initial reaction – positive or negative – and see what actually has changed. If nothing has happened the temptation is to blame the people concerned. But the communicator should first reassess his own communication to diagnose more precisely why it has failed. Did you really make clear enough the changes that were required? Did you check sufficiently thoroughly that everyone understood his part?

8 Communicate for tomorrow as well as today

Communication must be aimed primarily to meet the needs of a given situation in the present. If it is to be accepted by the receiver it must also be related to the common past – social, cultural and personal. Most important of all, however, it should be consistent with the long-term interests of the future. For certainly we have to live with the consequences of today's communication in our tomorrows, be it for good or ill.

In practical language communicating for tomorrow means the ability to speak to the purpose and aims of an organisation, or individual – what they hope to do and be in the future. Of course the situation, the general conjunction of circumstances, will shape the lives of both corporations and individuals, but – as we look ahead – there is a degree of choice before us. Communicating about that choice, and the values which can act as compass bearings guiding us in an as yet unformed future, should complement the mass of daily communications which jump from moment to moment. Awareness of the future, a distinctively human characteristic, makes communication more difficult, but enriches it. Sometimes it takes courage to communicate for tomorrow, but if we can bring ourselves to do so the people of tomorrow will rise up and thank us.

9 Be sure your actions support your communications

Actions speak louder than words. If someone's attitudes or actions contradict his words, our tendency is to discount what he says. Thus, in industry, communication is no substitute for sound management practices on the one hand, and integrity on the other. Action in this context is a wide term, embracing a foreman showing new employees how to do the job at one end of the spectrum, to a chairman or managing director establishing proper systems or procedures for communication at the other end. An action is what you do, as opposed to what you say. Words should interpret what is done, and action should accompany words. The test of our words is whether or not we are willing, if the situation requires, to back them with acts.

Thus, if you wish to improve your communication it helps to understand this dynamic relation between word and act. Gifts of oratory or an elegant style are pleasing accessories, but it is action – what you do – which really gets the message across. Make your communication more about the central action; look on your actions more as communications. Eventually our words should become acts, and our acts our truest words.

10 Last, but by no means least: seek not only to be understood but to understand – be a good listener

The art of being a good communicant has occupied many pages of this book and some practical suggestions for improving your abilities as a receiver have been made. Now is a chance to turn back and check those suggestions against your own diagnosis of your 'training needs'. Few of us, for example, are perfect listeners. For not many of us understand how much we can give to others by the simple act of giving them our whole attention. The heart has its reasons, but often we are not attuned to listen to them. For the listener must penetrate to the other's meaning without forcing his way in. He has to listen to what is not spoken – the implicit meanings and the hidden undertones, what is left half-said or unsaid.

One method for improving our powers of understanding is to concentrate on asking questions rather than rushing in with comments. Questions should pleasantly extend a speaker, like searching returns on a tennis court. We can also improve our 'feedback': giving others an accurate idea of whether or not we are clear about their meaning, either verbally or by some non-verbal method such as a smile or a nod. Like justice, listening should not only be done: it should be *seen* to be done.

*   *   *

Like all arts, communicating should be a natural and largely unconscious activity. But in learning any art or skill there must be times when we are thinking consciously about it, or about some artificially isolated strand which goes to make up the whole. A textbook can give exercises, and they are as necessary for the beginner in communication as books of piano scales are for the embryo musician. But by the time we have left school or college we have already learnt a great deal about communication. And further progress can best be made by a form of 'action research', i.e. by seeking to change what we do by reflecting *before* and *after* some identifiable piece of communication, if possible with the help of others.

Courses on communication, such as that described in the preceding chapter, can assist by high-lighting the principles and the rules, as well as by providing opportunities for practice and observation. But not all of us will be able to attend them. Moreover progress in any art should lead to the student becoming his own teacher, so that we become our own target-setters and chief critics. Just as self-discipline should replace an imposed discipline, so artistic evaluation becomes more-and-more an internalised function of our better selves. Thus we do not have to be told if we have failed to communicate, or fallen short as listeners or readers: we are instantly aware of the fact. Such travellers may dispense with a guide-book altogether in time, or merely return to it in order to refresh their knowledge of a journey they once made.

As we become our own tutors, like any mature practitioner of an art, it is important not to neglect that other important function of a teacher – encouragement. Most of us have notched up many communication failures in our personal, social and professional life. But we have also known those times when the magic of a true communication happened. Doubtless we contributed only our small part to those experiences, but it is always instructive to analyse the reasons why they went so well. It does not follow that the same approach will work next time. Yet the process of analysing our successes in the light of the principles and rules set out above, will help to educate that inner teacher who alone can guide us to realise our full potential.

Besides its more tangible and mundane benefits – higher performance and salaries, better relationships – we should recall that the rewards of good communication include the endless delights of being understood – and understanding. For all artists are paid in the coinage of joy.

Conclusion

If you are to get results working with other people it is essential that you develop your abilities and skills in the three inter-related areas of leadership, decision making and communication. Whether or not you are actually the appointed or elected leader in a group does not matter. These skills can contribute directly to your personal effectiveness, be you leader or team member. They will enable you to get things done as a colleague and as a subordinate as well as when you occupy the hot seat of a leadership rôle. Of course there is other desirable knowledge and other relevant if more limited techniques, such as interviewing, that you can usefully acquire. But this book has focused on the 'big three', the concepts that are going to make a dramatic difference – for good or ill – to your career as a manager.

At this stage it needs perhaps to be reiterated that 'one cannot teach leadership – it can only be learnt'. An educational situation can be created in which you are able to make discoveries for yourself through group discussion and practical exercises. The ingredients in that situation need to be thought out carefully, so that the challenges that it poses are neither too easy nor too difficult. The responsibility for learning, however, still rests upon you. It is the same when you are reading a book such as this one for the purpose of self-development. You 'own' the problem of becoming a better leader. Everything depends upon the effort you make to *apply* the skills which are here outlined.

Part of that process of self-development in leadership should include a continuing reflection upon the nature of leadership. It is that process which will make you into an educated leader, not merely a trained one. For leadership can never be a matter merely of acquiring certain techniques or book knowledge. As Lord Slim used to say, 'leadership is just you'. It is what sort of person you are, as well as what you know and what you can do, which will lead to your acceptance as a leader in a free and democratic society.

Democracy without leadership is an ineffective form of government. The 'anti-leadership' ideas prevalent among many intellectuals and educationalists in the 1960s and 1970s are not so strong now, but they still surface from time to time. For the most part these ideas rest upon false assumptions or misconceptions about the nature of leadership. Good leadership always exists in a form appropriate to its environment, and a shape which is fitting in one situation may not be so in another. Usually when people condemn leadership they are rejecting a particular image of it culled from a situation different from their own.

The word 'good' has been used in connection with leadership in this book in the sense of proficiency rather than moral worth. A similar use of it is found in the New Testament sentence 'I am the good shepherd ...', where the Greek word for 'good' means 'skilled in the craft' rather than good in the ethical sense. Yet it is perhaps not possible in an age which has seen the word 'leader' debased by its equivalent words in German and Italian, *Führer* and *Duce,* to avoid raising ethical questions in connection with a subject such as leadership. Is the functional approach as described in these pages merely a cold method of analysing leadership and developing efficient but spiritually empty modern leaders?

One way of replying to this question would be to say that leadership is a morally neutral phenomenon which takes on good or bad overtones from the task which the leader seeks to achieve in co-operation with his group. A moral 'end' justifies the leadership 'means'; an immoral one condemns its leader first and foremost.

From the first I have gone much further than this view. I suggest that ultimately the personal moral goodness of the leader does matter as well. This belief may be rationalised along certain lines. Perhaps most work is wasted, or at least of only temporal significance, soon seeping away into the estuary sands of time. But other objectives and aims link up and can be eventually related, like tributaries flowing into a river, to the purpose of mankind. If the vision of the end of the purpose is seen in personal terms then it becomes increasingly important that leaders should exemplify as far as they can the qualities which are necessary if mankind is to draw near to that goal. Central among these qualities is the reality we call goodness.

This view may be strengthened if we perceive 'opposing forces' at work to prevent mankind from achieving its purpose, to disrupt its unity, and to reduce or destroy the individual, three 'areas' which here – as upon every lesser human stage – inter-act upon each other for better or for worse. In this context such evidence as we have that goodness is the quality in human nature above all others durable against the assaults of evil takes on a new significance. Certainly integrity and moral courage, the brother and sister of goodness, are often stressed as core qualities in the character of a good leader.

Leadership, it may be added in conclusion, may often draw a man or woman into situations in which goodness will be tested by loneliness if by no stronger evil force. Perhaps only those leaders who pass through their ordeal, refined or tempered, can contribute anything of lasting value to the progress of mankind, or even to that of one other human soul.

Appendix
Qualities of a leader

US Marine Corps
Integrity
Knowledge
Courage
Decisiveness
Dependability
Initiative
Tact
Justice
Enthusiasm
Bearing
Endurance
Unselfishness
Loyalty
Judgment
(Card MCS Form 719)

RMC Canada
Loyalty
Professional
Competence
Courage
Honesty
Commonsense
Good Judgment
Confidence
Initiative
Tact

Self-Control
Humour
Personal Example
Energy
Enthusiasm
Perseverance
Decisiveness
Justice
(Syllabus 1962)

US Army
Bearing
Courage (Physical and Moral)
Decisiveness
Endurance
Initiative
Integrity
Judgment
Justice
Loyalty
Tact
Unselfishness
(FM 22–100 Military Leadership)

BRNC (Dartmouth)
Faith
Courage
Loyalty
Sense of duty
Integrity
Humanity
Commonsense
Good Judgment
Tenacity
Fortitude
Physical and
Mental Fitness
Self-Control
Cheerfulness
Knowledge
(BR 2138)

FM Lord Harding
Fitness
Integrity
Courage
Initiative
Willpower

Knowledge
Judgment
Team Spirit
(Address to
RMAS July
1953)

RAF College
Efficiency
Energy
Sympathy
Resolution
Courage
Tenacity
Personality
(Amp 202)

FM Lord Slim
Courage
Willpower
Initiative
Knowledge
(Address to RMAS
14 Oct 1953)

Notes and bibliography

Chapter 1. *The nature of leadership*

1. C. Bird, *Social Psychology,* D. Appleton-Century, New York, London, 1940, pp. 378–9. Professor Bird of the University of Minnesota looked at approximately 20 studies 'bearing some resemblance to controlled investigations' which contained 79 traits. 'Surprisingly little overlapping is found from study to study. Actually, 51 or 65 per cent are mentioned once, 16 or 20 per cent are common to two lists, 4 or 5 per cent are found in three, and another 5 per cent in four lists. Two traits are common to five lists, and one trait, namely initiative, to six, and another one, high intelligence, to ten lists.' (p. 379)
2. G. W. Allport and H. A. Odbert, 'Trait-names: A Psycho-lexical Study', *Psychological Monographs,* No. 211, 1936.
3. R. M. Stogdill, 'Personal Factors Associated with Leadership: A Survey of the Literature', *Journal of Psychology,* vol. 25, 1948, pp. 35–71.
4. W. O. Jenkins, 'A Review of Leadership Studies with Particular Reference to Military Problems', *Psychological Bulletin,* vol. 44, 1947, pp. 54–79.
5. A. H. Maslow, *Motivation and Personality,* Harper and Brothers, New York, 1954. The diagram appears in CFP 131 (2) *Leadership for the Professional Officer,* a Canadian Forces publication.
6. On the subject of motivation, closely related to the satisfaction of individual needs in work, the research work of F. Herzberg, Professor of Psychology at Western Reserve

University, USA and his associates, is highly relevant. See
F. Herzberg, B. Mausner and B. B. Snyderman, *The
Motivation to Work,* 2nd ed. John Wiley & Sons, New York,
1959 and F. Herzberg, *Work and the Nature of Man,* World
Publishing Co., Cleveland, 1966. Miss Lisl Klein, a research
worker in industrial sociology, has written a thought-
provoking pamphlet on the subject, *The Meaning of Work,*
The Fabian Society, 1963. Dr J. H. Oldham's essay entitled
Work in Modern Society, S.C.M. Press, 1950, is the best
introduction to the theological understanding of work.

7. R. Tannenbaum and W. H. Schmidt, 'How to Choose a
   Leadership Pattern', *Harvard Business Review,* March-
   April, 1958.
8. R. Tannenbaum and W. H. Schmidt, *op. cit.*
9. C. A. Gibb, 'Leadership', *Handbook of Social Psychology,*
   vol. 2, ed. G. Lindzey, 1954.

Further reading

B. M. Bass, *Leadership, Psychology and Organizational
Behaviour,* Harper & Row, New York, 1960. The author,
Professor of Psychology at Louisiana State University,
discusses many of the 1,115 books and articles on leadership
and cognate subjects listed in his Bibliography. An
introduction to American research.
M. G. Ross and C. E. Hendry, *New Understandings of
Leadership,* Association Press, New York, 1957. A clear
discussion of the main theories about leadership and some of
the research upon it.

Chapter 2. *Looking at leaders*

J. M. Scott, *Gino Watkins,* Hodder & Stoughton, London, 1935.
Field Marshal Lord Slim, *Defeat into Victory,* Cassell, London,
1956.
J. A. C. Brown, *The Social Psychology of Industry,* Penguin
Books, London, 1954.
Lieut. General Sir Brian Horrocks, *A Full Life,* Collins, London,
1960.
T. E. Lawrence by his Friends, ed. A. W. Lawrence, Jonathan
Cape, London, 1937.

Further leadership case-studies may be found in the following books:

Paul Brickhill, *Reach for the Sky*, Collins, London, 1954. Includes description of the means used by Squadron Leader Douglas Bader (as he then was) to transform the morale of a Canadian Squadron back from Dunkirk.

Air Chief Marshal Sir Basil Embry, *Mission Accomplished*, Methuen, London, 1957, pp. 239–60. An account of his actions after taking command of 2nd Tactical Air Force in May 1943.

T. T. Paterson, *Morale in War and Peace*, Parrish, London, 1955. The author, now Professor of Industrial Administration at the University of Strathclyde, served as a radar controller on an RAF Station during the war and acted as a 'consultant' on morale problems to the Commanding Officer. The book illustrates graphically *inter alia* the relationship between 'task' and 'team maintenance'. A redefined aim restored unity between ground and air crews.

C. Woodham Smith, *Florence Nightingale*, Constable, London, 1950, pp. 152–25. The classic account of Miss Nightingale's work during the Crimean War.

G. C. Homans, 'The Small Warship', *American Sociological Review*, XI, 1946, pp. 294–300. Professor of Sociology at Harvard University and an authority on the social psychology of small groups, G. C. Homans served in the US Navy as a Captain during the Second World War, and described in this article the factors which contribute to high morale at sea.

Chapter 3. *Leadership selection*

1. H. Harris, *The Group Approach to Leadership Testing*, Routledge & Kegan Paul, London, 1949. The author started work with WOSBs in 1943 and was still engaged upon them in late 1946 when he wrote his book.
2. A. Arnold-Brown, *Unfolding Character: The Impact of Gordonstoun*, Routledge & Kegan Paul, London, 1962, p. 81. As a Captain the author served as an instructor at the Highland Fieldcraft Training Centre.
3. *Outward Bound*, ed. D. James, Routledge & Kegan Paul, London, 1957.

Chapter 4. *Developing leadership*

1. See Lt. Col. D. M. Ramsay, U.S. Army, 'Magagement or Command?' *Military Review,* September, 1961.
2. The Seventh Elbourne Memorial Lecture, 'Leadership', *The Manager,* January, 1962.

Chapter 5. *The nature of thinking*

1. R. Thompson, *The Psychology of Thinking,* Penguin, London, 1959, p. 27.
2. For example, T. Dobzhansky in *The Biology of Ultimate Concern,* New American Library, New York, 1967: 'Man transcends all other life because he is, for the first time, life aware of itself, (p. 68).
3. I. P. Pavlov, 'Bequest to Academic Youth', *Science,* vol. 83, 1936, p. 369.
4. For such value-judgements in the definition of creativity, see (for example) *The Creative Organization,* ed. G. A. Steiner, University of Chicago, Chicago and London, 1965, p. 83; J. W. Haefele, *Creativity and Innovation,* Reinhold, New York; Chapman and Hall, London, 1965, p. 6.
5. *Op. cit.,* p. 41.
6. Tractatus Logico-Philosophicus (English translation, 1922), Prop. 4121.
7. C. S. Lewis, *Surprised by Joy,* Geoffrey Bles, Barlavington, 1955, pp. 206–7.
8. From William Blake's poem, *Eternity.*
9. Especially *A Life of One's Own,* Penguin, London, 1952 (written under the pseudonym Joanna Field).
10. Helmut de Terra, *Memories of Teilhard de Chardin,* Collins, London, 1964, p. 67. Cp. the remark about Newton by a contemporary 'Sir Isaac in mathematics, could sometimes see almost by intuition, even without demonstration ... And when he did propose conjectures in natural philosophy, he almost always knew them to be true at the same time', quoted in E. N. Da Costa Andrade, *Isaac Newton,* Max Parrish, 1950, p. 107.
11. J. Hadamard, *The Psychology of Invention in the Mathematical Field,* Dover, 1945.
12. Preface to Max Planck, *Where is Science Going?,* trans. J. Murphy, Allen and Unwin, London, 1933.

13. J. Burnaby, *Amor Dei:* Hodder and Stoughton, London, 1938, p. 154.

Chapter 6. *Thinkers in action*

T. E. Lawrence

From *The Seven Pillars of Wisdom,* Jonathan Cape, London, 1935, pp. 188–96.

General Dwight D. Eisenhower

From *Crusade in Europe,* Heinemann, London, 1948, pp. 270–71.

C. S. Forester

From *Long Before Forty,* Michael Joseph, London, 1967, pp. 240–1.

Sir Lawrence Bragg

From 'Fifty Years a Winner: A Profile of Sir Lawrence Bragg', BBC television, 2 December 1965; and a letter to *The Times* in November 1968.

Chapter 7. *Decision making*

1. From 'Life at the Top', The *Observer,* 24 May 1970.
2. *Ibid.*
3. Albert Speer, *Inside the Third Reich,* Weidenfeld and Nicolson, London, 1970, p. 100.
4. P. Drucker, *The Effective Executive,* Heinemann, London, 1967, p. 124.
5. P. Drucker, *The Practice of Management,* Heinemann, London, 1955, p. 355.
6. Reported in *The Times Business News,* 29 November 1968.
7. S. Weil, *Waiting on God,* Routledge and Kegan Paul, London, 1951, p. 56.
8. Lewis Carroll, *Through the Looking Glass* (1871), Dent, London, 1954, p. 224.
9. Robert L. Thorndike, 'How Children Learn the Principles

and Techniques of Problem Solving', National Society for the Study of Education, *Forty-ninth Yearbook, Part 1*, University of Chicago Press, Chicago, 1950, p. 196.

10. Nicholas G. Nicolaidis, *Policy-Decision and Organization Theory*, USC Bookstore, Los Angeles, John W. Donner Memorial Fund Publication No. 11, 1960. This study was summarised and enlarged by John M. Pfiffner in his article, 'Administrative Rationality', *Public Administration Review*, vol. 22, Summer, 1960, pp. 125–32.

11. P. Drucker, *The Effective Executive*, Heinemann, London, 1967, p. 113.

Chapter 8. *Problem solving*

1. G. Martineau, *Napoleon's St Helena* (translated from the French by F. Partridge), Murray, 1968, p. 47.
2. See K. Duncker, 'On Problem Solving' (translated Lynnes Lees), *Psychological Monographs*, no. 270, 1945. See also his article: 'A Qualitative (Experimental and Theoretical) Study of Productive Thinking (Solving of Comprehensible Problems)', *Journal of Genetic Psychology*, 1926, vol. 33, pp. 642–708.
3. *Ibid.*, pp. 108–9.
4. *Ibid.*, p. 24.
5. R. E. Adamson and D. W. Taylor, 'Functional fixedness as related to elapsed time and set', *Journal of Experimental Psychology*, vol. 47, pp. 122–6.
6. L. Hudson, *Contrary Imaginations*, Methuen, New York, London, 1966.
7. For an early formulation of the phases, see J. Dewey, *How We Think*, D. C. Heath, Boston, 1933.

Chapter 9. *Creative thinking*

1. J. W. Haefele, *Creativity and Innovation*, Reinhold, New York; Chapman and Hall, London, 1962, p. 261.
2. J. Field, *A Life of One's Own*, Penguin, London, 1952, p. 87.
3. *Ibid.*, p. 94.
4. *Ibid.*, p. 100.
5. *Ibid.*, p. 128.
6. Reported in *The Times*, 20 February 1970.
7. Book review published in *The Sunday Times*, May 1968.

8. J. D. Watson, *The Double Helix,* Weidenfeld and Nicolson, London, 1968.
9. K. Seelig, *Albert Einstein,* Europa Verlag, Zurich, 1954.
10. E. N. Da Costa Andrade, *Isaac Newton,* Max Parrish, 1950, p. 102.
11. R. Butler, *Creative Development,* Routledge and Kegan Paul, London, 1962, pp. 72–3.

Further reading

J. L. Lowes, *The Road to Xanadu,* Houghton Mifflin, New York, 1940. This is a classic study of the origins of Samuel Taylor Coleridge's poem *Kubla Khan.* It shows that the main images in the poem had been dropped into 'the deep well' of his mind by the poet long before the famous dream in which he conceived it as a whole.
A. Koestler, *The Act of Creation* (Hutchinson, London, 1964). In this large tome (708 pages) Koestler introduced the term 'bisociation' in order to make a 'distinction between the routine skills of thinking on a single plane, as it were and the creative act, which ... always operates on more than one plane' (p. 35).
W. I. B. Beveridge, *The Art of Scientific Investigation* (Revised edition, Norton, New York, 1957). Professor Beveridge wrote his book mainly as a guide to research students. He was Professor of Animal Pathology in the University of Cambridge. In an appendix (pp. 160–6), the author gives seventeen examples of scientists noticing and using 'chance' occurrences.
Creativity, ed. P. E. Vernon (Penguin, London, 1970). A representative and easily available collection of readings on the limited psychological research into the subject. It is divided into six parts: Pioneer Empirical Studies; Introspective Materials (including an excerpt from Henri Poincaré's classic account of his creative processes as a mathematician); Theoretical Contributions; Psychometric Approaches; Personality Studies; and Stimulating Creativity.

Some experimental investigations into creativity

Relatively little experimental work has been carried out by psychologists. In 1969 Professor John Cohen of Manchester University's Department of Psychology remarked in a letter to the author: 'All in all, I don't think that creativity is a subject about which a great deal is known to scientists. I imagine that poets and artists have more understanding of what it is all about.' The following examples of sparse material are grouped according to the main research method employed.

1. Analysis of questionnaires filled in by particular groups:
Musicians. J. Bahle, 'Eindfall und Inspiration in Musikalischen Chaffen'. The reference to (and discussion of) this article may be found in J. W. Haefele, *op. cit.*, pp. 221–2, 277.
Mathematics. J. Hadamard, *The Psychology of Invention in the Mathematical Field*, Princeton University Press, Princeton, NJ, 1945.
Inventors. J. Rossman, *The Psychology of the Inventor*, Inventor's Publishing Library, Washington, 1931.
Scientists. R. B. Cattell and J. E. Drerdahl, 'A Comparison of the Personality Profile (16PF) of Eminent Researchers with that of Eminent Teachers and Administrators, and of the General Population', *British Journal of Psychology*, vol. 46, 1955.
W. Platt and R. A. Baker, 'The Relation of the Scientific Hunch to Research', *American Journal of Chemical Education*, vol. 8, 1931.
C. W. Taylor and R. L. Ellison, 'Predicting Creative Performance from Multiple Measures', in *Widening Horizons in Creativity*, ed. C. W. Taylor, Wiley, New York, Chichester, 1964. Excerpts from it appear in *Creativity*, ed. P. E. Vernon.

2. Creators 'thinking aloud' while at work:
C. Patrick, *What is Creative Thinking?*, Philosophical Library, New York, 1955.
W. E. Vinacke, *The Psychology of Thinking*, McGraw-Hill, Maidenhead, 1952.

3. Deductions from creativity tests given to the general public:
J. P. Guildford, 'Traits of Creativity', in *Creativity and Its Cultivation*, ed. H. H. Anderson, Harper, New York, 1959.
J. W. Getzels and P. W. Jackson, *Creativity and Intelligence*, Wiley, Chichester, 1962. See also Sir Cyril Burt's critical review of it in the *British Journal of Educational Psychology*, vol. 32, Nov., 1962. Both are reprinted in *Creativity*, ed. P. E. Vernon, with other excerpts illustrating later research along these lines.

4. Psychological tests given to outstanding individuals:
Three articles by Anne Roe: 'A Psychological Study of Physical Scientists', *Genetical Psychology Monograph*, no. 43, 1951. 'A Psychologist Examines Sixty-Four Eminent Scientists', *Scientific American*, vol. 187, 1952. Reprinted in *Creativity*, ed. P. E. Vernon. 'A Psychological Study of Biological Scientists', *Psychological Monographs*, no. 331, 1955. See also A. Roe, *The Making of a Scientist*, Dodd Mead, New York, 1952.

5. Some current research projects:

Princeton University has a special laboratory investigating creativity. Sam Glucksberg, head of the research group, described its approach in *Think*, March-April 1968, the journal of IBM (USA).

Research into creativity is in progress at the Institute for Personality Assessment and Research in the University of California. The Director, Professor Donald W. Mackinnon, wrote articles on its work in *Productive Thinking in Education* (Washington, National Education Association, 1965) and *Personnel Administration*, January-February, 1968. Excerpts from his own research article, 'The Personality Correlates of Creativity: A Study of American Architects', first published in *Proceedings of the Fourteenth Congress on Applied Psychology*, vol. 2, Munksgaard, 1962, have recently been reprinted in *Creativity*, ed. P. E. Vernon.

Chapter 10. *The nature of communication*

1. Jane van Lawick-Goodall, *In the Shadow of Man*, Collins, London, 1971, last chapter.
2. Sir James Gray, *The Listener*, 3 September, 1959.
3. Michael Argyle, *Social Interaction*, Methuen, London; Atherton Press, New York, 1969. See also *Non-Verbal Communication*, ed. R. A. Hinde, Cambridge University Press, Cambridge, 1971.
4. Reuel L. Howe, *Herein is Love*, The Judson Press, Chicago, 1961, p. 102.
5. Published by Management Publications Ltd for the British Institute of Management.
6. William G. Scott, *Human Relations in Management*, Richard D. Irwin, Homewood (Illinois), 1962, pp. 196–203.
7. *Human Communication Theory: Original Essays*, ed. Frank E. X. Dance, Holt Rinehart and Winston, New York, 1967, pp. 295–6.
   A Case History of Poor Communication
   Cecil Woodham-Smith, *The Reason Why*, Penguin, London, 1958, pp. 228–37. For a fuller discussion of the 'reason why', see H. Moyse-Bartlett, *Louis Edward Nolan and his influence on British Cavalry*, Leo Cooper, London, 1971, especially Chapter 10.

Chapter 11. *Effective speaking*

1. John Casson, 'Are You Getting Through', *Industrial Society,* November, 1970.
2. See *Training for Decisions,* Chapter 1.
3. Quoted in R. Lewin, *Montgomery as Military Commander,* Batsford, London, 1971, p. 11.
4. *Nelson's Letters,* ed. G. Rawson, J. M. Dent, London, 1960, p. 457.
5. Quoted in *Training for Decisions,* p. 45.
6. Bertrand Russell, *Portraits from Memory,* Allen and Unwin, London, 1956.
7. John Casson, *op. cit.*
8. *The Observer,* 16 August 1970.
9. *Daily Express,* 5 January 1972.
10. *The Practice of Management,* p. 340.

Chapter 12. *Better listening*

1. Rosemary Stewart, *Managers and Their Jobs,* Pan Books, London, 1970, p. 150.
2. Ralph G. Nichols, 'Listening, What Price Inefficiency?', *Office Executive,* April, 1959. Mr Nichols is Head of the Department of Rhetoric at the University of Minnesota.
3. Ralph G. Nichols, 'How good are you at listening?', *Teamwork in Industry,* April, 1969.
4. Robert T. Oliver, quoted in D. A. Barbara (see below), p. 111.
5. *Op. cit.,* p. 112.

Further reading

Dominick A. Barbara, *The Art of Listening,* Charles C. Thomas, Springfield, Ill., 1958.
Ralph G. Nichols and Leonard A. Stevens, *Are You Listening?,* McGraw-Hill, New York, 1957.

Chapter 13. *Clear writing*

1. Rosemary Stewart, *op. cit.,* p. 38.
2. Michael Ivens, *The Practice of Industrial Communication,*

Business Publications, London, 1963, p. 146.

3. *Fortune,* November 1950.

4. G. H. Vallins, *Better English,* Pan Books, London, 1953, p. 8. As an example of the kind of textbook available for the young person training for entry into industry or commerce at technical colleges, see P. Little, *Communication in Business,* Longman, London, 1965 (2nd edn, 1970).

5. Sir Ernest Gowers, *The Complete Plain Words,* HMSO, London, 1954, p. 91.

6. Philip Oakes interview with Geoffrey Grigson, *The Sunday Times,* 23 January, 1972.

7. Sir Arthur Quiller-Couch, *The Art of Writing.*

8. W. W. Wells, *Communication in Business,* Prentice-Hall, Englewood Cliffs, NJ, Hemel Hempstead, 1968, p. 133.

9. *Timon of Athens,* Act 1, Scene i.

10. Gowers, *op. cit.,* p. 3.

Case History: Lincoln's Letters

Quoted in John D. Glover and Ralph M. Hower, *The Administrator: Cases on Human Relations in Business,* Richard D. Irwin, Illinois, 1957 (3rd edition), p. 256.

Further reading

For English readers:
H. W. Fowler and F. G. Fowler, *The King's English,* Oxford University Press, 1906 (Third edn, 1931).
H. W. Fowler, *A Dictionary of Modern English Usage,* Oxford University Press, 1926.
Eric Partridge, *Usage and Abusage: A Guide to Good English,* Penguin, London, 1973.
G. H. Vallins, *Good English: How to Write It,* Pan Books, London, 1951.
G.H. Vallins, *Better English,* Pan Books, London, 1953. Bound editions of both books by G. H. Vallins were produced by André Deutsch Ltd.
Sir Ernest Gowers, *The Complete Plain Words* (Revised edition by Sir Bruce Fraser), HMSO, London, 1977.

For American readers:
Rudolph Flesch, *The Art of Plain Talk,* Harper & Row, New York, 1946.
Rudolph Flesch, *The Art of Readable Writing,* Harper & Row,

New York, 1949.

Stuart Chase, *Power of Words,* Harcourt, Brace, New York, 1954.

Norman Shidle, *Clear Writing for Easy Reading,* McGraw-Hill, New York, 1951.

For reference:
The Oxford English Dictionary (in *Concise* or *Shorter* forms) and *Webster's Dictionary* are invaluable to anyone who wants to improve their use of words.

The Oxford Dictionary for Writers and Editors, compiled by The Oxford English Dictionary Department, 1981. For the spelling of tricky words and personal and place names, for dates of famous men and women, for the meaning and correct form of abbreviations and frequently used foreign words and phrases, for the elucidation of technical terms, and for many other practical purposes in the office and the study, the *Writers and Editors Dictionary* is a most helpful guide.

P. M. Roget, *Thesaurus of English Words and Phrases.* Originally published in 1852.

Chapter 14. *Meetings: the leader as chairman*

1. See Chapter 5, 'Sharing Decisions', in *Training for Decisions,* 1971.
2. From Bacon's essay 'On Counsel'.
3. *The Times,* 12 January 1972.

Chapter 15. *Communicating in large organisations*

Eisenhower case history
Dwight D. Eisenhower, *Crusade in Europe,* Doubleday, New York, 1948, pp. 314, 420–2.
1. *Communication in Industry,* ed. C. Chisholm, Business Publications, London, 2nd edn, 1957, pp. 22–3.
2. Peter F. Drucker, *The Practice of Management,* Heinemann, London, 1955, pp. 370–1.
3. D. S. Pugh (*et al.*) 'Organisation Structure, Organisational Climate, and Group Structure: an Exploratory Study of their Relationships', *Occupational Psychology,* vol. 45, no. 1, 1971.
4. This point is well illustrated in Stephen Crane's famous novel of the American Civil War, *The Red Badge of Courage.*

Index